Sydney Bellingham's

Canada

Sydney Bellingham's

Canada

People, Places, and Events in the Middle Half of the Nineteenth Century

William Hesler

Fitzhenry & Whiteside

Published in Canada by Fitzhenry & Whiteside,
195 Allstate Parkway, Markham, ON   L3R 4T8
Published in the United States by Fitzhenry & Whiteside
311 Washington Street, Brighton, MA   02135

2 4 6 8 10 9 7 5 3 1

Library and Archives Canada Cataloguing in Publication
Hesler, William, author
Sydney Bellingham's Canada : people, places and events in the middle half of the 19th century / author, William Hesler.

Includes bibliographical references and index.
ISBN 978-1-55455-415-7 (softcover)

1. Bellingham, Sydney, 1808-1900. 2. Canada--History--1841-1867.
3. Canada--History--1867-1914. 4. Canada--Politics and government--19th century. 5. Canada--Social conditions--19th century.
6. Canada--Social life and customs--19th century. 7. Politicians--Canada--Biography. I. Title.

FC471.B44H47 2018   971.04092   C2018-901883-6

Publisher Cataloging-in-Publication Data (U.S.)

Names: Hesler, William, author.
Title: Sydney Bellingham's Canada / author, William Hesler.
Description: Markham, Ontario : Fitzhenry & Whiteside, 2019. | Includes bibliography and index. | Summary: :"Historical portrait of
nineteenth century Canada, with emphasis on the people, places and events which figured in the experiences of an Irish-born entrepreneur,
lawyer, newspaper editor, politician, and militia officer, Sydney Bellingham"– Provided by publisher.
Identifiers: ISBN 978-1-55455-415-7 (paperback)
Subjects: LCSH: Canada – History. | Bellingham, Sydney, 1808-1900. | BISAC: HISTORY / Canada / General.
Classification: LCC F1026.B455 | DDC 971 – dc23

Fitzhenry & Whiteside acknowledges with thanks the Canada Council for the Arts and the Ontario Arts Council for their support of our publishing
program. We acknowledge the financial support of the Government of Canada through the Canada Book Fund (CBF) for our publishing activities.

Design by Kerry Plumley
Printed in Canada by Copywell

www.fitzhenry.ca

For Jackson and Lauren

CONTENTS

MAPS

ILLUSTRATIONS

A NOTE ON CONVENTIONS

Distances are expressed in miles rather than kilometres as they were throughout the period covered by this book.

Amounts of money are sometimes expressed in dollars, even during the period before the dollar became the official monetary unit in Canada. While pounds, shillings, and pence were the legal tender, Canadians often converted them in their transactions and speech to their equivalent in American dollars. To add to the confusion, there were two sets of pounds in the currencies of account—one British and one Canadian—with different values against the U.S. dollar. Attempts to give the present-day value of money are necessarily very approximate, but because the British pound sterling was pegged to a gold standard in the second half of the nineteenth century, the values remain relatively constant throughout the period covered by this book. In 1840, £100 was worth about $15,000 in Canadian money today. By 1850, it had actually risen in value to $20,000, and by 1900, it was still worth about $18,500.

Place names in Lower Canada are expressed in French when the majority of the local population was French-speaking, even though they had common English equivalents, such as "Three Rivers." Following the same logic, towns like St. Andrews keep their English names, although today they are known by their French names. The same applies to street names, like St. James. Prior to 1867, Quebec City is referred to only as Quebec. The Province of Quebec did not come into existence until Confederation.

Honorific titles such as "Sir" have been dropped, unless they are useful in distinguishing people with the same first and family names, such as "William Bellingham." Another exception is for members of the peerage who were known mostly by their titular names, such as "Lord Durham."

PREFACE

Dear Reader,

I am starting this off with the salutation often used by writers in the nineteenth century because this book is about Montreal, Quebec, and Ontario in the middle half of that century. Let me explain how I was compelled to write the book, and why its focus is on a man whose name was Sydney Robert Bellingham. I had never heard of him until a few weeks before I embarked on this project. I also want to explain my interest in the County of Argenteuil, Quebec, which figures so prominently in the life of Sydney Bellingham.

The County of Argenteuil consists of about 800 square miles of farms, forests, lakes, and rivers. Its principal town, Lachute, is about an hour's drive from Montreal. Its southern boundary is the mighty Ottawa River. Its northern boundary is in sight of majestic Mont Tremblant.

I spent ten summers of my childhood at my parents' cottage on the shore of a lake in Argenteuil, that lake having the distinction of being located at the convergence of three of the present county's nine townships, Wentworth, Morin, and Gore. When I was studying law, I spent most of my weekends instead building a cottage on another lake in Argenteuil, whose seven miles of water bridge the Townships of Montcalm and Arundel. Two decades later, my wife Nicole and I shifted our country focus to a farm in the southwest corner of Arundel Township. It fronts on the Rouge River, which flows from north of Mont Tremblant and runs due south to join the Ottawa. The steep, forested hills of Harrington Township are our southern boundary.

In 2007, Arundel celebrated the 150th anniversary of its settlement. To mark the occasion, the descendants of some of the first settlers put together an enchanting collection of family histories. I confess I did not get around to reading them in depth until 2015. That is when I learned that the man who promoted the settlement of Arundel was Sydney Bellingham. Wanting to know more about him, I turned to the short biography by Robert C. Daley in the remarkable fourteen-volume *Dictionary of Canadian Biography*. It made me wonder why I had never heard of him before. It also convinced me that if I wanted to gain a sense of what life was like in Canada in the nineteenth century, Sydney Bellingham's experiences would provide me with an impressive variety of illustrations.

Sydney Bellingham came to Canada in 1824 from Ireland all by himself at the age of fifteen. He spent a couple of years as the working guest of a family of Anglo-Irish settlers in the dense forests which surrounded what is now the city of Peterborough, Ontario. He then served as an apprentice to a lumber merchant at Quebec, and when he turned twenty-one, he set up an import-export business of his own at Montreal. At the young age of twenty-nine, he was appointed a magistrate in that city. During the Rebellions of 1837 and 1838, he served as a captain in the Royal Montreal Cavalry and played a key role in the success of the British forces at the Battle of St. Charles. After peace came, he became a lawyer and then a newspaper editor. He was Vice-President of the St. Patrick's Society and a Governor of the Montreal General Hospital. He was instrumental in the building of one of

the first railways in Canada, located in Argenteuil. For six years, he sat in the Legislative Assembly of the United Province of Canada as the member for Argenteuil. After Confederation, he represented that county in the provincial Assembly for eleven years. In the middle of all this, he brought about the settlement of Arundel Township. He was on a first-name basis with Sir John A. Macdonald and many of the other political and business notables whose names we still recognize today. Of the many people he had met in Canada, nearly a hundred are included in the *Dictionary of Canadian Biography*.

Why had I never heard of him? Why did such an interesting life escape broader coverage in the historical record? Probably because, after fifty-four years in Canada, Sydney Bellingham returned to Ireland, where he died nearly a quarter-century later. Probably also because he left behind no progeny to sing his praises— at least not one bearing his name. He does, however, live on through his brief appearances in Jan Henry Morgan's three-volume *A Chronicle of Lower Canada*. Aptly described as fictionalized history, rather than historical fiction, the meticulously researched *Chronicle* brings to life the events leading up to and including the Rebellions of 1837-38.

This is not a history book. It is more like a collection of historical snapshots of the events Sydney Bellingham witnessed and the people he knew. It is not a complete biography either. There are gaps in the narrative, which my research has failed to fill. We owe much to Kaye Lamb, Dominion Archivist, who had the foresight in 1958 to have Sydney Bellingham's handwritten memoirs transcribed, but those memoirs were dictated when he was close to ninety years old. Some of his recollections are cloudy, and some are simply not accurate. But through the memoirs and his few earlier writings which have survived, we learn some new things about interesting people and events, at least enough to debunk some historical myths whose truth we frequently take for granted.

Sydney Bellingham was remarkably independent in thought as well as in deed. He had a great admiration for the people who, back then, called themselves *Canadiens*. His lack of prejudice and snobbery sets him apart from a lot of English-speaking writers of that era, and made him a keen-eyed observer with a fresh perspective on important events in Canadian history. That is another reason why I decided to write this book.

1. Bellingham Castle House in an early photograph predating its
renovation, from Struggle, 1914–1920 by John Evelyn Wrench, 1935

CHAPTER 1

COMING TO CANADA

*I*N THE NORTHEASTERN CORNER OF THE REPUBLIC OF IRELAND, there is a county—a border county—called Louth. In that county, near the shores of the Irish Sea, is a village called Castlebellingham. Until the early 1700s, it was called Gernonstowne. There was indeed a castle, and it belonged to one of Oliver Cromwell's lieutenants, a man called Henry Bellingham, but it was destroyed in 1689 by the army of King James II during his attempt to regain the English throne. In its place, in 1712, the family erected a large home that resembled more a manor house than a castle. Today, expanded and renovated to make it look indeed like a castle, it is a posh boutique hotel.

On August 2, 1808, in a cottage on the Bellingham estate, Elizabeth Walls, the daughter of an English clergyman and wife of Alan Bellingham, gave birth to her fourth son, Sydney Robert Bellingham. Early in 1822, when Sydney was only thirteen, Elizabeth died.

The Bellingham family traced its roots to the north of England, on the other side of the Irish Sea from County Louth. That connection explains the peculiar way they pronounced their name: *Bellin-jum*. The Bellinghams were Anglo-Irish, part of the English landed gentry that controlled Ireland after Oliver Cromwell's brutal invasion in the 1650s had left the native Irish dispossessed and disenfranchised. Alan Bellingham, like his father before him and many other Bellingham family members, had served as an officer in the British Army. King George III had made Sir William Bellingham, Alan's uncle, a baronet in 1796.

These were hard times in Ireland. The years of relative prosperity that flowed from the needs of the British government during the Napoleonic Wars halted when peace was established in 1815. The linen manufacturers in the north of Ireland were going bankrupt, there was little employment, and the peasantry was starving and restless. In 1818, Alan Bellingham's regiment was reduced to a single battalion. England no longer needed to call upon the Anglo-Irish gentry to serve as army or naval officers, and Alan Bellingham was unemployed and running out of money. He spent some of what he had left on Sydney's education but by the spring of 1824, that too had to come to an end.

Alan's younger brother, John Bellingham, was married to Eliza, one of the daughters of William Stewart, who lived in County Down, just to the north. Another of Stewart's daughters was the second wife of the father of Sydney's teenage sweetheart, Charlotte Froude. Thus, both through his uncle and his girlfriend, young Sydney Bellingham had connections with the Stewart family.

Thomas Stewart, William Stewart's son, emigrated to Upper Canada in 1822, taking with him his wife, Frances Browne, and their three young children. Frances, or Fanny Browne, was a prolific letter writer, and her letters from Canada were topics of excited conversation among the ladies of the Anglo-Irish gentry of that part of Ireland. Understanding that her letters would be circulated, she let it be known that she and Thomas would welcome visits from her friends' "idle boys." Sydney heard about the letters from Charlotte Froude, and it was not long before he was drawn to the idea of joining the Stewarts in Upper Canada. By all accounts, conditions there were far better than in Ireland. Land was free for the asking, and Sydney would be able to acquire some as soon as he turned twenty-one. The plan was that Charlotte would join him then. In the meantime, he could learn the necessary frontier skills from Thomas Stewart, his cousin by marriage. Sydney was not, however, an "idle boy." The few last gold sovereigns his father had spent on his schooling and tutoring had been a good investment. He was well read, handy with numbers, and conversant in French. He knew how to handle a horse, a gun, and a sword. Had he been born a generation earlier, he probably would have become a cavalry officer like Charlotte Froude's father.

Sydney's father, being left with few other options, agreed with the plan. Alan's military service had created contacts in Canada who might be persuaded to guide Sydney in the right direction. One of those contacts was a former high-ranking army surgeon, Dr. William Holmes, now residing at Quebec.[1] Letters were exchanged with Holmes and the Stewarts and tentative arrangements were made with other contacts in Canada. Sydney's father equipped the expedition with a supply of clothing, footwear, and other items, and Fanny Stewart's friends put together an assortment of gifts and a pack of letters for Sydney to deliver to Fanny and her family in Upper Canada. A collection was taken up, and the young adventurer received a purse of gold sovereigns to tide him over until he could make his own fortune.

Sydney left Dublin on May 10, 1824, bound ultimately for the Stewart homestead on the Otonabee River in Douro Township in Upper Canada. His passage was aboard the *New Draper*, a small 141-ton brig under the command of foul-tempered Captain Thomas Barwise. The *New Draper* had been launched in 1791. Her long life on the high seas would end on the rocks off the Isle of Man in the Irish Sea in 1880. Sydney shared the only passenger cabin with a

---

1   In the portion of this book that covers events prior to Confederation in 1867, "Quebec" refers to what today we call "Quebec City." Before the creation of the Province of Quebec in 1867, there was no need to make the distinction. What today we mean by the Province of Quebec was until then called Lower Canada or Canada East.

surgeon who was paying for his passage by acting as the ship's doctor. The surgeon had plenty of patients, with eighty other immigrants crammed into steerage. The trip lasted seven long weeks, the first two made worse by seasickness. The food consisted mainly of ship's biscuit and salt junk (salted beef), with porridge and molasses for breakfast. There was no fresh meat or vegetables. The only memorable events included the frequent sightings of whales, which had not yet been hunted to near extinction by the New Bedford whalers, and evenings when the steerage passengers fraternized with the crew on deck and danced a jig to the sound of a fiddle. Decades later, Sydney's only other reminiscence of the voyage was the stench of the ship's bilge water, made worse whenever the ship pitched and heaved in rough weather.

Things picked up once they reached the St. Lawrence, with the sight of a neat *Canadien* village every few miles. The houses impressed Sydney for their uniformity of style, with whitewashed square timbers and red shutters, and in nearly every village he could see in the distance, gleaming with reflected sunlight, the tin roof of a church. It was hard work for the crew during the last 300 miles before Quebec, trying to catch an easterly breeze or the incoming tide to propel them up the river, or lying at anchor during long hours of waiting out the ebbing tide. Those passengers who had seen only the rivers of Ireland or England were awestruck by the breadth of the great river and the number of days it took to get only as far as Quebec. The sheer immensity of the continent they were

entering was something that, until then, they had only tried to imagine.

Finally the *New Draper* reached Quebec and berthed opposite the town, at Pointe Lévis. The arrival of a ship like this one usually drew a small crowd of locals eager to sell fresh produce to the passengers or offer their services as porters and waggoneers. For the first time in nearly two months, the steerage passengers were able to wash in fresh water. They donned their best clothes: the traditional Irish peasant garb of knee britches with long woollen stockings and a swallow-tailed coat sporting bright metal buttons. The rather pretentious European style stood out against the more practical dress of the *Canadiens* and *Canadiennes* gathered at the dock, the men dressed in a jacket, waistcoat, and trousers fashioned out of homespun cloth called *étoffe du pays*, with the traditional cap called a *bonnet bleu*. From his very first encounter to the last, Sydney had respect and even affection for the *Canadien* people. Both upon his arrival and in the years that followed, he found the farming and labouring classes of Lower Canada to be honest and industrious, courteous but not subservient, good-natured as opposed to grumbling, and in contrast with other people, living their lives in a culture and tradition that eschewed violence. Throughout his half-century in Canada, among the members of the political and professional classes who impressed him the most for their combined integrity, eloquence, and learning, there were more whose first language was French than those who could trace their roots back to England, Ireland, or Scotland.

Shortly after disembarking, he crossed the nearly mile-wide river in a horse-powered ferry to Finlay's Wharf and set off in search of Dr. Holmes's house in Quebec's Upper Town. He recalled being impressed by the substantial stonework and the "venerable stamp of age" of the buildings. In fact, Quebec was already more than 200 years old. The house was on Rue des Jardins, bounded to the rear by the Ursuline Convent and facing the Anglican cathedral.

William Holmes was ten years older than Sydney's father. They had both been commissioned officers in the 5th (Northumberland) Regiment of Foot, which was garrisoned at various times throughout the 1790s at Quebec, Detroit, and Fort Niagara, followed by a brief (and rather inglorious) return to Lower Canada in 1814.[2] In 1801, Holmes was appointed Surgeon General of the British forces in North America. From an economic perspective at least, he had married wisely. Under French law, or more specifically, the Custom of Paris, married women in Lower Canada could own and inherit real estate. Married women in the rest of British North America could not. In 1807, he wed Margaret Macnider, the daughter of wealthy Quebec merchant and landowner John Macnider. Margaret was the young widow and heir of another wealthy merchant and

2 See Postscript.

landowner, James Johnston. Holmes's first wife, who had died in 1803, was also the daughter of a wealthy merchant, Samuel Jacobs. By 1824, Dr. Holmes was semi-retired, living off the income from Margaret's properties but still seeing patients and donating his services to the Ursuline nuns who ran the hospital. One of his projects was acting as Commissioner for the Relief of the Insane. These efforts, nearly fifty years later, influenced Sydney Bellingham's campaign (as the Member of the Quebec Legislative Assembly for the County of Argenteuil) to secure better treatment for the inmates of the Beauport Lunatic Asylum near Quebec City.

Dr. Holmes greeted Sydney warmly and was pleased to receive a visit from the son of a fellow officer. Sydney met Margaret and their daughter, the sixteen-year-old Arabella.

Sydney's memoirs of the visit mention only that the young girl was fair-haired, without further comment,

3. Horse-driven ferry at Lévis, c. 1820, sketch by John Jeremiah Bigsby , LAC, MIKAN 3028509.

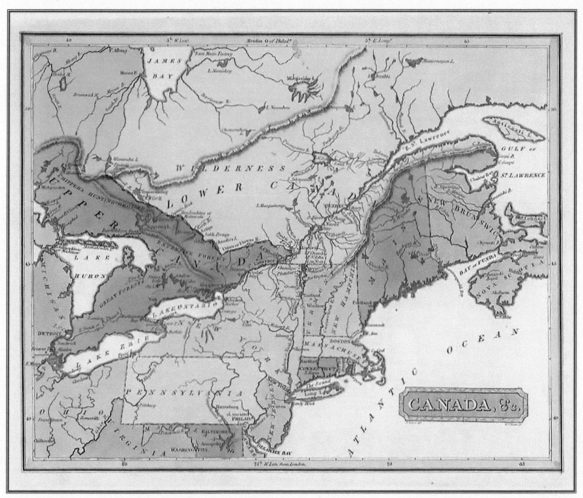

so we might assume that Sydney still had eyes only for Charlotte Froude, who was far away but not forgotten, at least not yet. Five years later, Sydney would marry Arabella Holmes. Like his future father-in-law, Sydney came to know the benefits of marrying into wealth.

After his first home-cooked meal in nearly two months, followed by his first night in a bed instead of a ship's hammock, Sydney was shown around the Upper Town of Quebec by his host. He was treated first to the splendid view from the governor's mansion, called the

Château St. Louis, which overlooked the St. Lawrence and Île d'Orléans from the site where the iconic Château Frontenac Hotel stands today. Then, with Holmes's servant François at the reins of a high-wheeled and comfortable gig called a *calèche*, or *marche-donc*, Holmes took Sydney into the countryside, where he owned farms located along both the Sainte Foy and Cap Rouge roads that led out of Quebec towards the town of Trois-Rivières. The farms looked neat and prosperous, a sign perhaps that Sydney's decision to come to Canada was a good one. As they drove by the Plains of Abraham, Holmes shared his thoughts on General Montcalm's fateful decision to leave the relative safety of the town's fortifications and engage Wolfe's forces in the battle that decided the future of the continent in 1758. He pointed out the Laurentian Mountains to the north and ventured that there was little prospect that the forest-covered lands distant from the river would ever be made part of civilization. This may have been when an idea was planted in Sydney's mind. Thirty years later, he would colonize a small portion of the Laurentian hinterland farther upriver.

Through Sydney's memoirs, we gain insight into the state of medical science in the first half of the nineteenth century. One of the things we learn early on is that through his experience with otherwise untreatable conditions, Dr. Holmes recognized the value of the placebo. Sydney recalled that during his brief first visit, the servant François was busily engaged manufacturing little pills that were placed in small boxes and distributed free of charge by Holmes to his patients. The pills were simply a mixture of yellow soap and flour, Holmes not letting on that he was counting solely on their effect on the imagination. They were, at least, harmless, unlike many of the potions and procedures of the day.

Sydney's memoirs are full of other reminiscences of Quebec, but most of them are from when he returned there in the years following his first visit. He mentions Montmorency Falls cascading over the escarpment a few miles downriver, clearly visible to those aboard any ship arriving or departing the city. There was the shrine at Sainte-Anne-de-Beaupré, just a bit farther down from the falls, with its stacks of crutches left behind by pilgrims from as far away as the United States. His memoirs reveal that even at that early date, some people believed the miraculous "cures" at Sainte-Anne-de-Beaupré were just temporary relief produced by "the force of imagination acting upon the nervous system," like Dr. Holmes's placebo pills. There was also the Huron community at L'Ancienne Lorrette, which provided Sydney with context for the observation that the early French colonists had treated the Indian population with greater respect and acceptance than the British and Americans would do. Another recollection was the rowdy behaviour of the crowd on Champlain Street, along the harbourfront, which he describes as "a nest of rum shops and dancing saloons." However, in July 1824, there was not enough time for him to lose his way there— at least not yet—because the day after his arrival at Quebec, he departed for Upper Canada.

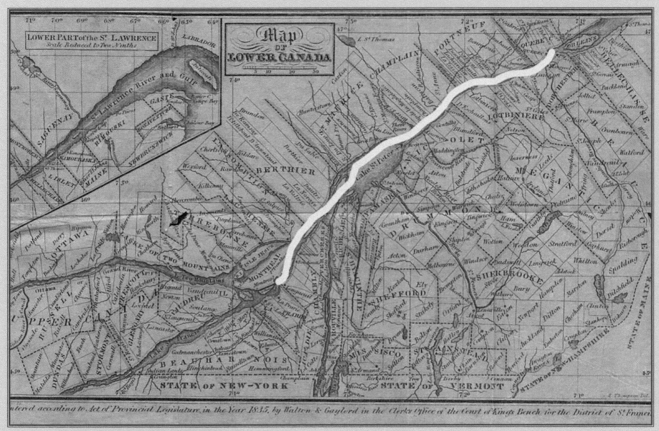

2. The journey from Quebec to Montreal aboard the steamer New Swiftsure, *from a map by Walton and Gaylord, 1835, LAC, MIKAN 4127087*

CHAPTER 2

UPPER CANADA

*A*FTER A VERY BRIEF STAY—AND REGAINING HIS LAND LEGS after so many weeks on the water—Sydney took his leave of the Holmes family and set out on the next part of his journey to Douro Township in Northumberland County, Upper Canada. Since 1791, the territory ceded by France to the British Crown had been divided into two separate colonies, each with its own government: Lower Canada (now part of present-day Quebec) and Upper Canada (now part of present-day Ontario). Douro was still an unsurveyed township in the wilderness on the east bank of the Otonabee River, near where the city of Peterborough, Ontario, now stands. It was the place where the family of Thomas Stewart had settled the previous year, and which Fanny Stewart described in the letters that had enticed Sydney to come to Canada in the first place. Sydney envisaged it as a little paradise where he could begin to make his fortune, on the way, perhaps, to greater things in the farther reaches of the Great Lakes.

In contrast with the tedious ocean voyage from Ireland, getting to Douro was an adventure in itself, and one that tells us a lot about the options available to the immigrant traveller in the 1820s. The desire of the British government to populate Upper Canada in the wake of the American Revolution, and the burgeoning lumber trade on the northern shores of Lake Ontario, provided the impetus for a few entrepreneurs and opportunists to supply various means of moving people and their belongings up the St. Lawrence to points beyond. Two hundred years earlier, Samuel de Champlain had visited Douro with his Huron allies, and if he had set out directly from Quebec in Huron canoes, he probably would have covered the 450 miles more quickly and with fewer complications.

Sydney and his cabin mate from the voyage across the Atlantic arranged to do the easy part—the trip to Montreal—by steamer. Steam navigation on the St. Lawrence was still in its early stages. John Molson's *Accommodation* was launched at Montreal in 1809 and is touted today as being the first steamer built entirely in North America, but it was more of a success as a novel topic of conversation than as a reliable means

of getting between Quebec and Montreal. Things had not improved that much by the summer of 1824, when Sydney and the surgeon spent three days with more than 400 other passengers aboard Molson's *New Swiftsure*, a smoky, wood-fired paddlewheeler, chugging slowly up the river, taking on cords of wood at Trois-Rivières or running aground on a mud bank in the shallow waters of Lake St. Pierre. Once freed, the *New Swiftsure*—which Sydney later described as being neither swift nor sure— was at least able to buck Saint Mary's Current where the river narrows on the approach to Montreal and get into the harbour while a cluster of sailing ships waited for an easterly wind to take them there. When he looked to starboard, his first view of Montreal as the steamer passed through the channel at Île Sainte-Hélène was John Molson's more enduring enterprise, the brewery. The harbour was then more of a muddy beach with a few simple wharves than a port facility.

The tightly packed stone buildings of the old town were clustered above the harbour with Mount Royal rising in the distance beyond the newer, rather ramshackle *faubourgs*, or suburbs, that had begun

to spread out from where the old fortifications had stood during the French regime. Looking in the other direction, from the harbour toward the southeast, the *Swiftsure*'s passengers could make out the other Monteregian Hills that popped up here and there from the otherwise flat, broad agricultural plain that Montrealers called "the South Shore." The name reflected the fact that the town, with scarcely more than 20,000 inhabitants, occupied only a small part of a very large island, one nearly ten times the size of Manhattan, in an archipelago surrounded by the waters of the St. Lawrence and Ottawa Rivers. The North Shore was on the other side, with another band of rich agricultural land separating it from the mountains of the central part of the same Laurentian Range that Sydney had seen at Quebec a few days earlier.

That first night in Montreal was spent at Mrs. Connelly's Hotel, a few blocks up from the harbour

3. The trip from Montreal to Lachine by stage, and from Lachine to Pointe des Cascades aboard the Perseverance *, from a map by Walton and Gaylord, 1835, LAC, MIKAN 4127087*

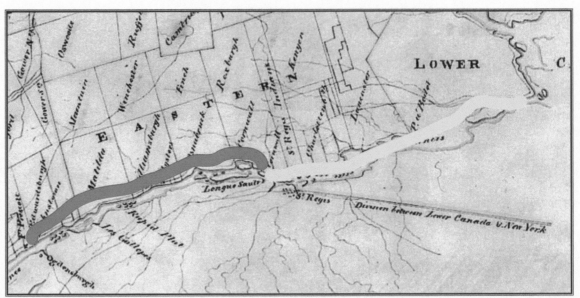

4. The journey from Pointe des Cascades to Prescott, from A Map of the Eastern Part of the Province of Upper Canada 1818, by Robert Pilkington, LAC, MIKAN 4129220

on St. François-Xavier Street, and not far from where Sydney Bellingham, barrister and solicitor, would hang his shingle after his admission to the Bar sixteen years later. Like many of the places Sydney found in Canada, Connelly's Hotel greeted him with the familiar sound of an Irish brogue.

The next morning, Sydney and the surgeon—who was on his way to see the wonder of the world at Niagara Falls—headed out by coach to Lachine, where they could resume travelling by water. It would be two more years before the completion of the Lachine Canal enabled steam-powered vessels to bypass the eight miles of rapids separating the harbour of Montreal

from the calmer waters of Lake St. Louis. This was the first of several canals on the St. Lawrence and on the Ottawa that would owe their existence largely to labour recruited from Ireland. Sydney and the surgeon covered the distance to Lachine in a nine-passenger stage, drawn over bumpy roads by a team of four horses. Sydney recalled in his memoirs driving through what was then bucolic farmland, but which today is mostly asphalt and concrete.

It is at this point in his memoirs that Sydney mentions his baggage. It seems that he had a lot of it, which necessitated arrangements with a freight forwarder to cart it separately, and not on the stage.

This is the first hint we get that his father had been able to equip the young adventurer with a fair amount of clothing and footwear, not to mention a gun. It deserves mention that he received a warning never to be separated from his baggage, and that this was one piece of advice he neglected to follow.

Arriving at Lachine, Sydney and the surgeon boarded the *Perseverance*, a small steamer, that took them about sixteen miles across Lake St. Louis to the next stretch of rough water on the St. Lawrence at Pointe des Cascades. On board the steamer they were entertained with historical narratives of events that had occurred nearby during the War of 1812. The narrator was a well-dressed Montreal lawyer who claimed to have been a volunteer in a militia battalion known as the Devil's Own. If true, we should mention that the 5th Battalion, Select Embodied Militia, got its nickname, not from prowess in battle, of which it saw very little, but

5. Durham Boats on the Rideau, c. 1838, watercolour by Philip John Bainbrigge, LAC, MIKAN 2896135

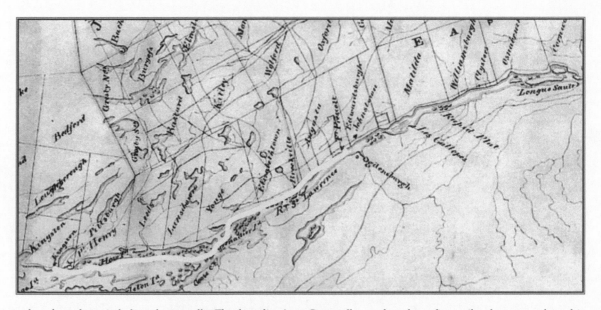

5. The journey from Prescott to Kingston, from A Map of the Eastern Part of the Province of Upper Canada 1818, by Robert Pilkington, LAC, MIKAN 4129220

rather from how it behaved generally. The battalion's one engagement was in a wilderness skirmish that later took on legendary proportions as "the Battle of the Châteauguay," during which Colonel Charles de Salaberry's 1,600 Canadians repelled an invasion by 4,000 badly led Americans intent on capturing Montreal. There is some speculation that events might have turned out differently if the American general, Wade Hampton, had not been drunk. Hampton's attempted invasion resulted in the loss of two Canadian lives. He resigned his commission shortly thereafter and returned to his plantation and 3,000 slaves in South Carolina.

From Pointe des Cascades, they travelled to Cornwall, another forty-five miles by water, but this time on board a flat-bottomed Durham boat that could be poled or hauled up the rapids where it could not be propelled by oars or sail. They could have covered the same distance by stagecoach; that they chose not to tells us something about how slow and uncomfortable travel by road must have been in 1824. Not that the ride up the Rapides des Cèdres was an easy cruise, with the boat bucking like an untamed horse, the spray from geysers of water hitting the rocks, and the shouts of the crew as they struggled to deal with the unpredictable current.

At Cornwall, they disembarked and travelled another fifty miles by stage to the head of navigation at

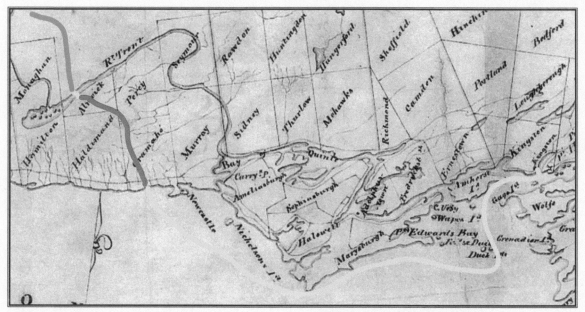

Prescott, bypassing the rapids of the Long Sault. On the way, they passed by farms and orchards that a century and a quarter later would vanish under the waters of the St. Lawrence Seaway. One of the passengers had lived in the area during the war and recounted how his mother had gone down to the riverbank to do some washing and a "cowardly Yankee" shot at her from the other side. The tale was the first of several explanations Sydney discovered for the animosity he found, particularly among Upper Canadians, for their American cousins.

Until this moment, Sydney had seen the Canadian forest only from a distance, and passing through it closely for the first time prompted a sense of awe in a young Irishman unaccustomed to the sight and smell of the giant pines and oaks through which the road penetrated like a tunnel.

At Prescott, they boarded a paddle steamer for the next 160 miles of their journey, to Cobourg, stopping first at Kingston to pick up passengers. It was the *Frontenac*, built near Kingston in 1816 and the first passenger steamer on Lake Ontario. Like the *Accommodation*, the *Frontenac* was a commercial failure. Sydney remarked in his memoirs that the ship had few passengers and attributed this to the expensive fares, but that it was

6. The journey from Kingston to Douro Township, from A Map of the Eastern Part of the Province of Upper Canada 1818, by Robert Pilkington, LAC, MIKAN 4129220

slower than a sailing ship must have also weighed in the balance.

The French had originally established Kingston in 1685 as Fort Frontenac, to guard the entrance to the St. Lawrence from Lake Ontario. During the War of 1812, it was one of the main bastions of defence against American attack, and the principal British naval base on the Great Lakes. When the *Frontenac* docked at Kingston with Sydney aboard, the town had a population of about 2,500 in addition to a sizable British garrison. Two years later, to avert the possibility of being cut off from Lower Canada by an American blockade of the St. Lawrence, the British began the construction of a canal linking the town to the Ottawa River, 120 miles to the north.

At Cobourg, Sydney and his travelling companion of many weeks parted company, the surgeon remaining on board the *Frontenac* to continue on to Niagara. It was here that Sydney's voyage by water, aboard five very different vessels, finally came to an end. For the next two years, Sydney Bellingham would travel mainly by foot. Cobourg lies at the midpoint of the north shore of Lake Ontario. It was originally a collection of small settlements clustered around a good harbour and a millstream, making it attractive to loyalist refugees from the American side of the lake in the aftermath of the Revolutionary War. One of those early settlements was called Hardscrabble, which tells us something about the plight of those who were forced to leave their farms and homes in the new United States. By 1824, Cobourg was still very much a frontier town serving as the jumping-off point for settlers north of the lake. The Stewarts had passed through Cobourg the previous year on their way to their new homestead in Douro Township, thirty-six miles inland. It was the first time in his life that Sydney had spent a night in a town not much older than he was.

It was at Cobourg that he planned to meet up with his baggage, but it had not yet arrived. He had made arrangements for it with the boss of the Durham boat outfit at Pointe des Cascades, a certain Finchley. In those days, freight forwarders and baggage handlers took their jobs seriously—their business depended on their reliability. Sydney could have waited a few days more before setting out for Douro, but being truly alone for the first time since he left Ireland, he resolved to make it on foot to the Stewarts' the next morning with only the clothes on his back, the purse of gold sovereigns his father had given him, and the packet of letters addressed to Mrs. Stewart by her relatives and friends in Ireland. There was a small general store in the little town that was the settlers' only local source for tools, clothing, seed supplies, and whatever food they could not produce on their own. The owner was James Gray Bethune, the son of a prominent loyalist clergyman. Bethune was well connected, through two of his brothers, with the Montreal mercantile scene. More than just a storekeeper, he served as the local

justice of the peace, postmaster, forwarding agent, and banker. The Stewarts had come to know Bethune well as a consequence of Thomas Stewart's being delayed in Cobourg by what they called "lake fever," a form of malaria encountered in that part of Upper Canada at the time. It was Bethune who arranged for Sydney to be taken the first few miles inland by wagon and who undertook to forward his baggage, if and when it arrived. Fanny Stewart had mentioned Bethune in her letters, which made Sydney think he could trust him enough to leave most of his gold sovereigns on deposit with him before setting out for Douro. As matters turned out, and contrary to what we might expect, it was a wise decision.

The first three miles of the wagon track inland from Cobourg were dotted with farms, but signs of settlement quickly faded as the track continued on through the forest. For the first time in Sydney's young

6. Cobourg, Upper Canada, in 1840 *watercolour by Philip John Bainbrigge, LAC, MIKAN 2836287*

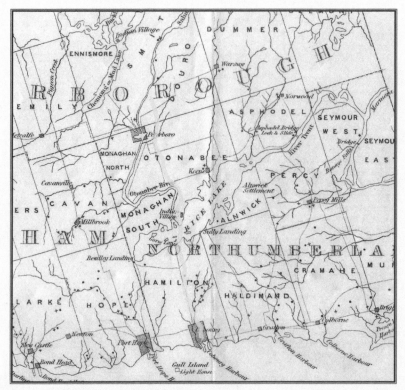

7. The route from Cobourg to Douro, from W. H. Smith's *Canada*: Past, Present and Future, *1851*

life, he was in a complete wilderness. The wagon soon came upon a tree that had fallen across the track, requiring the driver to dismount and clear it away with an axe. The fallen tree was a clear sign that no one else had recently ventured along the track. Twelve miles from Cobourg, they reached the shore of Rice Lake, a fairly shallow body of water twenty miles long and three miles wide, named for the vast quantities of wild rice harvested there by the Mississauga people. All this would change years later, when the water levels were raised to make the lake part of what became known as the Trent-Severn Waterway, a 240-mile link for small boats between Lake Ontario and Georgian Bay in Lake Huron.

On the shore of Rice Lake, they came to the only building for miles around, a log shanty serving as a

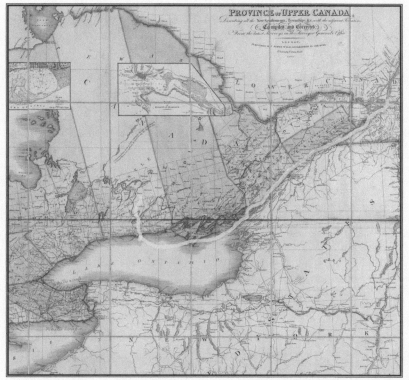

tavern owned by an American liquor merchant named Hulburt. Hulburt might be described either as an enterprising expatriate or as a fugitive from something or other. He agreed to row Sydney across the lake to Otonabee Township, and from there guide him five miles on foot along a path through the bush to the homestead of a certain Charles Rubidge. Rubidge had served in the Royal Navy under Horatio Nelson, had been wounded twice, and at the end of the Napoleonic Wars found himself laid off on half pay. He styled himself as "Captain" Rubidge, although he had never risen above the rank of lieutenant. His logic was that, had he been able to remain in the navy, he would by then have become a captain. Much later in life he applied the same logic to claim he would have reached the rank of admiral. From this, we would not be faulted

8. The journey from Montreal to Douro, from A Map of the Province of Upper Canada *1836, LAC, MIKAN 3722680*

for thinking that it was seniority, rather than merit, that mattered most in those days. Rubidge's situation must have been bad enough for him to take up the Crown's offer of 600 acres of free land in the dense pine forests of Otonabee, where he immigrated with his wife and three children in 1820. His naval experience helped him learn how to work with tools in building a log cabin and clearing the land, but Mrs. Rubidge must have found the new lifestyle rather more demanding than that of a naval officer's wife in the tea salons of Plymouth. Rubidge would later play an important role in the settlement of the area surrounding what is now the city of Peterborough, but he appears to have been a hard man, with no real empathy for the settlers themselves and the personal hardships they endured. In any event, his *laissez-faire* attitude regarding the well-being of the fifteen-year-old son of a fellow officer nearly brought an abrupt end to Sydney Bellingham's Canadian adventure, and his life.

At this point, having seen Cobourg and Rubidge's log cabin and having travelled through the forest on a dirt track in between, Sydney must have wondered what was in store for him at his journey's end, and whether it would fit the image in his dreams. If this was as good as it got for a man with a successful career as an officer in the Royal Navy, what would it be for Thomas Stewart, the son of a bankrupt Irish linen merchant?

In one of her letters to her friends in Ireland, Fanny Stewart had described Rubidge as their new friend,

so Sydney arrived at his door with at least that much by way of an introduction. Rubidge, without much enthusiasm, let him stay the night, fed him some bread and milk, and sent him on his way for the final fourteen miles through the bush to the Stewart farm. Rubidge apparently felt it was enough to tell Sydney that the trail was well "blazed," but Sydney had never heard the expression before and had no idea that it meant he had to carefully follow the axe marks on the trees. He later blamed his Irish pride for not asking. Shortly after setting out, he came to a watery swamp, and rather than wading across where the blaze marks showed the way, he tried to go around it to the right. Soon he was lost, travelling in circles, wandering farther and farther away from the trail. It was a hot July day. There were swarms of blackflies and mosquitoes. Both legs of his light cotton trousers were torn open in his struggle to wade through the swamp. He stumbled through patches of nettles and poison oak. He tried screaming for help, but there was no one to hear him for miles around. By nightfall, he was half crazy with panic and fatigue, crouching for shelter in the hollowed-out trunk of a giant burnt pine tree. Somehow he managed to lose a couple of the gold sovereigns he had kept with him upon his departure from Bethune's store. What little sleep he got was interrupted by the peculiar sounds of a porcupine. Before dawn, he was back on his feet, staggering around until the mid-afternoon, when by pure chance he found himself in the clearing of a small

homestead. It belonged to a Scottish Highland family called McIntyre.

Sydney's condition was not just hunger and exhaustion. His legs had multiple lacerations that, like the insect bites, became infected. It took him ten days in the care of the McIntyres to recover to the point where he was able to resume his trek. This time Donald McIntyre guided him. To rejoin the path to Douro, they turned westward towards Rubidge's log house, where they met up with him, and Rubidge was made to realize

7. The Stewarts' home in the forest, sketch by M. Haycock, from Our Forest Home, *by Frances Stewart, 1902*

the folly of letting the boy go into the bush alone.

That afternoon, still guided by McIntyre, Sydney caught his first glimpse of the Stewart homestead. To say that it was not what he had imagined would be an understatement. Perhaps he, or his father, would have been more circumspect about Fanny Stewart's cheerful musings about Upper Canada if they had known that in order to obtain title to his 1,200 acres of free land, Thomas Stewart would have to attract other settlers to Douro.

Located about three miles north of Otonabee Township, near the eastern bank of the river bearing the same name, a small clearing had been made and a log house built by hired labour less than a year and a half earlier. What Sydney saw as he approached from the forest was an area of about ten acres littered with the blackened stumps of trees and scarcely resembling anything that anyone in Ireland would call a field. The house was large but crudely built of logs of at least a foot in diameter, with the gaps between the logs chinked with wood chips and moss. There was a roof made of wood shingles and a stone fireplace. There was a large kitchen at one end and a bedroom and sitting room at the other. A ladder led to a loft above the main floor, the floor itself consisting of loose timber.

Thomas Stewart was thirty-eight. His wife, Frances, or Fanny, was thirty. His biography says that he had fallen on hard times when the textile firm he was a partner in went bankrupt, but Sydney gives us more detail in his memoirs. The fate of the firm resembled that of much of the Irish linen trade when the market for uniforms dried up at the end of the Napoleonic Wars. What Sydney adds is that its owner, Thomas's father, had died, leaving each of his sons a good inheritance, but Thomas's older brother, who was trustee, had gambled away both their fortunes. The story, according to Sydney, goes on to say that Fanny sold her jewels to finance their new life in Upper Canada and that she had a small annuity of £100 to sustain them over the years. Being partially crippled as the result of a childhood accident, Thomas walked with a cane and had to spend most of the annuity on hired labour rather than do much of the work himself like Rubidge. Sydney describes Stewart as a pleasant man but unsuited to homesteading in the bush.

He describes Fanny as charming, highly connected in Anglo-Irish society, and with refined tastes. Her new lot was not an easy one. After being deserted by the maid she had brought with her from Ireland, she had to acquire the frontier woman's skills of baking bread, washing clothes, and making soap and candles. One of her connections in Anglo-Irish society was with the Edgeworth family, and she may well have acquired a taste for writing from her much more famous friend, the novelist Maria Edgeworth. Another of her friends and frequent correspondents was Louisa Beaufort, also an author. In 1889, Fanny's letters to family and friends in Ireland were published in the book *Our Forest Home*. They reveal an articulate, educated woman of culture, but one who was also strong and persevering. She appears to have been sustained in the ordeal of homesteading not just by a strong religious faith, but also by her exchanges of letters with the Old Country—those exchanges sometimes taking as much as six months to make the journey both ways. One of her great delights was to receive each year, thanks to Bethune's forwarding arrangements, a shipment from Ireland of the sort of refined things she could never procure on the frontier. In July 1824, one such shipment accompanied Sydney, albeit delayed on the last stretch when his baggage went astray. As for Sydney, she described him as "fine, lively, good-tempered, very manly, and at the same time boyish and merry."

Stewart had gone first to York (now Toronto), which served as the seat of colonial government, to secure a grant of 1,200 acres and another grant of 1,500 acres for his brother-in-law Robert Reid. Fanny's connections in the Anglo-Irish establishment provided letters of introduction to the lieutenant governor that made things go smoothly under the "Family Compact" system, which favoured "people of quality," and in many respects was modelled on the Protestant Ascendancy that controlled economic, political, and social life in Ireland. But there were strings attached. Stewart and Reid could only obtain full title to the land on the condition that they induce relatives and friends of similar "quality" to settle near them. That reality may have influenced the tone of Fanny's letters home, which were far more cheerful than actual circumstances would have dictated. She was perhaps more objective in her description of York, which although she was well received there, she described as "not a pleasant place." It was after Sydney came to Douro that Fanny's letters began to reflect reality, feelings of loneliness, and even thoughts of returning to Ireland.

The farm consisted of a small plot that had been cleared by hand and surrounded by a split-rail fence. The ground was still full of tree roots, making it impossible to use a plough. There were two cows and some pigs, which foraged for wild leeks in the surrounding woods. The meals consisted mostly of porridge, pea soup, and dried pork, supplemented by the occasional partridge from the forest or fish caught in the stream. There was also venison obtained through barter with the Indians. There was no post office, no clergyman, and no doctor for forty miles. The previous year, the Stewarts' youngest daughter, Bessie, had come down with dysentery attributed to eating uncooked corn. Donald McIntyre, then working for the Stewarts, volunteered to fetch a doctor from Cavan on the other side of the Otonabee, but when the doctor arrived four days later, it was too late. Whether he could have done anything for the child is doubtful in any event. A few weeks later, Fanny gave birth to another daughter, the first white child born in Douro.

After surviving for weeks with his clothes in tatters and shoeless, Sydney was finally reunited with his baggage, which says something about the ability of Bethune to take care of things. The thicker clothing was especially appreciated in the evenings, not just to fend off the chill, but as some protection from the swarms of mosquitoes, blackflies, and sandflies that managed to evade the smudge pots that were kept burning around the house.

One of Sydney's chores during his time with the Stewarts was to retrieve a cow or pig that had wandered too far into the woods. One day, hearing the squeals of a pig just outside the fenced enclosure, he found it in the clutches of a bear. He drove the bear off with a stout tree branch and ran back to the house to retrieve the double-barrelled carbine that had arrived in his baggage. Setting out in search of the bear with Cartouche, the family dog, he was surprised when the bear found him first—or rather found the dog— whose life was spared when Sydney let the bear have both barrels from twenty paces. He thought he had missed, since the bear ran off to the banks of the Otonabee and swam to the other side. A few days later, he learned that a farmer had found the bear's rotting carcass. In addition to bears, the feeling that the forest contained danger was reinforced at night by the howling of wolves.

With the coming of winter, work on the Stewart farm shifted to the forest, and Sydney prided himself on becoming an expert axeman. They made firewood and potash from the birch and maples, and shingles from the cedars. Robert Reid had arrived earlier at Douro, and being far more suited to the frontier life, was better able than Stewart to teach Sydney the skills of the homesteader.

One thing we learn about Sydney through his account of life in the backwoods is that, although he left Ireland when he was only fifteen, he came to Canada with more education than most of the people he met in Douro. We do not learn exactly where he acquired it, but we do know that it was good enough to make young Sydney Bellingham the go-to man when the community needed someone with an education. In early 1825, he was dispatched to the western side of the river to canvass the more settled Townships of Cavan and Monaghan for signatures on a petition for the construction of a bridge. The experience gained in the process served Sydney Bellingham, Esq., well many years later when he was canvassing the backcountry of Argenteuil County for votes for a seat in the Canadian Parliament or the Quebec Assembly.

Something revealing of both his nature and his education is to be found in a poem he wrote in 1829 to mark the anniversary of little Bessie's passing:

ELEGY ON LITTLE BESSY STEWART

No marble marks thy lowly grave,
    No stone thy modest tomb,
But hemlock wild o'er thee doth wave,
    With branch of sombre gloom.
Soft is thy slumber, infant child,
    And still thy tranquil sleep;
Unheard by thee the tempest wild
    That o'er thy tomb may sweep.
What though the soil unhallowed be,
    That marks thy sad decay,
Thy sleep is soft beneath these trees,
    On shady "Hemlock Brae."
Stranger, if there thou chance to stray,
    To Bessy's tomb draw near,
Awhile thy wondering footsteps stay,
    Nor check the rising tear.

S. R. Bellingham

Another learning experience—likewise one he might not have had were it not for his education—was as a chain bearer during the survey of settlement lands conducted in the area in the winter of 1824–25. A chain bearer was a surveyor's assistant, or apprentice. The job involved trekking through the townships on snowshoes and sheltering for the night in temporary huts made of branches, but it paid the princely sum of a dollar a day, plus rations, for nearly three months. The survey was part of a grand scheme by the British government to bring a large number of impoverished Irish settlers into the area around Scott's Mills, under the leadership of Colonel Peter Robinson. Robinson was a New Brunswick-born veteran of the War of 1812, a successful York businessman, and a member of the Legislative Assembly of Upper Canada. Earlier immigration policies had been designed to fill a population vacuum and to occupy land mainly to secure it from the threat of further American aggression after the events of 1812 to 1815. This one was engineered in reverse—relieving the pressures of overpopulation in Ireland, now seething with the threat of insurgency. Whether or not it was a success from the perspective of the British government, it was successful enough from the local perspective to result in the renaming of Scott's Mills as Peterborough, in honour of Peter Robinson. The honour appears to have been well deserved. Sydney described him as "a thoroughly competent officer, of agreeable manners and thoroughly familiar with bush life and the colonizing of Crown Land." Thirty years later, when he set out to colonize Arundel Township in Lower Canada, the exact same description could have been accurately applied to Sydney Bellingham.

The influx of so many settlers around Peterborough created a boom for people like James Bethune, Thomas Stewart, and Charles Rubidge, but it also caused problems. Particularly in the townships west of the Otonabee, settled mainly by Protestant Orangemen who were forced to pay their own way, the arrival of a large number of impoverished Irish Catholics, with their expenses paid by the government, was not a recipe for friendly relations over the next few decades.

When they obtained their grants in 1822, Thomas Stewart and Robert Reid were promised some sort of control over settlement in the region, and as part of the government-sponsored immigration program in 1825, they were persuaded to relinquish that control to Robinson. As a reward, they were each given land in the new townsite, and Sydney received half an acre in what today would be the centre of Peterborough. Sydney's parcel went unattended after he left Douro for Lower Canada, and when he returned three years later, he found that the Crown Land agent had expunged his name from the register. That is not surprising, given that Sydney could not validly obtain Crown Land until he was twenty-one. In 1830, although by then living in Montreal, he obtained a grant of 400 acres in Douro.

Thirty years after his involvement as a surveyor's apprentice as part of Peter Robinson's grand settlement program at Peterborough, Sydney would embark on his own settlement program, but on a smaller scale, in the Townships of Arundel, Montcalm, Wentworth, and De Salaberry in Lower Canada.

Early in March of 1826, an enterprising Sydney Bellingham undertook his first commercial endeavour—making maple sugar—which helped replenish his dwindling supply of cash. He began the summer once again assisting Colonel Robinson's settlement measures and exploring. One of his later recollections, perhaps because it was so unexpected in what was still mostly wilderness, was meeting a gang of workers making charcoal for the short-lived smelting operation east of Douro at Marmora. The Marmora smelter began as a source of pig iron, to be used as ballast for navy ships on the Great Lakes, but floundered when the threat of war with the United States diminished. Many years later, Sydney sponsored a bill in the Canadian Parliament in support of the revival of the ironworks.

Later that summer, he expanded his horizons with what he later called a walking tour—first back down to Cobourg, and from there another seventy-five miles to York. About a fifth of the distance to York was on corduroy roads, which were muddy, swampy tracks surfaced with logs on account of the poor drainage and primitive construction. That helps explain why until the arrival of the railway in the late 1850s, travel by boat on Lake Ontario remained the preferred way of getting to Toronto.

At York, Sydney called upon the Honourable James Baby (born Jacques Bâby, pronounced *Bah-bee*), a powerful politician and landowner of old *Canadien* stock and a member of the "Family Compact," which effectively ruled Upper Canada at that point in time. One might wonder how a young backpacker, not quite eighteen years old, could be so bold. It is here that it might be helpful to examine Sydney Bellingham's pedigree in more detail.[3]

Sydney's father, Alan Bellingham, was for a very short time the second baronet of Castlebellingham. Sir Alan succeeded to the title when Sir William Bellingham, his uncle, died without heirs in 1826. The baronetcy had been created in 1796 as a reward for William's service, first as private secretary to Prime Minister William Pitt the Younger and then as a senior bureaucrat on the administrative side of the Royal Navy. His prominence was such that in 1792, Captain James Vancouver, while exploring the Pacific coast of North America, gave his name to the bay where the city of Bellingham, Washington, is located today. Sir William had another nephew who, like Sydney's father, was also called Alan. In 1795, this other Alan Bellingham was a lieutenant in the 24th Regiment of Foot at Detroit, then still part of British North America. In that year, he married Monique Bâby, one of Jacques Bâby's numerous siblings, then only sixteen years old. The following year, the British finally surrendered Detroit, as well as the aspirations of their Indian allies, to the Americans. The new couple moved first to Montreal and then to Quebec. In 1801, Alan Bellingham, who by then had been promoted to captain, returned to take up

residence at Castlebellingham, where he had inherited the estate upon the death of his father, Colonel Henry Bellingham. Monique later joined him there with their three young children, including William, their only son, who was born earlier that year. Alan, who by all accounts had always been a bit of a rogue, abandoned Monique in 1815 and moved to London, where he died in 1821, making young William the presumptive heir to the baronetcy. Litigation then ensued between Monique and Sir William over her late husband's estate. Struggling financially, Monique eventually settled her dispute with Sir William and moved to Lyme Regis, the resort town on the southwest coast of England that figures in the novels of Jane Austen. She never saw Canada or her brother Jacques again. Thus, by this convoluted route, Sydney was related by marriage to Jacques Bâby, but whether the Bellingham name evoked feelings of warmth and welcome in Bâby's heart remains another point on which Sydney's memoirs are silent. Philippe-Bâby Casgrain, writing in 1888, mentions that a young Bellingham, whom he presumed to be Sydney, tracked down Monique in 1830.[4] Equipped with a letter of introduction, this young Bellingham asked to marry the eldest of her surviving daughters, also named Monique, but as we shall see later, the overture was declined. Sydney's memoirs mention trips to Ireland,

---

3   See the genealogical tables at the end of this book. That there is at least one Alan Bellingham in each of the seven generations does not make it easy to discern who's who.

4   Philippe-Bâby Casgrain, Mémorial des Familles Casgrain, Bâby et Perrault du Canada. Quebec City: C. Darveau, 1898–99, 124.

Scotland, and England in 1829 and 1830, but perhaps in deference to Arabella, there is no mention of having visited Monique at that time.

He continued his walking tour as far as Niagara Falls, stopping overnight at farms along the way. He remarked later on the warm hospitality of the farmers and their families, who would accept no payment for his room and board and who were happy to see a stranger and get whatever news he could bring them. At the falls, he stayed in the newly constructed Pavilion Hotel, a large, clapboard structure, recalling later that the window of his room vibrated from the concussion of the cataract. The Pavilion was the jewel in the crown of a notorious Niagara huckster, William Forsyth, renowned for creating Canada's first genuine tourist trap and whose reputation is so drenched in rumour and innuendo regarding all kinds of activities and events that he might well have been a prototype for fictional characters in the same field of enterprise in twentieth-century Atlantic City or Las Vegas. The Pavilion burnt to the ground in 1839, recalling the fate of a competitor's hotel a few years earlier on a night when, strangely, Forsyth's son had taken a room there.

That autumn a chance encounter occurred that would shortly bring Sydney's sojourn in Upper Canada to an end and redefine his career plans. One morning he heard a voice calling out from the opposite side of the Otonabee and went down to see who it was. A well-dressed man shouted a request to be conveyed across the river. Sydney obliged by fetching him in a crude canoe that he had fashioned out of a large, half-burnt cedar log. The man had come all the way from Quebec at the request of a legal firm in Ireland, bearing a deed that required Thomas Stewart's signature. Sydney paddled him back across the river as soon as the paperwork was completed, but before he went on his way, the stranger told him that if he came to Quebec the following spring, he would give him a job. His name was James Hamilton, and he was a Quebec timber merchant active in the flourishing lumber trade. They shook hands on the deal, and Sydney left Upper Canada in May 1827 to take Hamilton up on his offer. The original plan to pursue his fortune farther west was forgotten, and Lower Canada would become his home for the next forty-seven years.

The short time Sydney spent with the Stewarts in Douro equipped him with the self-assurance and resilience he would need in his future business endeavours, and it fostered the development of an independent mind that would later reflect itself in his activities as a journalist and as a politician. This chapter in his young life would also prepare him for the events of 1837 and 1838, when he would have to show courage in the face of real danger.

Before we leave Douro, a few words would be appropriate about those whom Sydney left behind. Thomas Stewart and Charles Rubidge both received appointments as justices of the peace. They remained active in settlement projects in the Peterborough area, and Rubidge became the land registrar for the county. Stewart became recognized as a community leader and was named to the Legislative Council of Upper Canada in 1833. By the end of 1842, a frame house finally replaced the log cabin. At long last, he had obtained the relative prosperity and status that had been his goals in first coming to Canada. But he did not live to enjoy them for very long. Thomas died prematurely in 1847—one of more than 20,000 victims of the typhus epidemic that began that year among the emigrants fleeing the potato famine in Ireland and that spread as far as Peterborough. Fanny Stewart died in 1872 but lives on in her letters, which remain the object of historical analysis to this day. James Gray Bethune expanded his commercial and banking activities throughout Northumberland County but went bankrupt in 1834 and removed himself to Rochester, New York, on the opposite side of Lake Ontario, where he died a few years later. We will hear about his more successful brother, the Reverend John Bethune, in a later chapter.

*8. Timber cove at Quebec, drawing by W. H. Bartlett, from
Canadian Scenery, by N. P. Willis and W. H. Bartlett, 1842*

CHAPTER 3

RETURN TO LOWER CANADA

*I*N THE SPRING OF **1827,** SYDNEY BADE FAREWELL TO THE Stewarts and his Highlander friend Donald McIntyre and set out on foot to Cobourg. There he boarded a steamer for Kingston, and from there he continued downriver in a Durham boat carrying a cargo of a hundred barrels of flour to Montreal. The boat had what passed for a passenger cabin in the stern, entered by a trapdoor in the deck, and left in total darkness once the trapdoor was closed. It was equipped with two bunks, which passengers were expected to share. To his astonishment, the three other passengers turned out to be a woman and her two young daughters who were fleeing the violent abuse of a sergeant in the Kingston garrison. It was a peculiarly awkward situation, but Sydney prided himself on his good behaviour. Eventually, they arrived at Montreal, where Sydney took deck passage on a steamer bound for Quebec. The night was very cold, and on this occasion only the engines provided him with warmth.

Arriving at Quebec, Sydney was cordially received by his new boss at the offices of James Hamilton & Co., and given a room with bed and board on the floor above.

His tasks were essentially those of an office boy and runner at a meagre salary of £20 a year.

During the shipping season, between ten and twenty ships arrived each day, most of them departing within a few days with a cargo of timber. Many of them arrived with a cargo of settlers, like Sydney's ship in 1824. Some ships arrived in ballast, which occasionally was coal. As a result, the price of Newcastle coal at Quebec was lower than it was in London. Some days the departures included ships newly built at Quebec, with crews scrounged by recruiters called "crimps" who often pocketed most of the seamen's wages. The link between the transportation needs of the lumber trade and Quebec's thriving shipbuilding industry can be seen in Sydney's recollections of the *Baron of Renfrew*, a gigantic vessel built for the sole purpose of a single voyage so that it could be broken up upon arrival and its timbers sold along with the cargo. In effect, the *Baron of Renfrew* was a tax-avoidance scheme since, unlike the cargo, a ship's timbers entered port tax-free. The scheme failed when the unwieldy ship broke up prematurely before reaching London.

Sydney's memoirs reflect the impact that early unionization two decades later had on the business of the port of Quebec. The Ship Labourers' Benevolent Society, whose members were mostly Irish stevedores, used intimidation to drive out any *Canadien* labourers prepared to work for less, and saw to it that ships' crews were no longer allowed to assist in the loading and unloading of cargo. As a result, and encouraged by the deepening of the channel near Montreal in the 1850s, many shipowners chose to load their lumber cargoes there instead.

The business of James Hamilton & Co. involved matching orders that arrived from England and other European countries with the timber that was floated down in rafts from as far away as Lake Ontario and the upper reaches of the Ottawa River. Both shores of the St. Lawrence at Quebec were dotted with coves where the rafts were secured, allowing for inspection and measurement in a process called "culling." In these earlier days, most of the exported wood was only roughly finished, laboriously (and wastefully) fashioned into squared timber by hand axe. Some of the pinewood, however, was sawn into standard-sized planks, or "deals." Oak barrel staves were another product handled by the Hamilton firm.

Fanny Stewart's network of well-positioned Anglo-Irish friends included members of the garrison at Quebec, where Sydney stayed during an illness as a guest of Colonel Colley Lyons Lucas Foster. The description of Sydney's condition suggests he likely had malaria, the "lake fever" that had delayed Thomas Stewart's arrival in Douro. Sydney recalled evenings on the balcony of Foster's residence beside the Château St. Louis, listening to mildly embellished tales of military adventures on the Niagara frontier. Foster had become acquainted with Tecumseh, the Shawnee chief whose Indian confederacy made him a powerful ally of the British in 1812. Another of the favourite stories was how, in 1813 at the Battle of Stoney Creek, Lieutenant James FitzGibbon, with a company of only forty-seven men, tricked an American colonel into surrendering himself and his 462 troops. There was apparently no mention that FitzGibbon was able to surprise the American force as a result of the behind-enemy-lines actions of a local farmer's wife. Today, few Canadians are familiar with James FitzGibbon's name, but everyone has heard of Laura Secord.

Both from the events recounted in his memoirs and the reminiscences of others, the picture we get of the young Sydney Bellingham is that of an amiable, outgoing youth who made friends easily and knew how to deal with strangers. But it was at Quebec where he would face—probably not for the first time and certainly not the last—the hostility of a stranger, purely on account of his name. The occasion was his first visit to the imposing customs house to sign for a shipment of goods. Here

Stone by Sproule from an Original by W. S. Sewell.

for Hawkins' Picture of Queb[ec]

he encountered the evident hostility and glares of the collector of customs, Michael Perceval, a member of Quebec's powerful "Château Clique." Later, Sydney learned that this unpleasant individual was the brother of the late Spencer Perceval, who was Prime Minister of Great Britain from 1809 until his death. On May 11, 1812, Perceval was shot and killed in the lobby of the House of Commons by a disgruntled London merchant, John Bellingham (no relation). Many years later, Sydney would have to shrug off the buffoonery of a political opponent who routinely tried to implicate Sydney's family in the assassination of the British prime minister.

9. Château St. Louis, sketch by W. S. Sewell, from Picture of Quebec, *by Alfred Hawkins, 1834*

Towards the end of the summer in 1827, Sydney learned of the death of his father. The news came to him from a friend who had seen a newspaper notice. Sir Alan Bellingham died in Châtillon-sur-Loire in central France on August 26, 1827. It was rumoured he had gone there to escape his creditors. Only ten months earlier, he had inherited the title of baronet upon the death of his uncle, Sir William. Through Alan's death, Sydney's eldest brother, Alan Edward, became the third baronet. As the oldest male in the line of succession, Alan Jr. inherited the Bellingham estate under the rules of primogeniture. Since Alan Sr. had died intestate, it seems he left nothing to Sydney. The Bellingham family estate was recorded as including 4,186 acres in County Louth worth £4,291 a year, and if this passed from Sir William to Alan Sr., he would have had very little time to enjoy it before it landed in Alan Jr.'s lap ten months later. It is clear from Sydney's memoirs that he was very attached to his father, who had written him a short time before his death. Later in life, it was Sydney who arranged to acquire his father's gravesite in perpetuity, and in his will endowed the Protestant cemetery at Châtillon-sur-Loire with the sum of $1,000 for its continued maintenance.

An unexplained falling-out with Hamilton led to Sydney's spending the winter of 1827–28 as a boarder with the Gariépy family at L'Ange-Gardien, twelve miles downriver from Quebec. Two of his other family contacts at Quebec, the de Salaberry sisters, had sent him there. Their nephew was Colonel de Salaberry of Châteauguay fame, and they were related to Sydney through the Bâby connection. His stay with the Gariépys on their ancestral farm fronting on the St. Lawrence helped him adapt his English-tutored French to the different *Canadien* dialect, and it served to anchor the respect for French Canadians often reflected in his memoirs. During that time, through the prodding of a friend studying to become an Anglican priest, he flirted with the same career path. He spent the winter months studying Greek and Latin and passed an examination in the Greek testament under the approving eye of a future bishop, the Reverend George Jehoshaphat Mountain.

Before he could move on to the next step in that process, a conciliatory letter from James Hamilton arrived in April, and Sydney was once again back in the business world. That he briefly entertained becoming a clergyman is intriguing. The opportunities that calling offered for earning a secure living and gaining a respected position in society seem to have inspired the idea. Not once in his memoirs is there a reference to anything that would suggest he was a very religious man.

Hamilton's business had been growing rapidly, and Sydney was soon promoted from office boy to bookkeeper. Later in 1828, Hamilton sent him to open an office in Montreal. It is remarkable that a young man, still a year shy of his twenty-first birthday, would be entrusted with that responsibility from such a distance. Montreal was doing well commercially. John Molson's St. Lawrence Steamboat Company was increasing the flow

of goods and passengers, not just aboard its own vessels, but also by providing steam tug services to the sailing ships that still dominated trade. Those ships no longer had to wait for an easterly gale to get them past Saint Mary's Current and into the harbour. The new Montreal office dealt principally in the trading of bills of exchange and the purchase of potash and its more refined relative, pearl ash. Potash was at that time the settler's biggest, if not only, cash crop. It was produced by burning the hardwood trees cut down in clearing the land for farming and leaching the potassium carbonate out of the ashes. One acre of birch or maple could yield as much

10. Montreal Viewed from Mount Royal, *watercolour by T. Mower Martin, from* Canada, *by T. Mower Martin and Wilfred Campbell, 1906*

11. Hugh Allan's Ravenscrag, photograph by William Notman, McCord Museum, 4867, with permission

as $5, or the equivalent of the cost of hiring labour to do the clearing. Barrels of potash were sent down the St. Lawrence and the Ottawa to Montreal or Quebec, with most of it ending up in England where it was used in the textile, glassmaking, and porcelain industries.

Sydney turned twenty-one on August 2, 1829. It was then that he decided to set up his own business as a merchant at Montreal. In November, he sailed for Ireland on the *John Porter*—a fast, sturdy vessel owned by James Hamilton, which two weeks earlier had become the first ship to complete three round trips in a single season. Despite nearly foundering in a mid-Atlantic gale, it reached Dublin safely, and Sydney embarked on a tour of Ireland, Scotland, and England on the first of three business-development trips over the next few years. When he returned to Quebec, Sydney repeated what he had done on the occasion of his first arrival. He paid a visit to his father's old friend, Dr. Holmes. Not much had changed with Holmes, except that in 1827 his daughter Arabella had married one of Holmes's pupils, a young Dr. William Larue. Sydney undertook a second trip in November 1830, this time travelling directly to Scotland aboard the *Sophia*. He was shepherding the investment of his entire capital in a cargo of potash for sale at Glasgow, but it seems he may have been scouting for more than just business. He makes no mention of a side trip in his memoirs, but we know from another source that he continued on to Lyme Regis, the seaside town on the south coast of England where Monique Bâby

Bellingham had retreated with her daughters after being abandoned by her husband, Alan, at Castlebellingham. Armed with a letter of reference and the pretext of his visit in the summer of 1826 with Monique's brother at York, he wasted no time in asking permission to marry her daughter, whose name was also Monique. The request was denied. From a purely business perspective, as we shall see, it was a good outcome.

The spring of 1831 saw Sydney's new business expanding. His office was in the same courtyard as that of Adam Macnider, a prominent Montreal merchant. Macnider was a first cousin of Arabella Holmes. After less than three years together, Dr. Larue had died, and the young widow was staying with her cousin. As Sydney later put it, their "acquaintance grew into something more than friendship," and on October 28 they were married. They would remain together until Arabella died in 1887.

For the third November in a row, Sydney sailed for the Old Country, this time in the company of his new wife. They were aboard the *Canada*, a fine ship under the command of Captain Alexander Allan with his three sons acting as mates. The third mate, a young Hugh Allan, was destined to become one of the richest men in North America and the head of the world's largest shipping line. The mansion he built in 1863 on the upper slope of Mount Royal, with a splendid view of the city, the river, and farmlands on the South Shore, still stands as a monument to the days when Montreal was the centre of Canadian trade and commerce. Sydney and

Arabella spent the end of 1831 in Glasgow, long enough to explore the business opportunities, one of which led to a partnership with James Wallis, the young nephew of a Glasgow merchant. The firm of Bellingham & Wallis lasted for only a few years, but as we will see shortly, lives on in the case reports of the Judicial Committee of the Privy Council. Before we get to that story, however, there is more to be told about the extended honeymoon, which continued on through the west of Scotland and England, then to London, and back to Lyme Regis for another visit to Monique Bâby Bellingham. We do not know if Sydney had shared with Arabella the purpose of his previous visit.

The spring of 1832 found the young couple in Dublin, where they visited Sydney's brother O'Brien, a physician. In July, they visited the "Castle" manor house, where his great-aunt Lady Hester Bellingham entertained them. Hester was the childless widow of the first baronet, Sir William Bellingham, who had died in 1826, having acquired the estate from Monique Bâby following the death in 1821 of her estranged husband. Born Hester Frances Cholmondeley (pronounced *Chumley*), she was the great-granddaughter of Sir Robert Walpole, the first prime minister of Great Britain. Sydney described Hester as "very clever, full of humour and polished." His memoirs recount a grand dinner party at the Castle, hosted by the witty and headstrong dowager, during which his cousin Fanny Bellingham announced that she had taken the total abstinence pledge promoted by a radical temperance society known as Father Matthew's Knights of Temperance. Hester responded with, "I am very sorry, my dear Fanny, that you have been obliged to do so." If Julian Fellowes had scripted this story, central casting at the BBC would have picked Maggie Smith to play the part of Hester.

Hester may well have been the dominant presence at the Castle, but it was Sydney's oldest brother, Alan Edward, who sat at the head of the table. Alan Jr. had become the third baronet upon the death of their father, Alan Sr., in 1827. Neither would have succeeded to the baronetcy had it not been for the untimely death in 1822 of Monique's only son, William, while serving as a naval midshipman at the Cape of Good Hope. But there was yet another William—Sydney's younger brother—living at the Castle with his uncle and great-aunt. Sydney was only twenty-three, but he must have appeared sufficiently well established for Alan to suggest that William, then twelve years old, return to Canada as Sydney's ward. For the next five or six years, it would be Sydney and Arabella who took on the responsibility for feeding, clothing, and educating young William.

With William in tow, Sydney and Arabella returned to Quebec aboard the *Canada*, arriving on September 26. Four days earlier, the *Canada* had anchored at Grosse Isle for inspection of the passengers. The Grosse Isle quarantine station had been set up only a few weeks earlier to deal with a severe cholera outbreak that had spread like a firestorm since June, and that the local

population attributed to the arrival of impoverished immigrants from Ireland and Britain. By the end of the year, the epidemic would claim nearly 5,000 lives in Lower Canada alone and become one of the grievances against the colonial administration that would lead to civil unrest, which erupted into rebellion five years later.

Possibly because it felt safer, Arabella stayed with her parents in the Upper Town, while Sydney continued on to Montreal on board the steamer *Chambly*. Before he reached his destination, the passenger who occupied the lower berth in his cabin died of cholera. Had Sydney subscribed to the generally accepted view that breathing

12. Notre Dame Street and Church, *watercolour, by John Murray, LAC, MIKAN 2836035*

13. Papineau's house
on Bonsecours Street,
photograph by the author

stale air spread the disease, he must have felt lucky. On the other hand, he may simply have been a stickler for personal hygiene and averse to drinking water, the real source of contagion.

With the import/export business of Bellingham & Wallis prospering, the next couple of years were good ones. Montreal was coming into its own as the inland gateway to British North America, its future growth assured by its position at the hub of a large, fertile plain capable of supporting a population that would soon surpass Quebec's. Sydney and Arabella, with young William, moved into a rented house on St. James Street, which with the adjacent Notre Dame Street, was the prime real estate in town. Both streets ran parallel to the harbourfront, but some distance away on a spur of higher ground that was out of reach of floodwaters when the river overflowed its banks in the spring. The two streets sported some fine stone buildings at a time when many of the surrounding neighbourhoods still had structures of wood. Notre Dame Street was the site of a magnificent new Roman Catholic church bearing the same name, built in the Gothic Revival style, as well as the Anglican Christ Church Cathedral, the city hall, the courthouse, and Château Ramezay, the official residence of the governor under both the French and British regimes. Notre Dame, with its capacity of 8,000 parishioners, was then the largest church north of Mexico, dwarfing St. Jacques Cathedral on St. Denis Street. It stood as a subtle reminder that its owners, the Sulpician Order, held more sway over ecclesiastical affairs in Montreal than did the official diocesan hierarchy. For some years, Montrealers referred to Notre Dame Church as the "Cathedral," and the St. Jacques Cathedral as the "Bishop's Church."

Below Notre Dame Street, closer to the harbour, ran the older and narrower St. Paul Street, crowded with warehouses and buildings that served both as the shops and residences of an expanding merchant and artisanal class. The harbour itself now looked like a proper port facility, with ships tied up at large cut-stone wharves

rather than off-loaded at anchor by barges. Like St. Paul, Notre Dame, and St. James, the intersecting side streets running up from the harbour were paved in stone, providing the visitor with further evidence that Montreal was more than an upstart frontier town. At night, the streets of this part of town were lit, albeit dimly, by oil lamps and patrolled by a night watch.

Trouble was brewing, however. The lack of effective representative government, and even the absence of a fair share in the British-dominated ruling oligarchy known as the Château Clique, was pushing leaders of the French-speaking majority of Lower Canada's population towards confrontation with the colonial administration. Farmers toiling under the semi-feudal system of the seigneuries felt increasingly oppressed as absentee landlords raised their rents. The same issue was developing, without the linguistic divide, in Upper Canada, where the Family Compact held sway and settlers felt disadvantaged in the allocation of Crown Lands. The ravages of cholera in 1832 added fuel to the fire. The epidemic took 4,000 lives in Montreal from a population of less than 30,000 and struck again in 1834. In a spring by-election in 1832, a riot broke out during the polling at Place d'Armes, and three *Canadien* voters were killed on St. James Street when a magistrate summoned troops from the garrison to restore order. It was an act of unnecessary suppression that would set the tone for what was to follow. Ironically, two days later, the victorious candidate died of cholera.

It was in this climate of unrest that Sydney made

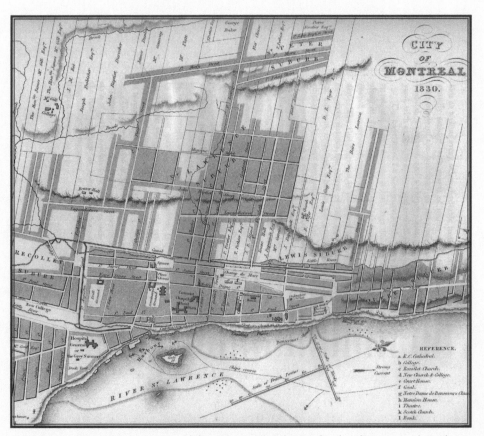

CITY OF MONTREAL 1830.

REFERENCE.
a R.C. Cathedral.
b College.
c Recollet Church.
d New Church & College.
e Court House.
f Goal.
g Notre Dame de Bonsecours Chap.
h Mansion House.
i Theatre.
k Scotch Church.
l Bank.

9. Bouchette's map of Montreal, from The British Dominions in North America, *1832*

his first venture into politics. He ran as a candidate in the eastern ward of Montreal during the general election in November 1834, but polled only 173 votes out of more than 800. In his memoirs, he ascribes his being induced to run to his being "young and vain." He recalled the poll being conducted in the house of Jacques Viger,

with a hospitality luncheon served on the second floor. Viger, then the first mayor of the newly incorporated city of Montreal, was a highly regarded scholar and public office-holder known for his efforts to improve Montreal's streets, public spaces, and sanitation. His artistry gave Montreal its official coat of arms, bearing the symbols of its four principal communities: French, Irish, English, and Scottish, and its rather wishful motto, *Concordia Salus*, or "Salvation Through Harmony."

Louis-Joseph Papineau, Speaker of the Legislative Assembly and leader of the *Patriote* party, handily won the neighbouring western riding. In an inflammatory victory address, Papineau took aim at Dr. William Robertson, the magistrate who had called out the troops during the incident at the polls in 1832. Robertson, one of the founders of the Montreal General Hospital and McGill University's Faculty of Medicine, decided to demand satisfaction in accordance with the duelling protocol of the day. The man he chose as his second to present the challenge to Papineau was none other than Sydney Bellingham, who considered Robertson to be his "family physician." Sydney called upon Papineau at his elegant home on Bonsecours Street on the morning of December 6, 1834, but Papineau declined, stating that he had only attacked Robertson in his *public* persona, not his private one. Papineau, as we shall see, was adept at triggering men's violent instincts, but even more skillful in ducking the consequences. In his memoirs, Sydney takes a kinder view of Papineau, whose cultivated exterior he admired. Papineau sat him on his parlour sofa for an hour's worth of earnest but unsuccessful republican proselytization. The following year, Sydney became vice-president of the newly founded St. Patrick's Society—at that time non-denominational—which was one of the wings of the Montreal Constitutional Association set up in opposition to Papineau's *Patriote* movement.

Sydney had a few of his own storms to deal with in this climate of general unease. The first involved a firm at Quebec named A. C. Freer & Company, which dealt in the West Indies trade. A. C. Freer obtained a loan of £3,000 in cash from Bellingham & Wallis on the understanding that Bellingham & Wallis would receive £5,000 worth of West India produce. Wisely, Bellingham & Wallis required a letter of guarantee from Noah Freer, the father of A. C. Freer, the "cashier," or general manager, of the Quebec Bank and a member of the Château Clique. By the close of the season, A. C. Freer & Company had made good on only £1,300. In what appears to have been part of a scheme engineered by the older Noah Freer, A. C. Freer offered to replace the outstanding debt with a promissory note for the balance. As Sydney later put it, "We fell into the trap." A week later, A. C. Freer & Company announced their failure, and Sydney travelled to Quebec to call upon Noah Freer to make good on his guarantee. Freer's carefully scripted response was, "I regret very much what has occurred, but I understand that you novated the original agreement, and that I am no longer responsible." Novation is a doctrine of civil law under which a guarantor is released from the guarantee if the creditor replaces, or *novates* the original debt without the guarantor's consent. Bellingham & Wallis sued Noah Freer but lost at trial, again on appeal, and on further appeal to the Judicial Committee of the Privy Council in London.[5] the legal costs alone must have been substantial. Counsel for Bellingham & Wallis was Jean-François Duval, who many years later became chief justice of Quebec. Sydney was convinced that Noah Freer knew what was going on in his son's business, and that the money lost had ultimately gone to his own benefit. As Sydney put it, "we were the victims of an elaborate swindle and paid smartly for the first lesson on the doctrine of novation." He would later get a second lesson on novation—this time for free—as an articling student of law. The incident is recounted in his memoirs in a way that shows his disdain for the hypocrisy of people who make a show of their religiousness, for he describes Noah Freer as "a very pious, strict, churchman" and "puritanical." Freer's fingers were on the purse strings of the bank that financed many municipal government activities, and he became one of the most powerful men at Quebec.

There were other ups and downs in these early years of business. A Liverpool firm gave Bellingham & Wallis a large order for wheat from Upper Canada, but by the time the shipment arrived in Liverpool the wheat market had collapsed from oversupply, and the Liverpool firm reneged on the deal. Sydney and James Wallis decided to dissolve their firm on amicable terms, and in 1835,

Sydney entered into a new partnership with a well-connected Scotsman, Charles Dunlop. After two years, the firm of Bellingham & Dunlop was so successful that Sydney, richer by £4,000 ($660,000 in today's money), decided to commence business on his own. He could also afford to acquire a seventy-acre estate on the northern slope of Mount Royal and built a large house there called "Dunany Cottage," in honour of the house he had been raised in near Castlebellingham. The pendulum swung back in the spring of 1837 when a New York firm defaulted on a large shipment of flour and pork. The effects of the Panic of 1837 in the United States, and its resulting recession, were felt as far away as Liverpool, where Charles Dunlop's firm came to grief. Sydney had neglected to post a notice in the Official Gazette of the dissolution of his partnership with Dunlop, with the result that Dunlop's creditors came after Sydney in Montreal. Two years of litigation ensued, during which he at first lost, and then regained, possession of the Dunany property.

During this period, Sydney became friendly with Félix Vinet-Souligny, a wheat merchant and shipowner whose office was nearby on St. Paul Street. Vinet-Souligny, a veteran of the War of 1812, had amassed a fortune of £40,000 by the time he died childless in 1838. He left the bulk of his estate to a nephew, Louis Villeneuve—a priest who lived in Rivière-des-Prairies, a community on the north shore of Montreal Island. Sydney later got to know Villeneuve, whose story is told in a later chapter.

---

5 Sydney Bellingham and James Wallis *v*. Noah Freer, Privy Council decision of May 16, 1837, reported in *Reports of Cases Argued and Determined*. An interesting example of English Law Lords opining on French law, being foreign law in force "in a part of the King's foreign dominions."

History has showered great adulation on the entrepreneurs of nineteenth-century Canada who experienced only success, largely by being in the right market at the right time, and often at the expense of others. Sydney experienced both successes and failures in his early business endeavours, but he weathered the storms and went on to fight other battles. What is rather remarkable is that he got as far as he did before reaching the age of thirty. We have to assume that he might not have come that far that quickly without the financial support of Arabella's inheritance, but much of his success seems to be due to an engaging personality and a fair amount of personal courage, intelligence, and drive. No doubt he was ambitious, but the drive and ambition were not those of the lumber barons, shipping barons, and later on, railway barons, who amassed much greater fortunes on the backs of others. Sydney Bellingham navigated the rough-and-tumble business world he found himself in with the help of his own moral compass. In all his endeavours of which we can find a record, there are no signs of the almost gleeful exploitation of those less fortunate that appears to have been the business norm in that same world. He does not appear to have gained anything without a lot of hard work. As 1837 drew to a close, his moral compass would be put to the test during a period when duty and human decency came into conflict with each other, and when British fair play yielded briefly to the methods that the British Crown used so effectively to keep its global empire intact.

CHAPTER 4

REBELLION

THE BRITISH CALLED IT "THE CAPTURE OF QUEBEC." Viewed from a global perspective, what happened in 1759 was just one event—albeit a very important one— in the latest round of a centuries-long conflict between Britain and France. The *Canadien* population called it *la Conquête*, and from their perspective, it was indeed a conquest. The immediate aftermath was in keeping with what a conquered people might well anticipate, and the *Canadiens* could have been expected to fear the worst given what the British had done when they uprooted and scattered their Acadian cousins just five years earlier. But all that quickly changed. By 1774, in many respects, life had returned to where it was before the British takeover, with the language, the laws, and the religion of the entire population protected under the *Quebec Act*, a statute of the British Parliament that gave the *Canadiens* more political and religious rights than many people in England, and certainly most of the people in Ireland, enjoyed at that time. Perhaps the biggest change—and the seeds of later troubles—lay in the arrival of English-speaking merchants, most of

them opportunists, who were chasing after the spoils of conquest and who believed it was their birthright to do so in an environment that was exclusively English, Protestant, and governed by the Common Law.

One factor in the restoration of the *status quo ante* was the desire of the colonial administration to create some sort of stability to balance unrest in the thirteen older colonies to the south. Part of it might have been just good luck. Throughout world history, governors appointed to rule over imperial conquests have not been very nice people, at least not from the viewpoint of the people they govern. The British military governor of Quebec, Jeffrey Amherst, fits that classic paradigm, but he was gone by 1763. Amherst is best remembered for his later military exploits, including the strategic use of the smallpox virus during his suppression of Pontiac's rebellion in Ohio. There are places named after him in Canada where petitions have been circulated for a change of name. However, Amherst's three successors from 1764 to 1795 were of an entirely different calibre, and that is where the good luck occurs.

The first civil governor of Quebec was James Murray, a Scot who felt more affinity for the *Canadien* population than for the new English mercantile element, and who basically ignored the instructions he had been given to anglicize the new colony. Lurking in Murray's past was his family's connection with the Jacobite Rebellion of 1745 and the traditional belief that the French were Scotland's natural allies in her conflict with the English. His successor, Guy Carleton, had worked with Murray and followed the same approach. Carleton was Anglo-Irish, with good first-hand knowledge of how Britain should not treat the inhabitants of conquered territory. Sir Frederick Haldimand was a Swiss-born Francophile, whose name before he joined the British Army as a career soldier was François-Louis-Frédéric Haldimand. When Haldimand's term was up, Carleton, soon to become known as Lord Dorchester, returned for another ten years as governor-in-chief of British North America.

So, as conquests go, this one got off to a fairly benign start. But then things began to deteriorate. Part of this was the inevitable conflict between two cultures, which even if nothing else had been at play, would have taken a few more generations to become more or less manageable. The influx of English-speaking loyalist refugees from the American Revolutionary War and its aftermath aggravated the situation. Things improved for a while with the creation of two separate provinces, each with its own elected assembly—predominantly English Upper Canada and predominantly French Lower Canada—

through the adoption of the *Constitutional Act* of 1791. But the real problem in Lower Canada during the early decades of the nineteenth century was just a variation on a theme that was to be played out elsewhere. In 1830, there were insurrections in France, Belgium, Switzerland, and Italy. In 1836, Spain finally renounced its possessions in Continental Latin America after decades of struggles for independence.

In 1838, the same year as the second outbreak of rebellion in Canada, the Chartist movement in England and Wales was gathering steam, leading to riots and bloodshed over the next decade. Later on, in 1848, there would be insurrections in nearly every country in Europe. Racial or language differences were a significant factor in very few of these events. The fundamental causes were social, political, and economic.

Much has been written about political theories and thinking in Canada during the first half of the nineteenth century. However, to understand why events of social and political upheaval occur, it is important to focus on the circumstantial evidence that reveals how the bulk of a population was actually *feeling*, as opposed to what the politicians and pundits were *thinking and writing*. In the 1830s, there were no fewer than sixty newspapers published in Lower Canada, although their circulation was confined mostly to Montreal and Quebec, and more than half of them were English. As noted by Sydney in his memoirs, the vast majority of the rural population, which accounted for nearly 90 percent of the total population of 670,000, never read a newspaper. The newspaper archives tell us a lot about what the writers were thinking, but very little about how the people were feeling. The *Quebec Act* of 1774 may well have restored the *status quo ante*, but the only people who were content with the *status quo ante* were the privileged seigneurial class—the Château Clique and the Roman Catholic clergy. The bulk of the population remained discontented over the payment of seigneurial dues and church tithes, and unhappiness grew as the financial burden of those impositions increased. An expanding agrarian population found it difficult to acquire land. To make matters worse, the mid-1830s were marked by disease in the wheat crop and poor harvests generally. There was hunger on a scale not seen since the siege of Quebec. Financial crises in the United States and Britain had an impact on the economies of Lower and Upper Canada, as Sydney experienced first-hand in his struggling import and export business at Montreal.[6] The devastation wreaked by the cholera epidemics of 1832 and 1834 left scars of resentment towards the "intruders" who had brought the disease with them and against the colonial authorities who had allowed it to spread. On the political front, the *Constitutional Act* of 1791 had promised "the very image and transcript" of the British Constitution[7] but had failed to deliver on one key element—truly responsible government, with the executive branch answerable to an elected legislative branch and an independent judiciary. When Louis-Joseph Papineau, the elegant and eloquent—some would say enigmatic—leader of the *Canadien* party first campaigned for change, he advocated not for the republicanism and the break from Britain that he later espoused, but for closer adherence to British constitutional principles.

People were not getting what they thought they were entitled to. The early 1830s was a period of intense and evolving debate over what was wrong with the system and how to fix it. In the hustings and in the newspapers, at dinner parties and in the taverns, two irreconcilable views emerged. On one side, the supporters of Papineau's *Canadien* party drifted away from British constitutional principles and came to advocate American-style republicanism or even the more radical French revolutionary republicanism. The *Canadien* party became the *Patriote* party, the new name evocative of revolutionary determination. By the late summer of 1837, the more radical party members began calling themselves *Fils de la Liberté*, or Sons of Liberty, modelled on Samuel Adam's American Revolutionary theme. On the other side, the arch-conservatives and even some reform-minded people, fearful of what had happened in the United States and France, labelled themselves "Loyal Constitutionalists". Many of them wanted reform—but not at any price, and certainly not through chaos. The bulk of the population, however, were neither attuned to, nor

---

6 See Chapter 3.
7 The description given to the act by the first lieutenant governor of Upper Canada, John Graves Simcoe, likely based on the intentions of its author, Home Secretary (and future prime minister of Britain) William Wyndham Grenville in an exchange of drafts with Carleton in October 1789.

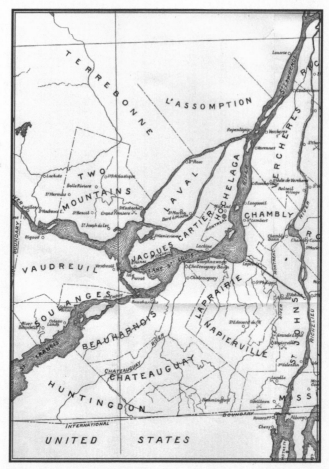

10. Geographic context of the rebellions of 1837–38, from William Kingsford's *The History of Canada, 1898*

interested in, the subtleties of refined political theory and discourse. What mattered to them was that the system was not working. They were having hard times while others prospered. They had a sense of unfairness and a belief that they were being exploited. It is revealing that their anger was directed not just towards the English-speaking ruling elite, but also towards the members of the small government bureaucracy with whom they interfaced on the local level. The cry often heard was *À bas les bureaucrates!* Down with the bureaucrats! All of this was aggravated by feelings of rancour towards immigrants and refugees. Some of the parallels with political upheaval in the twenty-first century are striking.

Later generations of Quebec writers have tried to depict what happened in 1837 and 1838 as the rising of a people, but it was not that. Much of the *Canadien* population remained indifferent to the cause and were opposed to the violence. For many, the switch to British rule had spared them the horrors of the French Revolution. Geographically, the armed conflict was confined to the Richelieu Valley and border area east of Montreal and to the County of Two Mountains to the northwest, leaving the other regions relatively untouched. There were rebel agitators, including some of the principal leaders, whose first language was English. In the same year, there was a rebellion in Upper Canada, where practically everyone's first language was English. The rise of an organized and militant backlash by certain English-speaking Montrealers, fearful that their voices would be drowned out if the Legislative Assembly gained the supremacy the *Patriote* majority sought for it, made it easy to conclude that the conflict was simply a matter of French versus English. The likelihood is that the rebellion would have occurred even if there had been no "Loyal and Constitutional" societies set up to resist it. In a nutshell, the rebellion happened because of a deteriorating political system that paid only lip service to the concepts of representative and responsible government and seemed rigged in favour of the interests of the pseudo-aristocracy of the Château Clique. Although far more complex in its social dimension, what happened in Lower Canada was not that much different from the revolt in Upper Canada against the regime of the Family Compact. On a much smaller scale, and minus the violence, there was similar agitation in Nova Scotia.

In January 1839, the man who had very briefly been governor the previous year, John George Lambton (Lord Durham), submitted the report he had been commissioned to write on the causes of the rebellion. One of his recommendations was a return to the original policy of assimilation through the union of the two provinces. Notwithstanding his reform-minded recommendations on responsible government, his often-quoted reference to "two nations warring in the bosom of a single state" was a gross over simplification, and the assertion that it was "a struggle not of principles but of races" was dead wrong. Those were not his only mistakes. Durham viewed French Canadians as a people without a significant culture of their own. They certainly were shorthanded when it came to poets, painters, and sculptors, but what Durham overlooked was that, compared to the general populations of Great Britain and Ireland at the time (of which this sheltered aristocrat probably also knew little), the *Canadiens* could be described as a more *civilized* people. Sydney's memoirs contain a number of observations in support of that

EARL OF GOSFORD.

comparison. As he recounts, the whole mess could have been avoided—and indeed almost was—through the efforts of an old school chum of his father.

Archibald Acheson, the second Earl of Gosford, was a liberal-minded Irishman of Scottish descent with a reputation in Ireland for fair dealing and conciliation. When he became governor-in-chief of British North America in August 1835, people hoped he could apply those talents to resolving the growing political crisis in Lower Canada. Gosford was a *bon vivant* who had brought with him a vast quantity of claret, champagne, and sherry. As Sydney put it, "He found his way down

14. Archibald Acheson, Earl of Gosford, artist unknown, LAC, MIKAN 4312918

the throats to the hearts of members of the Quebec Assembly and other prominent leaders." Sydney got Gosford's version of events first-hand when he visited him a few years later in Ireland. Gosford had worked out a compromise with Papineau on the list of grievances drawn up by the Assembly and known to historians as the "Ninety-Two Resolutions."

The Assembly's principal demands included the creation of an elected Legislative Council to replace the appointed body made up mainly of English-speaking members of the Château Clique who routinely blocked the initiatives of the Assembly whose members were

15. Louis-Joseph Papineau, lithograph by Maurin, Paris, from Canada and Its Provinces, *by Adam Shortt and Arthur G. Doughty, ed., 1914*

elected, mostly French-speaking, and had only limited control over the public purse. Another key demand was to make the governor's Executive Council, or cabinet, responsible to the Assembly, in line with the promises implicit in the *Constitutional Act*. Gosford's efforts at compromise were torpedoed, and his credibility irrevocably damaged, when the lieutenant governor of Upper Canada, Sir Francis Bond Head, leaked a copy of instructions from the Colonial Office that purported to show that Gosford had no authority to agree to such a compromise. According to Sydney's memoirs, Gosford told him that when he met with William IV at Windsor to receive his appointment, the king agreed that he should receive new instructions from the Colonial Office giving him the power to effect a compromise with the *Patriote* party and address the grievances set out in the Ninety-Two Resolutions. If this is indeed what Gosford told Sydney, we could be pardoned for doubting its veracity, given that William was known to be averse to any devolution of powers in Lower Canada. In any event, Head's disclosures convinced the members of the *Patriote* party that Gosford had duped them. During the uproar that followed, the moderate side of the party lost its grip on the Assembly, and those who believed that nothing could be gained peaceably embarked on a campaign that openly advocated rebellion. For the rest of his life, Sydney would attribute the tragedy that fell upon Lower Canada in 1837 to the meddling and treachery of Francis Bond Head, whom he described as "an aggressive Tory …

who encouraged racial antagonism between English and French." Fifty years later, when writing a congratulatory letter to Félix-Gabriel Marchand upon his becoming premier of Quebec, Sydney's rancour towards Head was still strong enough for him to slip in a remark about the false report Head had caused to be sent to Papineau.

Before the storm broke, one of Lord Gosford's day-to-day appointments, which he made shortly after his arrival, was to designate Sydney Bellingham a magistrate, or justice of the peace.[8] At the time, in addition to their legal functions, magistrates wielded considerable authority in municipal matters, and it would not be wrong to consider them as agents of the executive power of the Governor. Although we might not think of them that way today, in 1837, they were very much part of what the *Patriote* crowds were targeting when they chanted, "*À bas les bureaucrates.*" Sydney does not disclose how his appointment came about, but we can safely assume who called upon whom. Just as the fearless seventeen-year-old backpacker had knocked on the door of James Bâby at York in 1826,[9] we can imagine the brash twenty-nine-year-old merchant calling at the governor-in-chief's official residence and introducing himself as the son of the late Sir Alan Bellingham. Perhaps he sent off a letter before calling, but how he knew of the schoolmate connection with his father is a mystery. By this time, however, Sydney had been able to acquire

---

8   April 13, 1837.
9   See Chapter 3.

some loyalist credentials. He was vice-president of the St. Patrick's Society, one of the wings of the Montreal Constitutional Association that was formed in opposition to the increasingly republican tone of the *Patriote* political doctrine. The appointment, along with a magistrate's stipend, came at the right time for Sydney, who was still reeling from the financial consequences of his former partner Charles Dunlop's insolvency.[10] It is doubtful that a man of his young years would ever have received such a position without the family connection, and that he got it is a good illustration of how things worked in the days of the Château Clique. In any event, a minor appointment to a quasi-judicial function resulted in a brief change of career—not the one Sydney had asked for, but one that would draw him onto the battlefield.

Years of verbal clashes among the educated elite eventually evolved into large public assemblies with a raucous and seditious tone, and in early November 1837, those events in turn boiled over into mob violence between mainly French-speaking and mainly English-speaking factions in the streets and squares of what is now Old Montreal. It was the same pattern seen countless times before and since all over the world: as soon as the legitimacy of the established order appears to be seriously challenged, the disgruntled and the disadvantaged vent their own frustrations in the only way they think will be noticed, and then hooligans looking for some sport join in, especially in a harbour

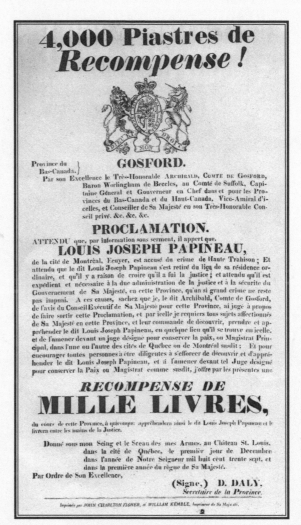

16. Reward poster for the arrest of Papineau, from Canada and Its Provinces, *by Adam Shortt and Arthur G. Doughty, eds., 1914*

See Chapter 3

town with a large transient population and an inordinate number of taverns.[11] It would have been very easy for an observer, looking only at the clashes of the two mobs in Montreal on November 6, 1837, to conclude that there were "two nations warring in the bosom of a single state," but that oversimplification ignored the politics leading up to what was essentially a sideshow. The two opposing mobs were a relatively benign manifestation of the classic "we" versus "they" tribal impulse, and it is likely that most of the participants would have been at a loss to clearly articulate the threat they perceived from the other side. In this instance, moreover, the distinction between the "we" and the "they" was not purely racial or linguistic. Among the principal targets of the Constitutional mob were men with names like Bell, O'Callahan, Nelson, and Brown. Sydney witnessed the scene from the windows of his rented house on St. James Street. He does not describe it as a clash between gentlemen of the idealistic political class in top hats, as some writers and artists have portrayed it, but rather as a mob that included "the lowest and most ignorant strata of society."

Although he played no part in what he witnessed from his window, the rioting indirectly drew Sydney into the conflict. In a futile attempt to nip the rebellion in the bud, a series of warrants were issued for the arrest of *Patriote* leaders, including Papineau. Magistrate Bellingham was summoned to the office of Charles Ogden, the attorney general, and received instructions to follow a company of soldiers to the village of Longueuil on the other side of the St. Lawrence. There they were to meet up with three prominent *Patriote* prisoners being escorted from the garrison at St. Jean by a detachment of the Royal Montreal Cavalry. Normally the task would have fallen to police constables, but Montreal had been without a police force for several months due to a lack of funds and political deadlock in the Legislative Assembly over the renewal of the City's charter. In the absence of a civilian police force, Ogden had effectively created one by deputizing volunteers from the Royal Montreal Cavalry, until then a part-time militia regiment. Sydney's participation was intended to give the operation the necessary trappings of civil authority, since martial law had not yet been declared. The magistrates had become the only legal authority for the execution of an arrest warrant, and few of them would have been willing and able to accept that role in a climate that threatened real violence. Sydney was still only twenty-nine and had acquired the skills of horsemanship expected of men of his comfortable means. He was also familiar with the villages and farming country of the South Shore, a favourite spot for young gentlemen of Montreal to indulge their passion for fox hunting. He and Arabella had visited the home of Gabriel Marchand at St. Jean. Marchand, a wealthy timber merchant and a member of Gosford's Legislative Council, was married to Arabella's aunt, Mary Macnider. On the morning of November 17, two companies of regular troops under major Henry Reid,

11 Nearly one hundred in a one-mile radius.

accompanied by a detachment of Ogden's deputized cavalrymen and Magistrate Bellingham and his horse, took the Hochelaga ferry across to Longueuil where they planned to rendezvous with the prisoner escort. The ferry was a large, hulled platform, propelled slowly across the water by a big, stern-mounted paddle wheel. Instead of steam, four horses harnessed to a revolving capstan on the deck powered the paddle wheel. Sydney knew some of the members of the Royal Montreal Cavalry, including Sergeant William Sharp, a former British Army trooper who owned a popular livery stable in Montreal, and Lieutenant Charles Oakes Ermatinger Jr., the son of a

17. *Fort Chambly, drawing by W. H. Bartlett, from* Canadian Scenery, *by N. P. Willis and W. H. Bartlett, 1842*

18. The encounter at
Booth's Tavern, sketch by
Henri Julien, 1888

prominent Montreal fur trader and an Ojibway princess.
Reid's orders were to wait by the ferry, but Sydney decided
to ride farther ahead to scout the situation. He soon came
upon a house where one of a small group of men was
loading a fowling piece. In inimitable Bellingham style,
he asked the man what they were up to, and the fellow
told him quite frankly that they were part of a group
that intended to intercept the arresting escort. It may

have helped Sydney that he was not wearing a uniform
or gentleman's riding clothes, but rather his preferred
homespun *étoffe du pays*, which he wore when riding and
that made him look like anything other than a magistrate
on a mission.

He rode on for another mile or so until he spotted
a barricade erected across the road, surrounded by a
much larger group of armed men. He wheeled about and

rushed back to the ferry to convince Reid to move out and engage the rebels at the barricade, but Reid stuck to his orders to stay put. With Reid's agreement, Sydney galloped to a farmhouse half a mile downriver, where he knew a man named Macdonald, and asked him to ride off and warn the escort of what was waiting for them at the barricade. We do not know if Macdonald agreed to do what he was asked, but if he did, it was too late. The escort, armed only with their sidearms and vastly outnumbered, was scattered by sniper fire from the barricade and nearby houses, and the prisoners were freed. Returning to the ferry, Sydney found it moving away from the wharf, but it returned to pick him up. On board the ferry were two members of the escort, one of them a badly wounded Sergeant Sharp. Also lying on the deck was Sharp's prize mare, bleeding from two bullet wounds. The other members of the escort found their way back to Montreal by a more roundabout route, some of them also having had their horses shot from under them. Among them were Lieutenant Ermatinger, wounded in the face from a blast of birdshot from a fowling piece, and a young John Molson Jr., with a hole in his cap from a bullet that grazed his head.

It was the first armed conflict of the rebellion. English-speaking *Patriote* Patrick Murray fired the first shot from behind the barricade near Longueuil. The general order to fire upon anyone escorting *Patriote* prisoners came from Papineau himself and marked the definitive moment in his personal espousal of

bloodshed as a means to his political ends. Just as the arrest warrants had backfired as a strategy designed to dampen the outbreak of armed rebellion, the ambush at the Longueuil barricade provoked the inevitable military response that eventually crushed it.

The day after this first encounter, Sydney and another magistrate, Pierre-Édouard Leclère, received instructions to search out and arrest those who had ambushed the prisoner escort. Leclère was not averse to taking risks. In 1834, he had fought a duel with Édouard-Étienne Rodier, actually a former classmate and close friend of Leclère. Leclère had taken offence at comments made in a newspaper Rodier owned, *L'Ami du Peuple*. Fortunately, despite the goading of their seconds, the two men managed to miss their targets, probably intentionally. Leclère was a law-and-order type who, before the outbreak of the rebellion, had worked strenuously against the *Patriote* cause in his capacity as superintendent of police. During the rebellion, the network of spies and informers he created with Charles Ogden, the attorney general, operated essentially as a secret police. One of the names on their arrest warrants was Rodier's, but Rodier fled to Vermont.

This time, in addition to fifteen troopers of the Royal Montreal Cavalry under Captain Eleazar David, they had the support of four companies of the 1st Regiment of Royal Scots, one of the most battle-hardened infantry units of the British Army, under the command of Lieutenant-Colonel George Augustus Wetherall. They

19. Rebel forces celebrating at St. Denis, drawing by Henri Julien, LAC, MIKAN 2995479

were to proceed as far as Fort Chambly along the Richelieu River at a point fifteen miles east of Montreal, where Wetherall was to set up a base of operations for securing the Richelieu Valley, the focal point of the insurrection. The Richelieu River runs northward nearly eighty miles from Lake Champlain to join the St. Lawrence at the town of Sorel. Along its fertile banks in the 1800s were numerous seigneurial farms and relatively prosperous villages, all enjoying the convenience of the river and good roads to connect it with the population centres of Montreal, Trois-Rivières, and farther on, Quebec. The Richelieu Valley's proximity to Montreal was a major factor in that area's rapid transformation into a hotbed of insurrection. Crop failures in the early 1830s may also have been a factor, along with concerns over the growing English-speaking populations to the east and south. Fort Chambly had originally been built to defend New France, first from the Iroquois and later from the British

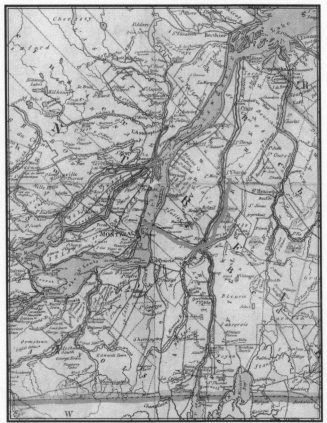

coming down the Richelieu from Lake Champlain and the Hudson River. A small British garrison had been maintained at Chambly after the fort was regained from American invaders in 1776.

Tagging along on foot with the mounted troopers was a volunteer whose identity serves as a good example of how conflict can attract participants whose presence at first appears bizarre and improbable. His name was James Burke. Burke, better known by his nickname Deaf Burke, was the current English heavyweight champion prizefighter. He was staying briefly in Montreal on his way back to London from New Orleans. Burke had gone

11. The march on St. Charles, from part of a map of Lower Canada by L. J. Hebert, 1838, LAC, MIKAN 4127086

20. Dr. Wolfred Nelson, drawing by Jean-Joseph Girouard, LAC, MIKAN 3635406

to the United States when he was unable to find work in England following the death of one of his opponents after ninety-nine rounds of merciless pummelling, for which Burke was tried and acquitted on a charge of manslaughter. The home crowd in New Orleans, fearing the same thing was going to happen to the local favourite, the Irish pugilist Sam O'Rourke, stopped the fight and ran Burke out of town. During his stopover in Montreal, the garrison had adopted Burke, more as a mascot than as a soldier, but his ability to put up a fight was considered an asset.

On the way to Fort Chambly, the detachment

Sydney had joined searched the houses from which the troopers had been fired upon, but found them deserted. They interrogated the neighbour of Olivier Fournier, a local blacksmith who had removed the handcuffs from the rescued prisoners, but Fournier had vanished. Closer to Chambly, the advance guard Sydney was riding with came upon a group of armed riders and chased them into the woods, taking two of them prisoner. Sydney came into close contact with one of the mounted rebels, took aim with his pistol, and fired. In his memoirs, he expresses his relief at having missed. This tells us something about Sydney Bellingham. Most other men telling their war stories many years after the fact would have expressed frustration or disappointment at having failed to dispatch their adversary.

A bit farther on, the guard came to Booth's Tavern where, they had been told, a large group of rebels had assembled. Surprised by the strength of the military response, most of the rebels had bolted; four were taken prisoner. Their interrogation revealed the names of those who had ordered the attack of the previous day, including a Dr. Timothée Kimber. As we shall see, the medical profession was well represented among the leaders of the rebellion. The interrogation also disclosed that a force of about 1,500 rebels was being assembled at St. Charles, fourteen miles downstream from Chambly, and that Papineau was farther downriver at St. Denis, where another large force was encamped under the command of Dr. Wolfred Nelson, another leading *Patriote* agitator.

Their mission completed, Sydney and Leclère hurried back to Montreal during the night, and early the next morning presented a detailed written report to Ogden. On the ride back, Sydney was hampered by the presence of Deaf Burke, who had asked for help. Sydney mounted Burke on one of the horses taken from the rebels, but discovered that he was not as good a rider as he was a pugilist.

There must have been something about rural taverns that made them points of rebel assembly. A mere three weeks later, another Bellingham would seek out a rebel gathering at another tavern, at the outset of another rebellion. The results, however, would be very different.

Sydney made a second trip to Fort Chambly four days later, this time bearing a letter from the commander-in-chief of the British forces in North America, General Sir John Colborne, ordering Wetherall to march on St. Charles, which had been selected as the rebels' military headquarters. The rebel plan was to use it as bait to draw Colborne's forces out of Montreal long enough for the first ice floes to prevent their return by boat. They would then be picked off as they broke into small detachments to defend the countryside against spreading rebel attacks. Colborne was happy to oblige, except that his plan was to consolidate and bring all his strength to bear on St. Charles in a two-pronged advance, one from the north led by Lieutenant-Colonel Charles Gore, and the other from the south under Wetherall. Colborne was a veteran of the Peninsular War against Napoleon's armies in Spain and Portugal, and under the Duke of Wellington again at the Battle of Waterloo, at which Colborne was credited with being instrumental in Napoleon's defeat. A regimental surgeon who served under Colborne in both Spain and Lower Canada likened him, in character and appearance, to the duke himself.

In contrast with the British military leadership, the rebel forces at St. Charles were led by a man they elected as "General of the Army of the South," Thomas Storrow Brown, a thirty-four-year-old radical Montreal hardware merchant with no previous military experience whatsoever. Ironically, Brown's first attempt to evade Ogden's arrest warrant had taken him to the Hochelaga ferry on the morning of November 17, where he found Sydney's party already embarked for the crossing to Longueuil. He wisely slipped away and reached the South Shore by another route. Brown had nearly been clubbed to death during the Montreal riots on November 6 and he was still feeling the effects. He recovered quickly in the luxurious comforts of the manor house belonging to local seigneur and member of Gosford's Legislative Council, Pierre-Dominique Debartzch, which had been commandeered as the rebel command post. Brown spent a frantic couple of days directing the erection of fortifications from where he could engage the enemy on the southern side of the village, and scrounging food, arms, and ammunition from local sources. Following a technique used in the Peninsular War, Colborne dispatched spies to keep him informed of the situation

on the ground and alert him to what he would be up against at St. Charles. Meanwhile, Papineau and other rebel leaders, including the Irish-born Dr. Edmund Bailey O'Callahan, had set up a kind of strategic nerve centre farther downriver at the village of St. Denis. The location selected was the old headquarters of the 5th Battalion, Select Embodied Militia—the notorious "Devil's Own"— that Sydney had heard about aboard the steamer on his way to Douro Township in 1824.[12] Papineau, not accustomed to the hardships of a man on the run, had taken up guest residence at the comfortable home of Dr. Nelson, known in the community not just as a physician, but also as the prosperous owner of the local distillery.

Sydney was one of three dispatch riders carrying Colborne's attack orders to Wetherall; each rider travelled separately by different routes in the expectation that at least one of them would make it through. To improve his chances, Sydney was fitted out at the ordnance store of the Montreal garrison with a carbine, a sabre, and two pistols. These were not a magistrate's usual accoutrements, but in this instance, the armed dispatch rider had to be a magistrate in order to clothe the operation as a request to the military to come to the aid of the civil power. Technically, the ensuing Battle of St. Charles was the result of a requisition, signed by two other Montreal magistrates, calling for military assistance in response to Brown's seizure of Debartzch's manor house. Early on the morning of November 22, Sydney

---

12 See Chapter 2.

once again took the horse ferry across to Longueuil, only to find that this time the wharf had been carried away in a gale. He and his equipment made it to the shore in a canoe, and fortunately his horse turned out to be a good swimmer. Sydney rode non-stop to Fort Chambly, which he reached around eight o'clock that night, and delivered Colborne's orders to Wetherall. They required Wetherall to set out immediately for St. Charles with five companies of infantry, twenty troopers of Captain David's Royal Montreal Cavalry, and two field guns with a detachment of Royal Artillery under Captain John Glasgow. Sydney was to accompany the expedition in his role as magistrate, but by now he must have felt more like a man on a military mission than the representative of the civil authority.

The expectation was that Wetherall would engage Brown at St. Charles the very next morning, and that Gore would march from Sorel and attack from the other side of the village. Encumbered with their field guns, both Gore and Wetherall had to contend with freezing rain, muddy roads, and bridges and ferries knocked out by the rebels. By ten o'clock the following morning, Wetherall had made it only as far as the village of St. Hilaire, halfway to St. Charles. His men were exhausted, rain-drenched, and suffering from the cold. Their rations of only one day's sustenance were nearly exhausted as well. Wetherall made the decision to rest for the day at St. Hilaire, where his men could be billeted and fed at Château Rouville, the estate of local seigneur Jean-Baptiste-René Hertel de Rouville, who was a member of the Legislative Council. Later, de Rouville was suspected to have been a rebel sympathizer.

During the night, Wetherall learned that the advance of Gore's men had been blocked and badly mauled in the course of a day-long engagement at St. Denis by a well-positioned force of rebels under the leadership of Dr. Nelson, who was proving himself to be rather adept in his new role of military commander. Gore's defeat and withdrawal to Montreal via Sorel was completely unexpected—just as his attack on St. Denis had come as a surprise to Nelson. Matters were made worse by the loss of Gore's field gun, which the retreating soldiers were unable to drag through the mud. Wetherall asked for volunteers from the militia cavalry to ride back to Fort Chambly for reinforcements to make up for Gore's withdrawal, but there were no takers. He needed someone who knew the countryside, so he summoned Sydney, explained the situation to him, and acknowledged that he had no authority to ask a magistrate to embark on a risky military mission through territory infiltrated by enemy marksmen. Sydney accepted nonetheless, unaware that all three of Colborne's dispatch riders carrying new orders to Wetherall had been intercepted earlier that day. One of the volunteer cavalry troopers, another Anglo-Irishman whose name was John Lovell, agreed to join him. They commandeered a scow at gunpoint from a rebel sympathizer and crossed the river with their horses in the dark. Spread out with a hundred yards between

them so that the other could get away if one of them fell, they were shot at on the way to Chambly, but arrived there safely around four o'clock in the morning. Sydney aroused Major John Warde, who had been left in charge of a reserve company of grenadiers, and they devised a plan to get downstream to Château Rouville by boat so that they could pick on which side of the river to take up position if attacked. Warde's reserve reached Château Rouville without incident, bringing Wetherall's combined force to about 420 officers and men.

Meanwhile, Brown had been preparing the southern approaches to the village of St. Charles,

22. Thomas Storrow Brown in later life, BAnQ

setting up advance pickets along the road and snipers in adjoining houses. Papineau and Nelson showed up to deliver rousing speeches to the rebels clustered around Debartzch's manor house. Papineau's metamorphosis from principled politician to ruthless military commissar had reached the point of warning the men that anyone who retreated from the impending battle would be dealt with severely by the rearguard. One could reasonably speculate that Papineau's increasingly shrill tone arose out of a fear that if he did not forcefully advocate bloodshed, he would be eclipsed in his role as leader by the likes of Nelson.

Earlier in the day, Colborne became alarmed at the extent of the rebel preparations, which were reported to him at Montreal by one of his spies, a court bailiff whom Brown had caught onto but naively believed to have converted to the rebel cause. With Gore's force retired from the field, Colborne decided to recall Wetherall's men as well, but this time not a single dispatch rider made it through. It is one of the more interesting "what ifs" of Canadian history to ask what might have happened if at least one of Colborne's three messages had reached Wetherall and the battle of St. Charles had never taken place.

With no word from Colborne, Wetherall decided on his own to set out for St. Charles on the morning of November 25, fearing that further delay might leave him stranded as winter closed in. Wetherall's men, buoyed by their respite at Château Rouville and drier weather, came in sight of the village around noon. Brown's advance pickets fired on them without much effect and were driven off, leaving the houses and outbuildings they had appropriated to be torched by the soldiers. When he reached one such scene, Sydney dismounted and ran into the barn in a vain attempt to free the cattle tied up inside, but he was driven out by the flames and the smoke. He remounted his horse and made off as quickly as he could but came under fire from Wetherall's rearguard, who had mistaken him for a rebel on account of his clothing. The firing stopped when Captain David shouted out, "That is Mr. Bellingham, the magistrate!"

Wetherall fetched an old man watching the advance from the doorway of his house, and speaking to him in French, sent him off to invite Brown to a parley. The old man never returned, and Wetherall decided to bring matters to a head by ordering Captain Glasgow's artillery to lob a few shots into the village. Brown was completely taken by surprise, having learned from one of the captured dispatch riders that Colborne had sent orders recalling Wetherall, but not realizing that none of Colborne's dispatches had actually been delivered. Desertions had left Brown with no more than 250 men. Supplies of guns and ammunition to be procured in Vermont had failed to materialize. His poorly armed men were spread out along the wood-and-mud redoubt that had been thrown up around Debartzch's manor house at the village entrance, with a few other men hidden in the woods to the left. Having still received no reply to his offer of a parley, Wetherall moved his men to within range of the redoubt, where there ensued a vigorous exchange of fire lasting nearly two hours. Needing an *aide de camp* to deliver his orders to the division nearest the woods on his extreme right, Wetherall decided that Sydney would again be a good choice. Sydney obliged, this time coming under fire from the rebels, who thought that the rider dressed in *étoffe du pays* was a traitor. Returning to Wetherall, he found his new commander's horse had been shot from under him and offered him his own. Captain David also had his horse shot from under him. Wetherall's bugler, positioned a few feet away, had

23. The Death of Colonel Moodie at Montgomery's Tavern, *artist unknown, from* Toronto: Past and Present, *by C. Pelham Mulvany, 1884*

taken a musket ball in the face. Sydney took cover with some of the soldiers in a dry ditch facing the redoubt and found the man next to him groping a fatal musket wound in the abdomen.

Inevitably, the moment came for a final advance on the rebel positions. Wetherall instructed Warde to order the Royals to fix bayonets and charge the redoubt. Some of Brown's men scattered, but a group of about fifty made as if they wanted to surrender, reversing their muskets in apparent submission. When the Royals hesitated, the rebels, or at least some of them, took aim and fired, killing one sergeant and wounding a few of the men.

The response from the Royals was merciless. When the bayonetting and firing stopped, 150 rebels lay dead or dying. Lovell and another trooper rounded up the few prisoners taken as they made a break for the river. The wounded—soldier and rebel alike—were taken to the church presbytery and attended to by the army surgeon, who was Wetherall's nephew. Only three of Wetherall's men had been killed, and about twenty were wounded. Discarded powder cartridges had started a fire in the dry, uncut November hay, and the conflagration consumed the clothing of some of the rebel casualties. Later in the day, because he could speak French, Sydney was asked to accompany two women who had come to retrieve their dead. The following morning, he was one of the early risers who had to use their pistols to shoot pigs that came to feast on the corpses. The whole experience must have been traumatic for a man whose only brush with the prospect of a violent death had been facing a bear in the forests of Upper Canada.

Before the fight was over, Brown had left the scene to meet up with Nelson at St. Denis and join the preparations there to resist an attack they expected to come from Wetherall. That, at least, is the explanation Brown later gave in his memoirs. The attack never came. Wetherall decided instead to return to a position of strength at Fort Chambly. In any event, support for Nelson and Brown at St. Denis evaporated overnight. Papineau had awaited the outcome from a safe distance and then fled to Vermont with his sidekick, O'Callahan, the two

of them disguised as monks and speaking nothing but English. In the days to come, Brown, Nelson, and other rebel leaders likewise dispersed across the border.

The Richelieu Valley remained in a state of unrest for the next few weeks, but the threat of another major engagement had passed, at least for the duration of the winter. The 150 rebel deaths at St. Charles had a very sobering effect on all but the fanatics, who continued nonetheless to play up the victory at St. Denis. Gore returned there in early December with eight companies of infantry and put the torch to Nelson's house and to other houses from which his earlier force had been ambushed. More burnings by Gore's men, but without his authorization, followed the discovery of the body of Lieutenant George Weir, one of Colborne's dispatch riders. Weir had been stabbed and shot to death by a mob in St. Denis after being taken prisoner by Nelson's men. His body had been tossed into a stream and covered with rocks. Sydney knew Weir, who was one of the officers aboard the ferry to Longueuil on the day the rebels liberated the St. Jean prisoners. Weir's murder was one example of how the beast in men can quickly come to the surface, even among a population renowned for its peacefulness. As we shall see, the consequences were not limited to the unfortunate residents of St. Denis.

In the weeks that followed, the mood in Montreal was one of fear and paranoia. Despite the outcome at St. Charles, there were concerns that the rebels would gain the upper hand before reinforcements could be

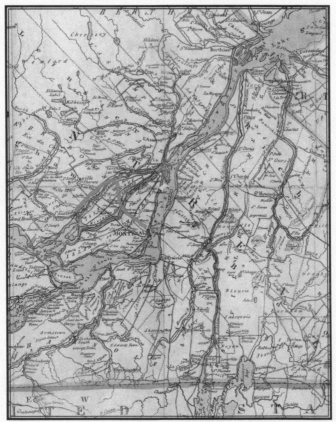

brought in from Nova Scotia and New Brunswick. Rebellion had broken out in Upper Canada, further stretching the military resources. Not for the first or last time, there were rumours of a possible invasion by American sympathizers. On December 5, 1837, the Court of Special Sessions of the Peace met in Montreal and passed a resolution asking for the district to be placed under martial law. Sydney was one of twenty magistrates attending the session. Later in the day, Governor-in-Chief Gosford signed the order.

On the same day, Sydney's younger brother, William, was taken prisoner by rebels—not along the

12. The march on St. Eustache, from part of a map of Lower Canada by L. J. Hebert, 1838, LAC, MIKAN 4127086

24. Sir John Colborne, from Canada and Its Provinces, by Adam Shortt and Arthur G. Doughty, eds., 1914

Richelieu but on Yonge Street on the wooded outskirts of Toronto, 350 miles away. After Sydney and Arabella had brought William back with them on their return to Montreal from their visit to Castlebellingham in 1833, they enrolled him in Upper Canada College, a school for boys in Toronto founded in 1829 by Sir John Colborne when he was lieutenant governor of Upper Canada. The rebellion led by William Lyon Mackenzie in Upper Canada and the *Patriote* rebellion in Lower Canada shared similar causes and objectives, but despite some communications between Mackenzie and Papineau, the two events were more coincidental than coordinated.

Compared to what took place at St. Denis, St. Charles, and later at St. Eustache, the "Battle" of Montgomery's Tavern was almost farcical. Mackenzie had mustered a gathering of armed sympathizers at the tavern located near what today is the corner of Yonge Street and Eglinton Avenue. Colonel James FitzGibbon, the War of 1812 hero Sydney had heard stories about when he was Colonel Foster's guest at Quebec a decade earlier, commanded the militia forces being cobbled together in the centre of town.[13] On the morning of December 5, two young law students who were riding with FitzGibbon, George Brock (a nephew of the lamented general of 1812) and nineteen-year-old William Bellingham, volunteered to go farther up Yonge Street to scout Mackenzie's position. William could not have known that three weeks earlier his older brother had been rooting out rebels at Booth's Tavern near Longueuil. This time, however, things turned out differently. Mackenzie's patrol nabbed George and William and kept them prisoner until FitzGibbon dispersed the rebels two days later. William later testified at the trial of one of the rebels and provided another with an affidavit attesting that he had been treated well. On the same day that William was captured, a retired British Army colonel seeking to raise the alarm had not been so lucky when he fired off his pistol to scare away the rebels blocking his way near the tavern. Mackenzie was blamed for shooting Colonel Robert Moodie, but in his account of the incident he claimed to have been several

miles away at the time, stating nonetheless that he "fully approved of the conduct of those who shot him."

With rebellions in both provinces, vigorous efforts were made to build up the militia units at Montreal, including the Royal Montreal Cavalry, which was immediately placed on the same footing as the regular British units. Sydney had made himself conspicuous to the military leadership, including General Colborne. He had demonstrated an ability to fend for himself and handle a horse in rough and dangerous conditions. With no military experience prior to the events of November, Sydney was appointed captain of a troop of fifty men of the Royal Montreal Cavalry on December 14, 1837, replacing Eleazar David, who had been promoted to major. Sydney replaced the *étoffe du pays* with the dark blue, red-and-gold-trimmed tunic and pantaloons of a hussar and kept the sabre, carbine, and brace of pistols. He remained with the regiment until the end of hostilities in December 1838. His captain's pay of about £250 per year enabled him to double the income he was receiving as a magistrate. In any event, after the declaration of martial law on December 5, the workload for magistrates on horseback was greatly reduced, but there was plenty of opportunity for cavalry officers to keep busy.

After St. Charles, the focal point of the rebellion shifted quickly from the Richelieu Valley, twenty miles east of Montreal, to the County of Two Mountains, twenty miles to the west, where the Ottawa River broadens out to form the Lake of Two Mountains before

---

13 See Chapter 3.

joining the St. Lawrence. An area of fertile fields and orchards, its 22,000 inhabitants made it the third most populated agricultural county in Lower Canada. It was also one where resentment ran high, in part due to abuses by the seigneurial landlords. Another factor was that the *Canadien* population in the western half of the county had begun to feel the threat of encroachment by Scottish settlers at St. Andrews, less than twenty miles distant. The local *Patriote* sympathizers were stirred up by grossly exaggerated reports of rebel success at St. Denis, with claims that as many as 197 soldiers had been killed (the actual figure was six). Rebel bands set up their headquarters in the village of St. Benoît, under the leadership of Jean-Joseph Girouard, a member of the Legislative Assembly who was also a local notary and the grandson of an Acadian deportee. From there they took control of the mostly loyalist town of St. Eustache, whose stone buildings appeared to provide an excellent defensive position. William Henry Scott, Girouard's co-member for the county in the Assembly and a *Patriote* in his own right, vainly tried to head off an engagement with the British forces. Loyalist townspeople and farmers, both English and French, were driven from their homes. Scott's general store was sacked. Other stores in St. Eustache and elsewhere, including the Hudson's Bay Company post at the Mohawk community at Oka, were looted for gunpowder, lead, food, and liquor. A more diplomatic attempt to gain the support and arms of the Mohawks themselves was courteously rebuffed.

In a curious parallel with Nelson and Brown at St. Denis, the two principal rebel leaders at St. Eustache were another idealistic physician, thirty-one-year-old Dr. Jean-Olivier Chénier, and a Swiss-trained writer and agronomist, Amury Girod. Girod, who claimed to have served in Simón Bolívar's liberation army in South America, got himself elected as general of the Army of the North. Many of the rebel recruits who had flocked to St. Eustache were persuaded to return to their homes by more moderate *Patriote* leaders like Scott and the local clergy, and a force that at one point had reached 1,500 men dwindled to just 250. Chénier and Girod held firm. Even the news of the defeat at St. Charles had no effect. The rebel leadership did not, however, realize the extent to which Colborne was preparing to visit a similar calamity upon St. Eustache. By December 13, two brigades of 1,280 well-equipped regulars were ready to move out of the Montreal garrison and march north over narrow, snow-covered roads, with Colborne personally in the lead. The infantry included companies of the 24th Regiment of Foot, known to film buffs for their stand against the Zulu army at Rorke's Drift in 1879. The regulars welcomed 220 volunteers, including *Canadien* loyalists driven from their homes at St. Eustache. Maximilien Globensky, whose house in the centre of town, like Debartzch's manor at St. Charles, was now a fortified rebel strongpoint, raised one group of volunteers. It is an odd coincidence that, in the space of only three weeks, the homes of two wealthy *Canadiens*

of Polish extraction—both of whom were veterans of the Battle of the Châteauguay in 1813—would become targets of the Royal Artillery. Accompanying Globensky's St. Eustache Loyal Volunteers was a company of Royal Montreal Rifles, a volunteer force led by Sydney's former fellow magistrate, Pierre-Édouard Leclère.

In the meantime, on December 8, a troop of Royal Montreal Cavalry led by Captain Sydney Bellingham and Lieutenant Charles Oakes Ermatinger Jr.—the latter still bearing the scars of the ambush near Longueuil—had been sent out to reconnoitre the territory around St. Eustache. They were part of an advance force encamped

25. Siege of the Church at St. Eustache, *painting by Charles Beauclerk, McCord Museum M4777.5, with permission*

at St. Martin, a village from which they could secure the bridges the main force would have to cross, first from the Island of Montreal to Île Jésus, and then traversing Île Jésus to the mainland at Ste. Rose, a fair distance northeast of St. Eustache. Sydney was billeted with a welcoming *Canadien* family some five miles from St. Eustache. The parish priest was also happy to see him but appeared uncertain as to whether he or Sydney should be in command. One of Sydney's missions involved searching the banks of the river and destroying boats and canoes that might be used by the rebels to escape by water. We do not know to what extent he was successful, but in any event the river was frozen over by the time the boats might have been needed. During another foray close to St. Eustache, Sydney and his friend, artillery captain John Glasgow, were reconnoitering the approaches to the town when they were fired upon from the church steeple. While waiting for Colborne's forces to arrive, Sydney received a visit from James Holmes, a Montreal provisioner, bringing food supplies. Holmes, like other Montreal tradesmen, was fearful of an attack on the city and the plundering of his stores by the hordes of rebel sympathizers who were rumoured to be massing on the border.[14] That attack, of course, never came. But the day after talking with Holmes, Sydney found himself evicted from his comfortable lodgings, which were commandeered as the officers' mess of the 3rd Regiment

of Foot, an Irish military unit that had distinguished itself in the Peninsular War.

On the morning of December 14, while the volunteer forces were creating a diversion on the ice directly in front of St. Eustache, Colborne's army of infantry, cavalry, and artillery approached on the left flank and began to encircle the town with the intention of cutting off any chance of a rebel retreat. Seeing their predicament, a number of *Patriote* leaders fled from the rear of the town towards St. Benoît. Among them was Papineau's cousin, André-Benjamin Papineau. Girod, under the pretext of going for reinforcements, rode off to the *Patriote* headquarters at St. Benoît, where Girouard berated him for cowardice and had him forcibly escorted back to the battle. Even in the rather undisciplined Army of the North, a general in the heat of battle does not run off for reinforcements himself— he stands his ground and sends someone else. On the way back to St. Eustache, Girod managed to elude his irate colleagues and made off in a carriage towards the north. A few days later, he shot himself when his arrest by the militia appeared imminent.

During the battle that took place over the course of the afternoon of December 14, the cavalry units, including Sydney's troop, remained on the fringes, where they were to cut off any retreat to the west or the north. The large infantry force spent most of the time out of range of rebel sniping from the stone buildings clustered around the square in the centre of town. These included

---

14 The building erected by Macdonnell, Holmes & Company at the corner of Saint-Paul and Saint-François-Xavier figures prominently in the film *The Score*.

the church, the presbytery, a convent, and Globensky's manor house. A detachment of the Royals under Colonel Wetherall's son Ned penetrated the presbytery and set it on fire. The convent and Globensky's house suffered the same fate. The occupants in all three cases had managed to escape to the river before the fires could harm them, but Globensky and Leclère rounded them up as they tried to make it across the ice. It was a different outcome at the church. Chénier and about sixty of his men were positioned in the upper gallery, from which they maintained an effective sniper fire. They had destroyed the staircase—and their own avenue of escape—in order to prevent a possible rush on their position. Another detachment of Royals penetrated the church and set it on fire. This time nearly all of the occupants, including Chénier, were killed as they tried to save themselves by jumping from the windows.

By the end of the short December afternoon, seventy rebels lay dead. Three British regulars had been killed. About eighty houses in what had been one of the finest villages in Lower Canada were in ruins or burning. A makeshift hospital was set up in a tavern some distance from the conflagration. As he had done at St. Charles, Wetherall's nephew and the other army surgeons tended to the wounded, rebel as well as soldier. In this instance, however, there were reports that some of the rebel wounded were dispatched by men of the 32nd Regiment to avenge the murder of their late officer, Lieutenant Weir. In his memoirs, Sydney wrote nothing about the battle itself, which suggests he was not part of it, and probably glad not to have been, given the fate of the insurgents who were slaughtered when they tried to escape from the burning church. In the immediate aftermath, he witnessed the body of Dr. Chénier being brought from the street to the makeshift hospital in the tavern and laid on a table. He was close enough to the scene to be able to describe Chénier in his memoirs, and the tone suggests that he had a certain admiration for the man's courage. Sydney's account of what he witnessed is devoid of anything to support the assertion of some authors that Chénier's body was intentionally mutilated in revenge for the murder of Weir.

The officially sanctioned burning of a few selected rebel houses was followed by unauthorized reprisals— mostly by the local volunteers and other loyalists—for the burnings and pillaging they had suffered earlier at the hands of the rebels. The day after the battle, Sydney was patrolling the countryside to protect its inhabitants from this sort of mischief. He recounts in his memoirs one incident of having to defend a *Canadien* family from the reprisals of a band of loyalist plunderers. Meanwhile, Colborne and most of his troops had advanced to St. Benoît, where they expected to encounter stiff resistance. There was none. Notary Girouard urged his few remaining people to lay down their arms, and he and the other rebel leaders took flight. Colborne ordered the destruction of three houses, including Girouard's, before leaving for Montreal on December 16 with the Royal

Montreal Cavalry as his personal escort. The previous night, a volunteer force hastily raised at St. Andrews in the neighbouring Seigneury of Argenteuil had joined Colburne's regular troops. The St. Andrews–Carillon Volunteers had been cobbled together in the expectation that St. Benoît would be the major showdown, but they were not needed and were told to return home in the morning. But before they complied, it was once again the volunteers who ran amok, resulting in the almost total destruction of a village that, until the week before, had been home to more than 1,000 people.

The concentration of rebel forces in the Richelieu Valley and in the County of Two Mountains may have been part of a coordinated strategy to draw the limited military resources of the Crown out of the Montreal garrison in opposite directions when their mobility was compromised by the weather. If all went according to plan—including the expectation that the local populations would turn out en masse to support the core groups—the victorious and expanding rebel forces could then cross the winter ice to Montreal and take the city. The inexperienced rebel commanders appear to have been overly optimistic about their chances of defeating experienced career soldiers supported by artillery. Their strategy, based on sniping from behind barricades with hunting pieces, failed to take into account that it takes more time to reload a musket than it does for a disciplined soldier with a bayonet to run the effective range. They may also have assessed the British military capability

in Lower Canada on the basis of its composition and performance in the War of 1812, not understanding that the units they would be facing had been hand-picked to prevent a future invasion attempt by the United States. They clearly failed to consider that Colborne and many of his officers were experienced battlefield commanders who had faced far more daunting foes in previous encounters, as Colborne had done at Waterloo. They also miscalculated their estimates of local support. Acts of intimidation against those not rallying to the cause may have inspired many to feign support, but only while it appeared that the hard-core rebel leaders held the upper hand. Most of the *Patriote* leaders were idealists drawn from the privileged professional and political classes. Most of the *Canadien* population they were counting on for support were the descendants of generations of hard-working pragmatists whose main preoccupation in life was the welfare of their families.

Much of 1838 was uneventful, leading some writers to consider the outbreak that occurred towards the end of that year to be a second rebellion, rather than a continuation of what had already occurred. In the meantime, the rebel prisoners from St. Charles and St. Eustache had become a serious legal problem. Were they subject to prosecution before the civil courts, or to trial by military commission? Their lawyers' efforts to obtain release through writs of habeas corpus forced General Colborne, who had now become administrator of the province following Governor Gosford's return to

England in February, to suspend the *Habeas Corpus Act*. In June, on the pretext of honouring Queen Victoria on her coronation, the new governor, Lord Durham, ordered a general amnesty and the release of all but 15 of the 161 rebel prisoners then still in jail. Durham, born John George Lambton, and sometimes referred to as "Radical Jack," fell out of favour with Westminster as a result of his liberal views and actions and returned to England after resigning his position in October 1838. Durham's first wife, Lady Harriet Cholmondeley, was a cousin of Sydney's great-aunt Hester Cholmondeley Bellingham.[15]

In early 1838, Colborne summoned Sydney to ask how he could best express his satisfaction with his conduct. It was the sort of situation in which personal advancement was there for the asking. Instead, Sydney asked that consideration be given to obtaining a regular commission in the British Army for William, now a lieutenant in the Queen's Rangers militia at Toronto. In March 1838, Colborne summoned him again to advise that William Bellingham had been made an ensign in the 32nd Regiment, stationed at Toronto. William remained a career officer for the rest of his active life. Three generations of Bellinghams can trace their military careers back to that day in early 1838 when General Colborne asked Sydney what he could do for him. After his years of active service with the 32nd and 50th Regiments, William became colonel of the Louth Militia when he retired to Ireland. His son, Sydney Edwin, was a major in the Duke

of Cambridge's Own (Punjab) Regiment, but he died at the age of forty in Balochistan, near the Afghan border, in 1893. Sydney's residual heir, William's grandson Alan, also rose to the rank of major and was awarded the Military Cross for his conduct in the First World War.

After St. Eustache, despite a few relatively minor incidents, the rebellion appeared to have been crushed, but it broke out again in November 1838. Once again, the focal point was on the South Shore, but this time farther south, closer to the American border where the rebels could find arms and sanctuary, notwithstanding a neutrality proclamation by President Martin Van Buren that outlawed support for the rebellion. The practice followed by American authorities was to let Canadian rebels come and go as they pleased, as long as they did not cross into the United States with their arms. (A quarter-century later, Canadian authorities reciprocated by allowing American rebels to come and go as they pleased.) In January, following an ideological breakup in relations among key *Patriote* leaders at a conference in Middlebury, Vermont, the leadership passed to Dr. Robert Nelson, Wolfred's younger brother. Robert Nelson had been arrested earlier in the year and released on bail.

Starting even before the defeat at St. Charles, rebel leaders, including Papineau, had been busy trying to drum up support and acquire arms from American sympathizers in New York, Vermont, and Maine. Part of the strategy was to provoke a conflict between the United States and Britain, in concert with border

---

15 Pronounced Hester Chumley Bellinjum!

incursions by Mackenzie's supporters in Upper Canada. The governor of Maine was pleased to oblige, in the hope of grabbing disputed territory along the border with New Brunswick. On the night of February 28, Nelson crossed the Vermont border on the east side of the Richelieu with a sizable force, which by the next morning had dwindled to only 160 men. Undaunted, he issued a carefully drafted declaration of independence, setting himself up as president and commander-in-chief of a new republic. The other provisions were rather more enlightened, including the abolition of the seigneurial system, universal suffrage, abolition of the death penalty except for murder, and the end of the tithe and other state-supported privileges for the clergy. It was a package that the aristocratic Papineau would never have endorsed. The new republic lasted less than a day. A battalion of local militia under the leadership of Sydney's friend Major John Warde of the Royals drove the invaders back across the border, where the American authorities disarmed them. No casualties were reported. President Nelson spent the next few months in Vermont organizing a new form of resistance—an underground movement with secret initiation ceremonies and secret oaths of loyalty called the *Frères Chasseurs*. Over the summer, a number of secret *Chasseur* lodges were set up as far away as Quebec, in Montreal, and even in the County of Two Mountains, where the notary Girouard, recently released from prison under the amnesty, resumed his role as local rebel leader, but this time less openly. The

real *Chasseur* threat, however, was in the valley of the Châteauguay River, a modest stream that runs parallel to the St. Lawrence just a few miles southeast of the great river. This was the area where de Salaberry repelled the American invasion of 1813, as Sydney had learned during his trip aboard the *Perseverance* a few days after his arrival in Canada.[16]

In the early months of the new year, the Royal Montreal Cavalry remained active. Its role was to help restore order by maintaining a visible and mobile military presence in the countryside. By late spring, things had calmed down enough for Sydney to spend most of his time in Montreal. On the morning of May 22, 1838, he was exercising his horse on the outskirts of town when he met up with Sergeant Sharp. Sharp told him there was a rumour circulating that Major Warde had been shot in a duel that same morning. It was Warde whom Sydney had roused at Fort Chambly on his quest for reinforcements for Wetherall's forces at the Battle of St. Charles. Sydney replied that he knew Warde well, and that he was the last man he knew who would likely provoke a duel. Later that morning, the news around town was that Warde was dead, having been shot by Robert Sweeney at dawn at the old racetrack in what is now the borough of Verdun. Sweeney, a former lieutenant in the Royal Montreal Cavalry, was reputed to be an extraordinary marksman. The night before, Warde had sent a bouquet of flowers, with a hidden note, to a *Canadienne* to whom, to use

16 See Chapter 2.

Sydney's words, Warde had "been paying attention." By mistake, the messenger delivered the flowers to Sweeney's house, where he lived with his American wife, whom Sydney described as "an accomplished and attractive personage." Intercepting the note, Sweeney flew into a rage and drove directly to the officers' mess, where he confronted Warde, called him a coward and then a liar when he denied the charge, and challenged him to the duel. At the time, although duelling was technically illegal, a British officer could not refuse a challenge without ruining his reputation and career. Sweeney fled to the border but returned when the grand jury declined to indict him for murder due to a lack of witnesses, despite the fact that a number of notables had

26. Lord Durham, drawing by J. Stewart, from Canada and Its Provinces, *by Adam Shortt and Arthur G. Doughty, eds., 1914*

gathered at the racetrack to view the event. It was the last fatal duel in what became Canada.

Since the beginning of the year, Colborne's forces had nearly doubled through the arrival of regular regiments from New Brunswick and Britain. In June, two regular cavalry regiments arrived, leading Colborne to deactivate the volunteer regiments, including the Royal Montreal Cavalry, in August. Sydney drew what he thought would be his last captain's pay in July. But by October, reports from Colborne's network of spies led Colborne to reconsider the need for experienced militia cavalry officers who were familiar with the territory south of Montreal. In charge of coordinating Colborne's intelligence efforts was Pierre-Édouard Leclère, previously Sydney's fellow magistrate on the mission to Longueuil, and now the superintendent of police at Montreal. By early October, Leclère became aware of an elaborate *Chasseur* attack plan, which included not just military operations, but the targeted killing of magistrates, militia officers, and loyalist sympathizers. Despite Robert Nelson's lofty democratic ideals, this second insurrection had a nastier side to it than the first. To some extent, or at least in some quarters, the outcome of the first insurrection may have increased ethnic or linguistic hostility during the second, displacing purely political reform as the main rallying cry of the rebellion.

On the night of November 3, Robert Nelson crossed the border on Lake Champlain by boat and set out with his entourage to a planned rendezvous with *Chasseur*

forces at Napierville, thirteen miles north of the border. The plan was to march on St. Jean and overwhelm the garrison there by sheer numbers. At Napierville, Nelson had one of his men reread the declaration of independence which had fallen on mostly deaf ears back in February. While this was going on, *Chasseur* bands terrorized the loyalist population in the Châteauguay Valley, plundering farms for horses and cattle, breaking into homes, and in one instance, killing the head of the family. Another band went north to Caughnawaga, the Mohawk village on the St. Lawrence opposite Lachine. The plan there was to secure the neutrality of the Mohawks and take their guns and ammunition. The result was even less inspiring than the similar attempt at Oka nearly a year earlier. Some sixty-four *Chasseurs* ended up being paddled to Lachine in canoes, where they were turned over by the Mohawk warriors to a troop of the Royal Montreal Cavalry garrisoned there, and from there they were paraded to jail in Montreal.

Another raid took place farther up the St. Lawrence at Beauharnois, opposite Pointe des Cascades. During the night of November 3, a band of *Chasseurs* took over the manor of Edward Ellice, carrying off his son as a prisoner and holding his son's wife and her sister captive in the manor while their captors passed the night sampling the copious wine cellar. The fabulously wealthy Ellice Sr. not only had the distinction of being the local seigneur, but was also private secretary to Lord Durham, at that very moment on his way back to England. At dawn,

the gang that had taken over the manor house went to the river, where the steam ferry *Henry Brougham* had stopped to take on fuel on its return run to Lachine from Pointe des Cascades. The *Henry Brougham* had replaced the *Perseverance*, which Sydney took on the same route during his trip to Upper Canada in the summer of 1824.

Its sleepy passengers and crew were quickly rounded up and joined Mrs. Ellice and her sister as prisoners in the local priest's presbytery. The *Henry Brougham* was holed, grounding her at the dock and preventing her from being used to ferry troops from Montreal.

Three years earlier, at St. Jean, a grand ceremony had

27. The Rebels at Beauharnois, watercolour by Jane Ellice, LAC, MIKAN 2836920 marked the opening of the Champlain & St. Lawrence Railroad. One of John Molson's endeavours, it was Canada's first railway, providing a direct link between the St. Lawrence at Laprairie and the Richelieu River at St. Jean. It was an event of such importance that both Governor Gosford and Speaker of the Assembly Papineau were in attendance. At about the same time as the *Henry Brougham* was seized, a band of rebels destroyed a section of the railway in order to prevent its use in bringing troops from Montreal to St. Jean.

Reports of these incidents and of the massing of rebel forces on a coordinated basis at different points convinced Colborne that this second insurrection was well planned, and possibly in greater strength and better equipped than the previous one. Practically overnight, the village of Napierville had become an armed camp, as St. Denis and St. Charles had been, but now on a more tightly organized scale. On the morning of November 6, Nelson dispatched a force of about 100 men on horseback and on foot to the border area near Rouse's Point, New York, where they were to link up with other rebels and American sympathizers and return with a supply of weapons, including cannon, for the attack on St. Jean.

At this point, the rebel plan began to unravel. Interestingly, it was not Colborne's regular forces that came to bear on the rebels, but units of border militia. These amateur soldiers scattered the *Chasseur* force at Lacolle, leaving eleven *Chasseurs* dead and relieving them of the one cannon they had managed to bring across

the border. In the meantime, Colborne crossed the St. Lawrence with 3,300 regulars and additional volunteer cavalry units, including Sydney's Royal Montreal troop. The plan was to launch a three-pronged offensive against Nelson's encampment at Napierville, which Colborne believed to be at least 4,000 strong. However, news of the defeat at Lacolle and the failure of the plan to prevent reinforcements from Montreal had reduced the number of men at Nelson's disposal to a mere 500. He decided to abandon Napierville and move south to Odelltown, closer to the border. Along the way, he was seized by a band of his own men and released by another, no one knowing for certain whether his abductors were loyalist agents or *Chasseur* diehards trying to prevent him from fleeing to the United States. At Odelltown, converging volunteer forces drove the *Chasseurs* back towards Napierville, killing fifty of them. Before the battle commenced in earnest, Nelson took his leave and ran for the border. Meanwhile, in the Châteauguay Valley, local volunteers, backed by more experienced Highland militia units from the Cornwall area and Mohawk warriors, moved north towards Beauharnois, where they freed the civilians taken captive at the Ellice manor and on the ferry. By mid-November, the second uprising had melted away. Sydney and his troop spent the rest of the year patrolling the border from St. Jean, waiting for an attack of *Chasseurs* and their American sympathizers, which never came.

The second uprising, despite the more careful

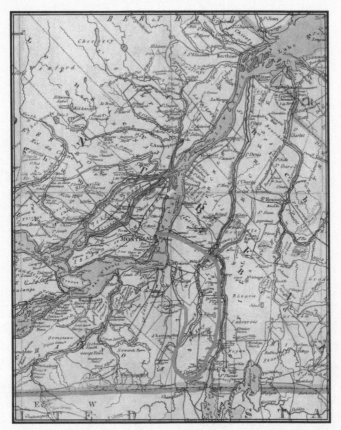

planning and coordination, may have been doomed to failure because of the overwhelming British regular forces assembled to deal with it. But those regular forces were never really brought to bear against rebel formations, not at Napierville nor anywhere else. The uprising had failed before the need arose to deal with it on that scale.

When it was all over, there had been only one fatality among the regular troops. The large rebel force that had convened at Napierville, and *Chasseur* bands elsewhere, simply faded away with news of the engagements with local militia in the border area and in the Châteauguay Valley. It was not really a matter of the militia units being

13. Expedition to St. Jean and the border area, from part of a map of Lower Canada by L. J. Hebert, 1838, LAC, MIKAN 4127086

superior in some way to the *Chasseurs*. Particularly at Lacolle and Odelltown, they were made up of amateur soldiers carrying their own equipment, and with the exception of a few officers, not even wearing a military uniform. It may be that many *Chasseur* recruits, including those pressured into joining, had more taste for a fight with the hated Redcoats sent over from Britain than with their Canadian neighbours. The neighbours spoke a different language, and for the most part, professed a different religion, but they were, after all, neighbours. Even the intruding Glengarry and Stormont Highlanders from the Cornwall area, although some had been regular soldiers before settling in Canada, were like many of the *Chasseurs*: men who worked the land and had families to look after. In addition, the Highlanders professed the same religion.

Attorney General Ogden had devised a method of bringing his concept of justice to those rebel leaders who had fled to the United States, some of whom continued to agitate from the other side of the border with impunity. A list was drawn up of the homes of the renegades, and the military were entrusted with the task of finding those homes and setting them on fire. In his memoirs, Sydney describes two incidents in which he was involved, apparently because of his ability to speak French. In the first, he was asked to accompany a Major Denny and a detachment of the 71st Highlanders to the village of St. Édouard, to the west of Napierville. Riding some distance ahead of the foot soldiers, they came to a large farmhouse that was the first on the list, and Denny told Sydney that he was to remain there "and not see anything removed" until the infantry had arrived and set it on fire. After Denny had moved on towards the next home on his list, the anxious lady of the house came out to ask Sydney what the soldiers were going to do. He replied that they were going to set fire to the house once they arrived, and that he was not to see anything carried away in the meantime. Orders being orders, but feeling a sense of repugnance, he told her that he would sit with his back to the premises and would thus be unable to see anything carried away. Half an hour later, the troops arrived to torch the house, but by then the old lady and her neighbours had emptied it of its contents. In the second incident, he was accompanied by his fellow officer in the Royal Montreal Cavalry, Charles Ermatinger, with orders from Major-General James Macdonell to set fire to the home and general store of another rebel leader. They found the premises occupied by the owner's wife and infant child, and the store well stocked with provisions. This time it was Ermatinger who was reluctant to carry out orders, so they returned to General Macdonell to report on the situation and hopefully gain a reprieve. The request was refused, and Macdonell insisted they carry out his instructions. They did so, saving only the baby's crib from destruction.

Just as had happened in the County of Two Mountains, the officially sanctioned practice of selectively destroying the houses of leaders of the rebellion was followed in the extreme by militia units, whose men embarked on a campaign of unrestricted reprisals against anyone suspected of being a rebel. The extent of the burning of homes and farms is difficult to estimate, but it took on major proportions in the later analyses by certain writers who sought to portray the rebellion not only as a struggle of a people, but one that was brutally suppressed. There was indeed collateral damage, but not a single civilian casualty, apart from the one loyalist farmer shot by the *Chasseurs* near Napierville. Looking at the whole period of rebellion, the total number of rebels killed has been pegged at 298, with half of those deaths occurring during the Battle of St. Charles, at the very beginning of the conflict. Compared to what the British Army showed itself capable of in dealing with other colonial rebellions both before and after, the extent of the suppression was relatively mild. Robert Bouchette, who was wounded on the Richelieu, taken prisoner, and transported to the Montreal jail pending exile to Bermuda, commented favourably in his memoirs on the way he was dealt with by the British regulars. The judicial retribution was also rather muted. Twelve *Patriote* rebels were executed. In the aftermath of the much less intense rebellion in Upper Canada, there were twenty-five executions of English-speaking rebels.

The failed rebellion may have had some positive impact in convincing the colonial authorities that responsible government had to be introduced in Canada, but the negative impact was far greater. On the economic front, the destruction of farms in the Richelieu Valley and in the County of Two Mountains aggravated an already dismal agricultural situation. Socially, the events of 1837 and 1838 served only to deepen the divide between French and English. If we examine the motivations of the principal rebel leaders, we can find among some of them a brooding hostility that only grew deeper after the rebellion was suppressed. Setting aside Papineau, whose motivations were probably too complex to lend themselves to a simple analysis, it is reasonable to conclude that many of the leaders who came from the professional class already harboured a deep resentment for the condescending and sometimes plainly insulting manner in which their English counterparts acted towards them. Why else would so many physicians and notaries become not just sympathizers, but leaders of the rebel cause? Notary Girouard might be the best choice to study in the search for an answer. Cool-headed in contrast with the fanatical Dr. Chénier, he was a cultivated man and relatively prosperous. Intellectually curious, he was a talented artist[17] and a generous benefactor to those in need. He may have harboured a grudge for the manner in which the British treated his Acadian forebears, but he also bore personal witness, as a member of the Legislative Assembly, to the high-handed manner in which the Château Clique played the political game in the years immediately preceding the rebellion.

---

17 He drew the portraits of a number of his *Patriote* colleagues while in prison, including the one of Wolfred Nelson, reproduced in this chapter.

We can rely on Sydney's memoirs to confirm the suspicion that *Canadiens* of equal social rank were often treated condescendingly and insulted by some English-speaking politicians and office-holders who believed they occupied a superior position of entitlement simply because of their Britishness. The superiority complex was encouraged by the final outcome in the ancient rivalry between France and Britain. The defeat of Napoleon after a quarter-century of war with France convinced at least some of British stock to believe they had a right to treat *Canadiens* as if they too were "the damned French." Sydney recounts how the colleagues of refined and educated *Canadiens* serving as regular officers in the British forces taunted them merely for being French-speaking. He gained this insight during his visit to the home of Monique Bâby in Lyme Regis in 1831, when he met her brother Daniel, then a major in the 24th Regiment of Foot, later retiring from the British Army with the very senior rank of lieutenant-general. Along with other *Canadiens* like De Salaberry, he had served under Wellington in the Peninsular War and had tasted personally the various epithets used by British-born officers in regard to the French. Sydney's Irish roots may help explain why he took a more egalitarian view, but his respect for the *Canadiens* was also the mark of an independent mind that did not fit well with the "we versus they" mentality of the tribe. Although there were many like him, it was, as he remarked in his memoirs, an age when racial and religious prejudice ran high.

Regrettably, it would take a few more generations of co-habitation before British condescension would fade from the Quebec scene, more as a result of demographic changes than personal enlightenment.

There were, however, members of the *Canadien* elite and professional class who were drawn to the *Patriote* cause, either as sympathizers or active participants, purely out of principled political conviction. One example is Robert Bouchette. The fourth son of the illustrious surveyor-general Joseph Bouchette, Robert was a fluently bilingual Anglophile. He was a lawyer, and like his father, a gifted cartographer. Much of the work that went into producing *The British Dominions in North America*, published by his father in 1832, was his. He had travelled to England, and, like his father, was well connected in Anglo-Canadian society. Yet in 1837, his name appeared on a list of proscribed *Patriote* committee leaders, with a warrant for his arrest. He fled to Vermont, then returned and was wounded in a skirmish on the Richelieu. Imprisoned and then exiled to Bermuda by Durham, he eventually returned to Lower Canada, and like so many other ex-*Patriotes*, resumed his career. His memoirs, which include correspondence written during the events themselves, and which are thus not diluted by after-the-fact rationalization, reflect a calm outrage at what he perceived as the denial of the rights guaranteed under the English Constitution. Bouchette did not feel threatened by the English. He felt threatened by the denial of responsible government.

The case of William Henry Scott also supports the argument that politics, rather than language or ethnicity, was the driving force behind the rebellion. Why else would a Scottish Presbyterian, a prosperous merchant in St. Eustache living a stone's throw from Globensky's manor house, espouse the *Patriote* cause and take the risks that caused him to lose his commission in the militia and be imprisoned for several months on charges of treason?

Ironically, it was the 1849 granting of royal assent to a bill to compensate those who had suffered losses during the rebellion, regardless of which side they were on, that finally confirmed that responsible government was a reality in Canada. In the meantime, a general amnesty proclamation issued in 1844 enabled "General" Thomas Storrow Brown to return to Montreal and resume business as a hardware merchant. Papineau came back from exile in France to do a bit more politicking and live out his days on his Seigneury in Argenteuil. Wolfred Nelson became a vice-president of the College of Physicians and Surgeons. He continued his role in Quebec politics, both in the Assembly and later as mayor of Montreal, but his brother Robert remained in the United States, where he practised medicine and tried his luck in the California gold rush. The boxer Deaf Burke returned to London to live in poverty and died there of tuberculosis in 1845. Eleazar David briefly went back to his law practice while retaining his association with the Royal Montreal Cavalry as a senior officer.[18] Pierre-Édouard Leclère gave up police work and moved with his wife and their seventeen children to St. Hyacinthe, where he worked as a notary and dabbled in agriculture. Lieutenant John Molson Jr. rose to the rank of lieutenant-colonel in the militia but became better known as a banker. Trooper John Lovell and Captain Sydney Bellingham of the Royal Montreal Cavalry remained close friends for the rest of their long lives, as well as allies in battles of a different sort, their weapon of choice being the printed word.

---

18 In 1840, he eloped to the United States with the wife of a captain in the 24th Regiment of Foot.

28. Robert Baldwin, photograph,
from Canada and Its Provinces, by Adam Shortt and Arthur G. Doughty, eds., 1914

CHAPTER 5

AFTERMATH

THE EVENTS OF **1837** AND **1838,** TO THE EXTENT THAT they were driven by so-called "racial" differences, only served to aggravate the divisions in the population, and the solution adopted by the British government made things even worse. That solution, in line with the more misguided portion of Lord Durham's report, was to return to the original policy of assimilation. The government believed that, in light of the great increase in Upper Canada's population, uniting the two provinces under a single assembly and executive would eventually submerge the French population in a sea of loyal, English-speaking Protestants and minimize the chances of another uprising. That was the plan, but it did not work. The *Act of Union* of 1840 only firmed up the *Canadiens'* resolve to preserve their identity. In addition, what the social engineers at the Colonial Office had not factored into the equation was that the divide between different political factions could trump language differences. Beginning with the alliance of Robert Baldwin and Louis-Hippolyte La Fontaine in 1841—a remarkable tale in itself that Sydney was moved to mention in his memoirs—a succession of alliances between French-speaking and English-speaking Reformers worked against the assimilation agenda. One result was the oddity of a supposedly united legislature, where initially only English could be spoken,[19] adopting different sets of laws, one for the old Upper Canada and another for the old Lower Canada with the latter written in both French and English. The Assembly also followed a practice called the "double majority," requiring new legislation to have the support of a majority of Lower Canada members and a majority of Upper Canada members. There were two attorneys general, one for Canada East and the other for Canada West. Eventually, it was as if the union had not really been implemented. Certainly, from a French-Canadian perspective it was far from ideal, but it would be hard to find a better example of principled people from different cultural and ethnic backgrounds working together in a fledgling democracy.

The tale Sydney recalled fifty years later is worth

---

19 English ceased to be the only official language following an amendment to the *Act of Union* in August 1848.

repeating. Robert Baldwin was a Reformer in what used to be Upper Canada. Louis-Hyppolyte La Fontaine was a Reformer in what used to be Lower Canada. In the mid-nineteenth century, party lines were not as clearly drawn, nor as firmly adhered to as they are today. Members of the Assembly who identified as Reformers were generally people who insisted on responsible government and were uncomfortable with the *Act of Union*. On the other side were the Tories, who were generally in line with the *Act of Union* and supportive of the ultimate authority of the Crown, as represented by the governor general. Some Tories were more liberal than others, and Sydney is a good example. But before we get to his political life, a word about Baldwin and La Fontaine.

Robert Baldwin was born at York in 1804. Like so many other people we have met on this journey, his background was Anglo-Irish. A lawyer, he was first elected to the Legislative Assembly of Upper Canada at age twenty-six and quickly became identified as an advocate of responsible government. Appointed to the Executive Council by Lieutenant Governor Head in 1836, he soon resigned when it became clear to him that Head would work against responsible government. Returning to politics in 1841 as a member of the new Legislative Assembly of the United Province, he resigned from the reconstituted Executive Council when Governor General Sydenham refused to appoint what Baldwin felt was a sufficient number of French-speaking members. Unilingual and lacking any real connection with Lower

Canada, his defence of French- Canadian interests appears to have been motivated solely by principle. In the general election of 1841, so skillfully manipulated by Sydenham, La Fontaine had been denied a seat through physical obstruction of the polls by an Orange Order mob in the County of Terrebonne, north of Montreal. Baldwin opened up a seat for him in a riding north of Toronto. In 1842, Orange Order mob violence prevented Baldwin from being returned to his seat near Belleville in eastern Upper Canada. La Fontaine opened up a seat for him in the riding of Rimouski in eastern Lower Canada. For nearly a decade, Baldwin and La Fontaine formed a unique political partnership. It was a decade in which Sydney Bellingham would flirt with politics, and as we shall see, his flirtations were somewhat fickle, like those of many other politicians at that time.

After the end of armed conflict in December 1838, Sydney turned away from his short but eventful military career and resumed civilian life. Charles Ermatinger replaced him as captain of the second troop, and the Royal Montreal Cavalry remained on regular duty for another thirteen years. During that period, one of its functions was to guard the U.S. border. At first, this meant watching out for further incursions by *Chasseurs* and their American sympathizers, but oddly enough the flow changed direction, with British regulars deserting the Montreal garrison to seek out a new life in the United States.

Sydney's experiences with the Freer and Duncan

failures, which had cost him dearly, had dampened his enthusiasm for the import/export business, and he turned his attention instead to the law. Perhaps he felt that a good knowledge of law would better equip him for an eventual return to trade, without the risk of repeating past mistakes. In any event, after articling with a pre-eminent Montreal lawyer, Alexander Buchanan, he was admitted to the bar of Lower Canada on March 23, 1840. His financial situation had stabilized when Arabella's mother died in 1838, leaving her 15,000 acres of land in the County of Bellechasse, located fifteen miles inland from the South Shore of the St. Lawrence opposite Quebec. The land included much of the Township of Buckland, created under the British regime, beyond the boundaries of the seigneuries that separated it from the river. Under the *Coutume de Paris*, although Arabella retained a half-interest in the couple's community of property, the management of that property rested exclusively with her husband.

Bellechasse is beautiful country, with the Appalachain Mountains to the east and the Etchemin River running through it on its way to the St. Lawrence. Before completing his articles, Sydney spent some time there to settle the inheritance, collect rents owed by the tenant farmers, and negotiate the sale of timber. Early in the winter of 1840, he set off alone for Bellechasse by sleigh. A less adventurous landlord would have waited for spring and the first steamer to Quebec, but all traffic on the river had ceased for the season, except in the places where it could be crossed by sleigh over the ice. It was sometimes possible to cross to the South Shore at Montreal, but the current there made that option a dangerous one. Instead, he drove his sleigh fifteen miles from the centre of Montreal to the northeast end of the island, where the ice was more predictable on the calmer waters of the Back River, and where he could more safely cross to the North Shore as he had done on the way to St. Eustache in 1837.

Until the advent of reliable railways, the country inn was as important as the road itself in the system of travel by land and to the mail service. The inn provided not just accommodation for the traveller, but also livery for the horses. The government encouraged the establishment of inns at regular intervals along the principal roads through the granting of lucrative liquor licences. At the inn where Sydney stopped for the first night, the innkeeper entertained him with an oft-repeated tale of how, many years earlier, the inn had briefly lost its licence. Governor General Sir George Prévost and his retinue had stopped there overnight on their way from Quebec to Montreal. The next morning, before leaving, he was handed a bill for £50, the equivalent of nearly $7,000 today. Complaining that he had never before been presented with such a monstrous bill, the innkeeper truculently replied that he had never before entertained a governor general. His licence was cancelled the following day.

After being given a far more modest bill, Sydney

continued on to a point about thirty miles above Trois-Rivières, where the St. Lawrence expands to form Lac Saint-Pierre and where the ice could again be trusted. Descending a steep hill in heavy snow, the sleigh, horse, and driver tipped and rolled from top to bottom, but without suffering any damage. He recalled in his memoirs the ingenious *Canadien* harness system that enabled the driver of a *calèche* or sleigh to quickly uncouple the horse and get back on the track. Crossing to the South Shore, Sydney proceeded along snow-packed roads for another ninety miles to Lévis, opposite Quebec. It was territory he had never seen before until he reached Lévis, where he had disembarked on his voyage from Ireland in 1824. Left untouched by the troubles of the previous years, the people reminded him of those he had lived with for a short time at L'Ange-Gardien. Some of them had a penchant for horse-dealing. Along the way, he traded his horse, which he described as a "nag," for a "three-minutes-a-mile trotter." In the soft snow, moving at that speed, snowballs built up in the horse's hooves and "were flung with great force into the face of the driver."

From Lévis, Sydney turned southeast to the village of Sainte-Claire, where he met up with Jean-Joseph Reny, the local notary. Sydney had brought with him a letter of introduction from one of the most influential bureaucrats of the day, Pierre-Louis Panet. Panet, a lawyer and son of a judge, was the chief road inspector for the district of Trois-Rivières, one of the three rural districts into which Lower Canada had been divided after the British occupation. The position was a holdover from the French regime, when the *grand voyer* was the final authority in the construction and maintenance of roads and bridges. The office was finally done away with at the end of 1840, when municipal councils assumed responsibility for roads and bridges. Maître Reny introduced him to his brother-in-law Charles Taschereau, another landowner in Bellechasse. The following day, Reny and Taschereau drove him to a spot on the Abenaskis River where they found a harvest of 20,000 saw logs assembled behind booms to be floated downriver to Lévis in the spring. Lévis timber merchants had cut the logs, without permission, on Arabella's land. This was a time when lumber companies raided timber from both Crown and private land, counting on the lack of government controls and gambling that absentee landowners would never hear about it. Over the next few days, acting on Reny's advice, Sydney retained a lawyer to place the logs under a court seizure. It could have represented a small fortune in the lumber market. However, after Sydney returned to Montreal and spring came, a flash flood destroyed the booms and the logs were swept away in a torrent of water, cascading down the Abenaskis to the Etchemin River, and from there to the St. Lawrence and beyond. After attending to the problem of the logs, Sydney was received as a guest in the home of Jean Bilodeau in the nearby village of Saint-Lazare. Bilodeau was a gentleman of means, and it was at his large house that Sydney received a procession of some 180 tenant farmers coming

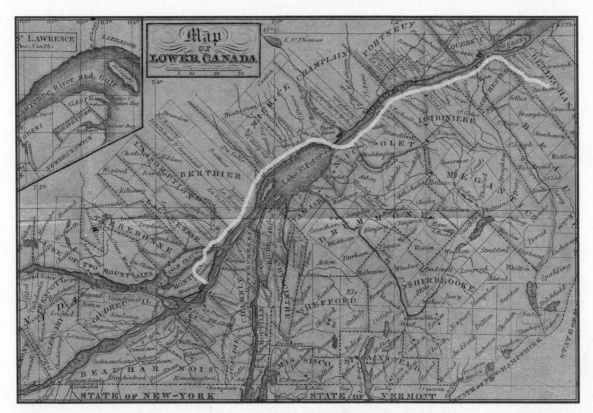

to pay their rents to the new landlord. He set himself up at a table in one room, with his account books and a stack of title deeds, while the tenants waited their turn in an adjacent room. His arrival had been dutifully announced by the posting of a notice on the door of the church, which tells us something about the role of the *curé* in ensuring that even business matters were conducted in an orderly fashion. It was, in fact, an annual ritual that the tenants were familiar with. Previously, they had dealt with William Holmes's land agent, and somehow word had gotten about that it would be easier to deal with the new administration. Perhaps from his knowledge of the plight of tenant farmers in Ireland, Sydney respected these hard-working people and felt that it was to them,

14. The trip to Bellechasse County, from a map by Walton and Gaylord, 1835, LAC, MIKAN 4127087

and not absentee landlords, that the French Crown should have given the land in the first place. It was they, after all, who had cleared and fenced the land, built the roads and bridges, and provided the labour and much of the resources that made it possible for a village like Saint-Lazare to boast a parish church and presbytery. The soil in this rear section of Bellechasse County was poor, and many of the tenants could not have provided for their families without working for the lumber companies during the winter months or trapping for furs in the backcountry.

The Township of Buckland was relatively new and not part of the older seigneurial territory. Although the British initially maintained the seigneurial system, they did not create new seigneuries. Crown lands newly opened up to settlement were divided into townships, the basic unit into which the non-seigneurial part of each county was divided. The Honourable Jean-Thomas Taschereau had owned Buckland for a short time. Taschereau, a judge at the Court of Queen's Bench at Quebec and owner of the neighbouring seigneuries of Joliette and Saint-Joseph, was enamoured with the seigneurial system and had structured the ownership and leasing of the Buckland freehold lots in a manner that mimicked it. In all but name, Sydney found himself effectively in the role of *seigneur*. Uncomfortable with this replication of a system he disliked, he was soon spotted as an easy mark for a *rabais*, or request for a discount, on rents that were already only about $4 per hundred

acres. From one tenant to the next (or from one tale of woe to another tale of woe), the parade, which lasted the better part of a week, yielded less in the end than what he would have received if he had left the whole matter in the hands of a more dispassionate land agent.

Sydney did what probably very few landlords would have done by socializing with the tenants and their families, attending their Sunday-evening card parties, smoking their homegrown tobacco, and even passing himself off as one of the faithful at Sunday Mass, sitting beside Bilodeau in his high-rent pew in the front row. He remarks in his memoirs on the civility and correctness of the *habitants*, and how a Sunday-evening conversation at the card table would rarely stray from topics that *Monsieur le Curé* would approve of if he were there. He writes that during his trips to Bellechasse he never witnessed a quarrel or an incident of drunkenness or violence, despite the absence in the area of a constable or any other strong arm of the law. No doubt he had great admiration for the peaceful nature of *Canadien* society, but he goes a bit overboard when he writes that he had never heard of a French Canadian accused of murder. He could not have avoided hearing about the trial of the *Patriote* François Jalbert for the murder of Lieutenant George Weir at St. Denis. Jalbert's acquittal by a mainly French-speaking jury caused a riot in Montreal. He also seems not to have heard about a gruesome murder in his own Township of Arundel in 1875, but which was revealed only after he had returned to Ireland.[20]

The only such incidents he mentions involved English-speaking villains. One of them was another murder in Argenteuil, this one in 1845, which had a most remarkable connection with the events he had witnessed during the rebellion. The victim was none other than Sam O'Rourke, the Irish prizefighter whose fans drove Deaf Burke out of New Orleans in May 1837. O'Rourke did not remain in the United States, and he did not return to Ireland either. He may have followed Deaf Burke to Montreal, but he eventually gave up prizefighting and took up farming near the village of Grenville on the banks of the Ottawa River, just twenty miles south of Arundel. O'Rourke had lent a horse and some money to a fellow Irishman, John Brady, and went to Brady's shanty one night to call in the loan. O'Rourke's body was later found in the Rouge River, along with his dead horse. We know from a report in the *Montreal Gazette* that Brady was arrested, but according to the Bellingham memoirs, he got away with the crime for lack of witnesses.

Despite a few oversights, Sydney was essentially correct in his observations about the non-violent nature of *Canadien* society. In contrast with most of the rest of North America, it has remained the same to this day. But the criminal justice system, which was the product of the British tradition, was a different story. Prior to the rebellion, fewer people were convicted of murder than were hanged for theft.

Sydney would return to Bellechasse, but as the years progressed he would rely increasingly on his notaries there and at Quebec to attend to the renewal of leases and his other business interests in Buckland Township. The Quebec notarial profession was then, and still is, a unique institution in North America, often misunderstood by people in the rest of Canada or the English-speaking world at large. The Quebec notary is essentially a lawyer who specializes mainly in real-estate transactions, contracts, wills, and family-law matters in a non-adversarial context. In the colony of New France, adversarial lawyers were banned, not to reappear until after the British took over. Under the French regime, the notary enjoyed a reputation for integrity and objectivity that was not then enjoyed by lawyers in France, or even by lawyers in Canada after French rule came to an end. Especially in a rural community, the notary enjoyed a level of prestige second only to the parish priest and was often an important figure in local politics. Rural notaries might also be the only local source of borrowed money, further enhancing their influence. The notarial profession not only survived the British takeover, but also attracted to its ranks new members from the English-speaking business and legal community. In the will he signed in Ireland in 1898, Sydney named two executors. One was his nephew and neighbour, Sir Alan Henry Bellingham. The other was a Quebec City notary he had not seen in more than twenty years, Edward Graves Meredith.

Edward Graves Meredith was the son of Chief Justice

---

20 See Chapter 8.

William Collis Meredith of the Quebec Superior Court. The Dublin-born Chief Justice Meredith, a veteran of St. Eustache, was related to Sydney through his marriage to Arabella's niece. After Leclère and Warde, he is the third person in Sydney's narrative—but not the last—to be involved in a duel. The surviving descriptions of this event, which appears to have occurred in August 1837, are somewhat confusing. It is possible that accounts of two separate duels have become conflated. One story has it that Chief Justice Meredith was known to regularly assist his colleague, Justice James Smith, up the stairs of the Montreal courthouse. It is explained that Smith was crippled when a pistol ball permanently lodged in his thigh during a duel with Meredith over a bill of costs when they were both young lawyers. The other story has it that the other young lawyer was James Scott, not James Smith, and that Meredith was often seen assisting his brother judge Scott up the stairs of the courthouse. It is indeed James Scott who is mentioned as the injured loser in a contemporaneous newspaper report of a duel with Meredith.[21] However, James Scott was never a judge. He was the son of William Scott, the member of the Legislative Assembly who later in 1837 briefly allied himself with the rebel side at St. Eustache.[22] If it was indeed James Scott who was Meredith's opponent, he was a formidable one, having previously lodged a ball in the thigh of Campbell Sweeney, the brother of Robert

Sweeney, who killed Major Warde the following year. Fortunately, duelling was not as rampant in Montreal as it might seem, but it was certainly one of the risks of annoying members of the Sweeney family. It was also obviously not an impediment to becoming a chief justice. Michael O'Sullivan, a prominent Montreal lawyer who had been De Salaberry's *aide-de-camp* at the Battle of the Châteauguay, became chief justice of Lower Canada, notwithstanding a duel in 1819 with Dr. William Caldwell. Caldwell was one of the promoters of what became the Montreal General Hospital. O'Sullivan, who was then a member of the Assembly, opposed the project. There were exchanges of heated words and later of five shots each, two of which hit O'Sullivan. He suffered for nearly twenty years from those wounds and died only two months after his appointment in 1838 as chief justice. It bears mentioning that Caldwell was the brother-in-law of Robert Sweeney.

From his travels to Bellechasse via the Back River crossing, Sydney got to know a priest who lived in a rather prosperous-looking house in the village of Rivière-des-Prairies on the northern edge of the Island of Montreal. He was Louis Villeneuve, the nephew and heir of Sydney's old friend Souligny.[23] One day, to quote Sydney, Villeneuve "was approached by a brother ecclesiastic of a higher rank." To make a long story short, Villeneuve's superior, a member of the powerful Sulpician Order, persuaded him to make the costly trip

---

21 *La Minerve*, edition of August 10, 1837.
22 See Chapter 4.

23 See Chapter 3.

to Rome and pay homage to the pope. The Sulpicians, who held the seigneurial rights to the entire Island of Montreal, maintained an office next to Notre Dame Church in Place d'Armes, two blocks from Sydney's office on Little St. James Street. It was housed in the large stone seminary building erected in the 1680s from plans drawn up by François Dollier de Casson, a former French cavalry officer turned priest who had a flair for urban planning and architecture. Sydney remarked in his memoirs how many of the original Sulpicians, who had been key participants in the early development of the town, had returned to France after the British takeover and how the Montreal branch of the order would have died off altogether had they not been replaced, at the invitation of the British authorities, by a fresh batch fleeing persecution during the French Revolution. The idea of British colonial authorities importing Roman Catholic priests as a stabilizing influence on the local population would have been hard for a lot of people in Ireland to understand following centuries of religious persecution and disenfranchisement in their country.

From their offices in the seminary, the Sulpicians administered their vast windfall property interests, with clerks and a notary on full-time staff. Villeneuve was invited to drop by the office prior to his departure for Rome, ostensibly to collect some letters of introduction to a number of Vatican notables. They urged him to make out a notarial will, in the event that he should meet with some misfortune during the voyage. As an added

precaution, he left the administration of his inheritance in the capable hands of the Sulpicians, who could be relied on to collect the income in his absence. Two years later, upon his return, he called at the office of the Sulpicians to collect his money. It was explained to him that what he had signed was not a will, but rather a deed of gift *entre-vifs*, and that he had given his entire inheritance to the order. In civil law, a gift *entre-vifs* (between living persons) can be valid only if made before a notary. One of the best-known lawyers of the day, Côme Séraphin Cherrier, was engaged to undo the deal, but all he could recover for Villeneuve out of his £40,000 was a pension of £80 a year. Villeneuve was forced to sell his house in Rivière-des-Prairies, lay off the servants, and move into humble accommodations in the old Sulpician seminary building on Notre Dame Street.

Having paid a brief visit to Bellechasse, our focus now shifts back to Montreal. Sydney won the first case he pleaded as a young barrister. It was a jury trial involving slander. The case itself was unremarkable, but the same could not have been said about either the presiding judge or Sydney's opponent, William Walker, about whom we will learn more in a moment. The judge was Joseph-Rémi Vallières de Saint-Réal, soon to become the chief justice at Montreal. Vallières had gained a reputation as a brilliant lawyer, wealthy landowner, social activist, and politician before becoming a judge. In 1814, he was elected speaker of the Legislative Assembly, and for several years he was Louis-Joseph Papineau's political rival. Considered by many as a man of genius, he was an independent thinker, and principled. But judicial independence was not then what it is now. When Colborne suspended habeas corpus during the Rebellion of 1838, Vallières considered the order unconstitutional and freed a farmer who had been detained as a suspected *Patriote* sympathizer without being formally charged. Furious, Colborne, with prompting from Attorney General Ogden, removed Vallières from the bench, whereupon he likely would have returned to politics and become a leading figure in the new Union Parliament had he not been reinstated by Governor General Sydenham in 1840.

Montreal was still very much a garrison town in 1840, and the officers and their ladies kept busy with a steady succession of balls, picnics, and a new activity that was all the rage in winter—the skating party. In the spring of 1840, the officers of the 24th Regiment of Foot organized a grand country picnic on the banks of the St. Lawrence at Lachine, and guests with carriages were expected to drive the wives of the men arriving on horseback. It fell to Sydney to escort Eliza, the charming wife of Captain Henry Harris of the 24th. He mentions in his memoirs that he had not the remotest idea that Eliza was planning to elope to Vermont with his old colleague from the Royal Montreal Cavalry, Major Eleazar David. It was the biggest scandal of the day. David forfeited his law career and high position in the military, but only for a few years. At the Battle of Chillianwallah in January

13, 1849, during the second Anglo-Sikh War, the 24th suffered horrendous casualties, and poor Harris was one of them. The regimental history describes him as "a tall portly old officer," which gives us a hint of why Eliza had eyes for Eleazar, who apparently cut a dashing figure in his cavalry officer's uniform. Shortly after Harris's death, Eleazar David married Eliza and they returned to Montreal with their five children.

In 1841, Sydney still held his appointment as a magistrate and sat as one of the members of the Court of General Sessions of the Peace, reviewing accusations of bullying at the polls in the first general election held after the *Act of Union* came into force. This was the election in which La Fontaine's supporters in Terrebonne had been blocked from voting. With Governor General Sydenham's blessing, if not at his instigation, gangs of anti-Reformer Orange Order goons interfered with the polling in a number of ridings in Lower and Upper Canada, but Terrebonne was a prime example of the kind of tactics used. It was the governor general who decided how many polling stations there would be and where they were to be located. Sydenham concluded that a single polling station would be sufficient for the County of Terrebonne, which had a population of about 20,000. The place he picked was at the northern end of the riding in a pocket of Scottish and Scots-Irish settlement, where the goons could easily intimidate any La Fontaine supporters bold enough to venture the many miles from their homes to the polling station. This was

just one incident among many in British North America throughout the mid-nineteenth century, with adherents of what was supposed to be a benevolent mutual aid society venting their hatred for their Catholic neighbours, both Irish and French. Election violence was not the only manifestation. In Cavan Township on the other side of the Otonabee from Douro, Orange vigilante gangs terrorized Robinson's Irish Catholic settlers and burned their farms a couple of years after Sydney left Douro to return to Lower Canada.

The charter of the City of Montreal, having lapsed during the legislative deadlock that preceded the rebellion,

29. Louis Hyppolite La Fontaine, from a painting in the Château Ramezay, from Canada and Its Provinces, by Adam Shortt and Arthur G. Doughty, eds., 1914

was finally renewed in 1841. Prior to the reinstatement of elected municipal government, magistrates managed city affairs. One of the problems they had to deal with was a creek, called the Little River, which ran along what would later be called Craig Street (today's Rue Saint-Antoine). Until 1842, Little River flowed westward past McGill Street, where it turned south, reversed course, and emptied itself into the harbour at Pointe-à-Callière, the spot chosen by the first French colonists 200 years earlier. There was a lot more to flush than just water. The creek, fed by other small streams, had become an open sewer. Its stench was blamed for typhus and cholera, and its swampy areas were a breeding ground for malaria-carrying mosquitoes. There were two schools of thought about what to do. The French-speaking magistrates, with whom Sydney sided, proposed using the streambed as an extension of the new Lachine Canal, bypassing Saint Mary's Current where the St. Lawrence narrows at Île Sainte-Hélène. John Molson's friends opposed that idea. Molson's steam-tugboat business made its money bringing sailing ships into the harbour against the current. In the end, the Molson faction won out, and the streambed became the route of a new main sewer, a tunnel seven feet in diameter, more than a mile and a half long, made of bricks. But unlike the Little River, it was supposed to flow in the opposite direction, from west to east, and empty itself in the St. Lawrence below Saint Mary's Current. It was designed with a slope of seven and one half feet over its entire length, on the assumption that the ground itself sloped in the same direction, parallel to the river. In reality, the ground sloped in the opposite direction, and the big sewer was almost perfectly level. It performed more as a sewage collector than as a means of sewage disposal and had to be cleaned out through manholes in the middle of the street. The stench and danger of disease only worsened as the city expanded and feeder lines were connected to the Craig Street tunnel. In the spring of 1848, one of the worst floods in Montreal's history occurred when the river dammed up with ice. The floodwaters surged up McGill Street as far as Craig and flushed the contents of the big sewer, spreading filth throughout the neighbourhood and into the basements of the buildings. Sydney recalled witnessing the event and worrying about a return of the cholera epidemic of 1832. The commercial heart of the city, situated on the ridge of higher ground that separated Craig Street from the harbour, was spared the floodwaters and the filth, but not the stench.

Sydney left the Buchanan firm shortly after his admission to the bar and went to work with another respected Montreal lawyer, William Walker. Walker had been a political opponent of Papineau and Robert Nelson, narrowly losing to them in the 1834 contest for the two-member riding in the West Ward of Montreal, when Sydney was a candidate in the East Ward. Walker was one of the founders of the Montreal Constitutional Association, the group formed to oppose the policies of the *Patriote* party. Walker, the fourth of Sydney's acquaintances who had been involved in a duel, walked with a limp as a result of an early-morning rendezvous with another lawyer, Campbell Sweeney, the brother of Robert Sweeney, who killed Major Warde in a duel.[24] Campbell Sweeney also walked with a limp, courtesy of James Scott. Scott, as we have seen, walked with a limp as a result of his encounter with William Meredith.

Despite his political activities, Walker was, first and foremost, a lawyer. Among his clients were a number of *Patriotes* facing trial in the aftermath of the rebellion, and he acted for his old political rival, Robert Nelson, in an early attempt to negotiate his return from exile. In 1840, Walker took on the added responsibility of editor of the Reformist *Times and Commercial Advertiser*, and in that capacity he was fiercely opposed to the Union of Upper and Lower Canada, as was Sydney. They shared a strong distrust for Governor General Lord Sydenham and his policy of cultural and linguistic assimilation. Sydney soon found himself working on the newspaper. In July 1842, Walker was elected to the Legislative Assembly and called upon Sydney to take over the task of editing the *Times*.

Sydney took to journalism with a passion. Setting aside the practice of law, which he considered incompatible with the duties of a newspaper editor, he devoted himself almost exclusively to the paper. In those days, journalistic independence was a rarity, if it existed at all, and the *Times* was clearly aligned with the Baldwin–La

Fontaine Reform movement, which had assumed power in September 1842. As a result of Walker's influence, Sydney went through a political conversion. Initially Tory in his political ties, his involvement with the *Times* had brought him into the Reformist camp dominated by the Baldwin–La Fontaine alliance. On November 29, 1842, Sydney wrote La Fontaine, soliciting financial support for the paper in response to Tory party attempts to cut off its revenues from the publication of government notices. Lord Sydenham had died the previous year from complications following a riding accident, and the more moderate Sir Charles Bagot replaced him as governor general. Bagot in turn succumbed to illness in 1843 and Sir Charles Metcalfe succeeded Bagot.

It may have been Sydenham's demise and the advent of more liberal governors that caused Sydney's political conversion to be short-lived. His conservatism was always more political than social. It was a conservatism focused on respect for the established order, but flexible enough to accommodate liberal values if they could be realized within that order. A meeting with Metcalfe triggered his drift back to moderate conservatism. Sydney had gone to Kingston, then the capital, to present the licensing grievances of a group of Montreal innkeepers and tavern owners. Metcalfe was locked in a political struggle with the Baldwin–La Fontaine faction. Although it had nothing to do with Sydney's mandate, the two of them spent time discussing the bigger picture. Metcalfe, who enjoyed a reputation for fairness in his previous

---

24 See Chapter 4.

colonial appointments in India and Jamaica, won Sydney over with his views against the policies of assimilation and anglicization that underlay the *Act of Union* and were characteristic of the earlier administration under Sydenham. *Canadien* politicians themselves were deeply divided in the debate that raged in the papers between the supporters of La Fontaine and those who admired Metcalfe's liberalism and good intentions. Part of the attraction may have resided in Metcalfe's support for moving the capital to Montreal and the granting of amnesty for participants in the rebellion. Sydney told Metcalfe that he would advocate his cause, even if it meant severing ties with the Baldwin–La Fontaine faction. On February 10, 1844, fending off accusations that he had betrayed the Reform movement, Sydney resigned as editor of the *Times* and published a valedictory letter explaining his support for Metcalfe. In the letter, he reaffirmed his beliefs in responsible government and in a fair share for French Canadians in the executive branch of government. In the years to come, he would continue to maintain his opposition to the Union and its goals of assimilation, believing that the Union was an unrealistic artifact created by the Colonial Office. More than thirty years later, he would oppose Confederation out of concern for the survival of French-Canadian culture, language, and institutions in an even broader agglomeration of British North American colonies.

Not long after Sydney's resignation as editor, William Walker died in April 1844 at the age of forty-six. The *Times* expired with him. Metcalfe resigned in November 1849 and soon became the third governor in a row to die from an incurable illness. James Bruce, better known as Lord Elgin, replaced Metcalfe. In May 1844, the capital of Canada was moved from Kingston to Montreal.

In 1845, Sydney travelled to Ireland, Britain, and France and did not return until 1847. We do not learn from his memoirs why he left nor what occupied him during that period, but his absence could be explained in part by the death of Hester Bellingham in 1844, which brought an end to her life tenancy at Bellingham Castle House and may have left Sir Alan Edward in need of some assistance in settling Hester's estate.

Upon his return to Canada, a new sight greeted Sydney as the paddle steamer from Quebec made its way past Saint Mary's Current into the harbour. This time, instead of John Molson's brewery, what focused the attention of passengers was the new Bonsecours Market, with its neoclassical domed architecture. Sydney resumed his legal practice upon his return, taking an office on Little St. James Street, a few steps from where the courthouse had been destroyed by fire on July 17, 1844. The fire was set by an accomplice of a man called Félix Mercure, whose trial for theft had been adjourned at the request of his lawyer, Lewis Thomas Drummond, of whom we will learn more later in our journey. Construction of a magnificent new courthouse began in 1851. "Little" St. James Street was the extension of "Great" St. James Street, eastward from the square called

Place d'Armes.[25] It was home to nearly fifty lawyers and notaries, as well as the head office of the St. Lawrence and Atlantic Railroad. During Sydney's absence, work was also completed on the new Pantheon-style building of the Bank of Montreal, one of several banks and insurance companies to set up their headquarters on Great St. James Street. It was built facing Notre Dame Church on the other side of Place d'Armes. Its planners were anticipating a boom in the banking business that would justify the expense, but their timing was off.

---

25 The eastern end of Little St. James Street disappeared in 1964 to make way for the construction of the present-day high-rise Montreal Courthouse.

30. Bonsecours Market, drawing by A. Deroy, LAC, MIKAN 2837616

These were not good times. Canada, and Montreal in particular, were feeling the effects of the new free-trade policies of the Peel government at Westminster, with the end of preferential tariffs for Canadian exports to Britain. Unemployment drove large numbers of *Canadiens* to emigrate to the United States. Later generations of separatist thinkers would blame the *Act of Union* for the exodus, but it had little or nothing to do with that.[26] The wheat and lumber producers of Upper Canada were just as affected by the loss of preferential tariffs and by the general economic depression in Europe and North America. Not until the 1860s did changes in the

31. Great St. James Street, c. 1843, drawing by John Murray, LAC, MIKAN 2837616

26 When he was Quebec's vice-premier and minister of finance, Bernard Landry claimed that had it not been for the *Act of Union*, Quebec would have today a population of fifty million.

seigneurial regime begin to improve the opportunities for a growing rural population that viewed the United States as an El Dorado in contrast with the moribund urban economies at home. Added to the economic and agricultural problems were other misfortunes unrelated to the *Act of Union*. Quebec was ravaged by devastating fires, not once but twice in 1845. In 1847, there was an epidemic of typhus among Irish refugees from the potato famine, killing thousands. Among the victims was Sydney's host in Douro, Thomas Stewart. In this depressed, and depressing, environment, the political debate between Tories and Reformers was incessant and vitriolic. Matters came to a head in 1849 in ways that were strangely similar to the events of 1837. It has been said that history does not repeat itself; it just rhymes. In this instance, April 1849 rhymed with November 1837, but the roles of the protagonists were curiously reversed. But before we get to the events of 1849, there is something about 1848 that we need to have a look at—something that does not fit the pattern of Sydney's political life, a sort of radical interlude that leaves us scratching our heads.

The year 1848 was a momentous one in Europe. It saw uprisings and revolutions in nearly every country on the continent. The United Kingdom was practically the only country spared actual violence—except for Ireland. In Ireland, there was a gun battle between the Irish constabulary and members of the "Young Irelanders" movement, in what was called the "famine rebellion" at Ballingarry. Sydney's travels in 1845 and 1846 had given

him a close-up view of what was going on in Ireland, with Daniel O'Connell's more peaceful attempts to bring about the repeal of the *Act of Union* of 1800 and set up a separate kingdom still under the British Crown, but with its own parliament. He saw first-hand the pitiful conditions culminating in the Great Famine that had yet to reach its peak. He heard of the "monster meetings" organized by O'Connell to peacefully promote repeal. After his return to Montreal in 1847, he became president of the Montreal Repeal Association, a short-lived collection of supporters of O'Connell's moderate campaign. He certainly was not the only Anglo-Irish Protestant with a conscience, in either Ireland or Canada, to back that cause. In a sense, Sydney's support for repeal of the *Act of Union*, which the British had forced on the Irish in 1800, was consistent with his rejection of the *Act of Union* the British had imposed on the *Canadiens* in 1840. Both sought the eventual disappearance of an ethnic minority through assimilation. But the following year, he moved further to the left in support of a young Irish-born Montreal barrister, Bernard Devlin. Sydney helped Devlin organize an O'Connell-style "monster meeting," but one that appeared to endorse the more radical Young Irelander movement. There were even rumours that Devlin was linked to the Irish Republican Union, a New York–based organization of Irish expatriates, some of whom proposed an invasion of Canada as a distraction in aid of a hoped-for rising in Ireland. The fact that Devlin later commanded the 1st Regiment of Volunteer Rifles of

Canadian Militia (precursor to the Canadian Grenadier Guards) against an Irish-American Fenian raid in 1866 suggests that the rumours were exaggerated.

In any event, not all Irish Montrealers looked favourably on Sydney's endorsement of repeal. His stance was particularly embarrassing to the Irish members of the Baldwin–La Fontaine ministry, like Francis Hincks, Lewis Thomas Drummond, and Benjamin Holmes, who were trying to reassure the governor general and the electorate that they were loyal servants of the Crown. John Henry Walker was an Anglo-Irish illustrator and engraver who published *Punch* in Canada, a short-lived attempt to replicate the famous British satirical magazine. In his "Lines Addressed to Mr. Bellingham," we read the following:

> Sydney Bellingham, of Bellingham,
> You never sought the public weal;
> Most intent you were on selling 'em
> That great humbug called Repeal.
> Anything to make a splutter,
> Suits the temper of your soul;-
> Writer (!) lawyer (!)—in what gutter
> Will you next contrive to roll?

These lines—and the rest of the poem—are typical of the vitriolic political discourse of the age, but the clash of views over what was happening in Ireland, combined with the usual divisions over matters of Canadian politics,

made for harsh words. What had pushed Sydney so far in one direction? The likelihood is that he was driven by anger over the conditions the British government had allowed to occur in his birthplace, which he had seen upon his visit there in 1845 and 1846, and anger over the parallels he saw in the economic decline the British government was permitting in Lower Canada. His involvement in the Montreal Annexation Association in 1849 corroborates the theory that the previously loyal servant, like others in the Montreal business elite, had become seriously disenchanted with the British Crown.

The year 1849 began with the introduction of legislation to indemnify those whose homes and farms had been looted or burned during the rebellion, regardless of which side they were on, as long as they were not among the few convicted of treason. Sydney, who had witnessed some of the officially sanctioned burnings first-hand, felt they had indeed been excessive, but that the imperial military authorities should bear the cost of indemnification, not the Canadian taxpayer. The views of other former Montreal Loyal Constitutionalists were less nuanced. On April 25, the granting of royal assent to the *Rebellion Losses Bill* triggered an immediate and violent backlash. Governor General Elgin's carriage was mobbed when he returned in haste to his official residence at Monklands[27] after giving consent to the bill, which had been passed in both Houses. Governor General Elgin's signature on the bill was the first clear

---

27 Now the Villa Maria school.

proof that responsible government had arrived in Canada after decades of struggle. The racist editor of the *Gazette*, James Moir Ferres, published a special edition calling upon all "Anglo-Saxons" in what was clearly an incitement to further rioting that night. Ferres, in contrast with his bigotry towards French Canadians, had a very generous view of what constituted the "Anglo-Saxon" race, which included not just English Montrealers, but the more numerous Irish and Scots as well. As many as 1,500 assembled on Champ-de-Mars in what must have been viewed by many as a strange repetition of what had happened in November 1837, except that this time the mob was not made up of two nations at war with each other, but the "Anglo-Saxon" nation at war with legislation passed by a democratically elected assembly, ratified by the Legislative Council, and sanctioned by the governor general. What made the situation even more different was that most of the members of both the Assembly and the Council were Anglo-Saxons, and the measure would have passed even without the double-majority rule.

There were a few rabble-rousing harangues by Ferres and others, and benefiting from the recent introduction of gas lighting on the city's streets and squares, the mob then marched to the Parliament Buildings in Place d'Youville. They used a fire wagon to ram through the locked doors. Ironically, it was a volunteer fire chief, a struggling frame maker named Alfred Perry, who later claimed to have been the one who set the buildings on fire by hurling a brick at a gas chandelier in the Assembly room. Sydney knew Perry, whom he described as a "dare devil" and one of the sort who are "always found to assume command of mobs." The buildings were completely destroyed, along with more than 22,000 books in the parliamentary library and part of the official archives. But Perry took great pride, as a true "Anglo-Saxon," in saving the mace, the symbol of British royalty. The violence continued over the next few days. The homes of Reformist members of Parliament were vandalized, and La Fontaine's was gutted. In contrast with the by-election riot of 1832, the military showed restraint in eventually restoring some semblance of order without a bloodbath. Some believe this restraint was because the soldiers were British and the mob was British. The violence flared up again with the arrest of the suspected arsonists in August. La Fontaine's home was again attacked, this time with gunfire exchanged with La Fontaine's friends standing guard inside. Seven attackers were wounded, one of them fatally. The house still stands today, showing the bullet marks on the stonework, but it is protected now as a heritage site and loomed over by high-rise luxury condominium towers. That throughout all this, there was no retaliation by a French-Canadian mob is further refutation of Durham's "two nations at war" theory. Deep resentment and hostility existed, but there was no war.

Montreal was rewarded for the stupidity of its "Anglo-Saxon" mob by losing its status as the capital of Canada; this was transferred to Toronto. The economic

32. The Burning of
Parliament, *oil painting
by Joseph Légaré, McCord
Museum M11588,
with permission*

situation in Montreal went from bad to worse. In June, the repeal of the *British Navigation Acts* opened up shipping on the St. Lawrence to vessels of all nations, with the result that Quebec, and Montreal-based carriers lost their privileged position in the competition for cargos. There was very little export trade, and the capital needed for new infrastructure was almost non-existent. There were only fifty miles of railway lines, compared to 3,000 miles in the United States. Real-estate values plummeted. By summer's end, the level of frustration was so intense in the Montreal business and professional community that it took only five hours to get the signatures of 325 of its more prominent members on a carefully worded manifesto, coyly advocating the annexation of Canada by the United States. Within ten days there were 1,000 signatures, including Sydney's. Whether they were all deadly serious or just bluffing, the signers included men like William Molson, John Abbott (a future prime minister of Canada), and A. A. Dorion (a future chief justice of Quebec). Abbott would later claim that most of the signers had no more intention of seeking annexation "than a petulant child who strikes his nurse has of deliberately murdering her." However, by July 4, 1849, the Stars and Stripes could be seen draped from some of the windows on St. James Street.

Sydney does not mention the Montreal Repeal Association or the Montreal Annexation Association in his memoirs, which is a bit surprising given that at one time he was secretary *pro tem* of the latter. Sydney, however, was much more than a passive observer. In June, he had circulated a prospectus for a newspaper that would support the cause, and although the paper was never launched, the prospectus served as inspiration for the manifesto terms. The previous summer, he had made the arduous journey to New York to gather support there, and his campaigning for Irish repeal plus his endorsement of annexation appear to have been bundled together. In December 1849, he wrote a letter to the association encouraging it to campaign in the Bellechasse region, where there was frustration over isolation from Quebec for several months of the year, and

the lack of a road linking it to the U.S. market. He felt there would be support for the movement, particularly in Irish settlement pockets of Buckland and Frampton Townships.

The irony of the annexation movement was that it was also a plank in the platform of Papineau's *Parti Rouge* movement. Former *Patriotes* and former Loyal Constitutionalists were now on the same page. Louis-Joseph Papineau had returned from exile in 1845 and was elected to the Legislative Assembly in 1848. He saw the chance for French-speaking Lower Canadians to preserve their identity through annexation in a manner similar to the Cajuns of Louisiana, and although only a minority agreed with him, reports by *Canadien* emigrants in the northeastern United States appeared to bear him out. Paradoxically, Papineau's goal of a new French-speaking state in the American Union was the exact opposite of the goal sought by some of the English-speaking Montreal annexationists, who railed against what they saw as increasing "French domination" and viewed the American Union rather as another avenue for assimilation. Initially regarded by many as a returning hero, Papineau's aura faded a bit when Dr. Wolfred Nelson publicly accused him of cowardice during the events at St. Denis in 1837.

Whereas two years earlier there had been fears of war between Britain and the United States over Oregon, now purely economic interests were driving political sentiment to the point where even loyalty to the Crown was becoming secondary, at least for the moment.

Along with the *Rebellion Losses Bill*, there was another piece of legislation adopted in early 1849 that saw the Baldwin–La Fontaine ministry on the same side as Papineau. Since 1834, Papineau had been writing and speaking out on the subject of the right of women to vote. One might expect that a man styled as a great advocate for democratic reform was a pioneer in the fight for women's suffrage, but that assumption would be dead wrong. His arch-conservative streak shows up not only in his views regarding the privileges of the Church and the seigneurial system, but also in his campaign to plug what he saw as a loophole in the *Constitutional Act of 1791*. In the February 3, 1834, edition of the Montreal newspaper *La Minerve*, Papineau wrote, "It is revolting to see women dragged by their husbands, and daughters by their fathers, often against their will, to hustings. Public interest, decency and the modesty of women demand that these scandals never reoccur." When Sydney ran as a candidate in the 1844 elections, it is safe to assume that Arabella voted for him. The prevailing interpretation of the act gave women like Arabella the right to vote, because under the *Coutume de Paris* that applied in Lower Canada, they could own property and thus meet the eligibility requirements. But Arabella could vote for him no more. On May 30, 1849, royal assent was given to a bill that baldly declared, "that no woman shall be entitled to vote at any such election."[28] It would be another ninety-

---

28 *12 Victoria*, c. 27, s. 46.

one years before that prohibition was lifted in Quebec.

The annexation movement faded after 1854, when the United States and Britain signed a Reciprocity Treaty that allowed Canadian raw materials and agricultural products to enter the United States duty-free. But in the years in between, things went from bad to very bad in Montreal. The population had grown to more than 55,000, and many inhabitants had no employment. The number of ocean ships visiting the port in 1849 was a fraction of what it had been five years earlier. The value of exports had shrivelled to less than a third of the meagre imports.

In June 1850, a fire broke out in the predominantly Irish neighbourhood of Griffintown, southwest of McGill Street, destroying more than 200 houses. Two months later, another fire ruined 150 houses in the neighbourhood east of St. Laurent Street. The city's population dropped by at least 4,000 as people sought their fortunes elsewhere, particularly in the United States. Incredibly, two more devastating fires broke out in 1852. The first occurred on June 7 and razed much of the core commercial area of the old town just above the harbour. For a while, it appeared flames would reach Notre Dame Church, and Hôtel Dieu Hospital had to be evacuated. The second conflagration on a hot and windy July 8 and 9 raged over a large area on both sides of St. Laurent Street, destroying Saint-Jacques Cathedral on St. Denis Street and threatening the Montreal General Hospital on Dorchester Street. It then flared up between Notre Dame Street and the eastern section of the harbour. The poorly led volunteer fire department could do little, especially since the water reservoir in St. Louis Square had been drained for repairs. Over 1,100 buildings were levelled and more than 10,000 people were made homeless.

In 1853, a riot broke out during a lecture by the Italian anti-cleric Alessandro Gavazzi. The military was called out. This time there was a bloodbath, with five people killed and dozens wounded, most of them outraged Irish Catholics. In 1854, cholera returned once again and took nearly 1,200 lives.

Throughout these unpleasant years, Sydney and Arabella had the good fortune—thanks to her very real fortune—of living comfortably on the opposite side of Mount Royal at Dunany Cottage, the mansion Sydney had built in what was then seventy acres of wooded countryside. During the summer heat, they could "take the waters" at Rivière-du-Loup, which was then a fashionable vacationing spot for the political and business elite 120 miles downriver from Quebec. Later, the town became known as John A. Macdonald's "summer capital," due to the amount of time he spent there.

The couple also took two trips to England and Ireland. Sydney's accounts of those journeys give us some insight into how transatlantic travel had become faster and more comfortable with the advent of the steamship, but there were still risks. The first incident was in 1850 aboard the *Conqueror*, a new vessel on her first trip from Quebec with a cargo of timber. Sydney and Arabella were the only passengers, comfortably lodged in a large poop cabin. After a pleasant voyage from Quebec to the Irish coast, the *Conqueror* ran into a violent gale and heavy rain as it entered the English Channel. A passenger steamer headed for Liverpool was seen bearing down on them but put up her helm at the very last moment, the sides of the two ships scraping against each other. Driven off course, the *Conqueror* found herself headed for the rocks off the Isle of Man in waves fifty feet high. Sydney opened the cabin door, catching a glimpse of the lighthouse on the Isle of Man, which appeared alarmingly close. The captain and the crew worked frantically to turn the ship around, one of them yelling to another, "We are going ashore!" He meant, of course, that they would soon be on the rocks, where certain death awaited them. Arabella, who had overheard what was said, but misunderstanding its portent and not realizing the seriousness of their predicament, asked Sydney what she should bring with her when they went on shore. It took a month before Sydney could get the scene out of his thoughts.

The second such incident was aboard the *Asia*, a luxuriously outfitted, sail-rigged paddlewheeler built in 1850 for the Cunard Line. The captain was C. H. E. Judkins, one of Cunard's longest-serving masters, but one almost universally disliked by his passengers. Crossing the Grand Banks in heavy fog, the *Asia* crashed into a fishing boat. Sydney heard the shrieks of the fishermen, but Judkins made no effort to turn the ship around and search for survivors, saying it would be pointless to attempt to do so in the fog. Then, halfway across the Atlantic, when a strong gale necessitated the reefing of the auxiliary topsail, one of the crew lost his footing and was tossed into the sea. Sydney ran to the poop deck, from where he could make out the crewman rising and falling with each wave, swimming as fast as he could to get back to the ship. The *Asia* was doing fifteen knots, and it would have taken her three miles to reverse course. Again, Judkins refused to turn the ship around, saying that it would be futile to try to find the man in those circumstances. The passengers raised a donation of £40 for the man's widow, who met them when they arrived at Liverpool. Judkins retaliated by closing off the saloon where the passengers met and turning out the lights.

Eventually, in 1855, the economic storm passed and the dark cloud that seemed to be hanging indefinitely over Montreal lifted. The 1854 Reciprocity Treaty spurred the economy, and by the spring of 1855, the harbour was busy again. Construction of Victoria Bridge, connecting the island city to the mainland and the longest in the world at the time, was well underway. So was legislation to abolish the seigneurial system. With lessons learned from the fires of 1850 and 1852, work began on a large new reservoir on Mount Royal, named after the fur trader Simon McTavish, and ordinances were passed to limit the construction of wooden buildings. Many of the fine stone buildings that characterize parts of Montreal today date from this renewal. And Montreal was gripped by a new fever—the railway-building craze.

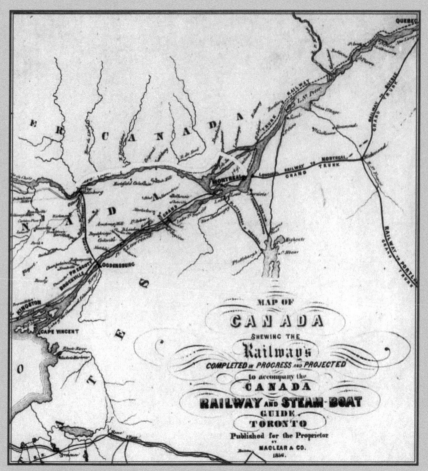

15. *Route of the Montreal and Bytown Railway, from a A Map of Canada Shewing the Railways, by Maclear, 1856, LAC, MIKAN 4128119*

CHAPTER 6

THE RAILWAY

A BOOK THAT WANDERS THROUGH SOME OF THE HISTORY of Canada in the nineteenth-century would be on the wrong track if it did not contain at least a few paragraphs on railways. Fortunately, railways were a complete chapter in the life of Sydney Bellingham.

In 1849, when the signers of the Annexation Manifesto bemoaned the pitiful extent of track mileage in Canada, there were only two railways leading out of Montreal. In a sense, neither of them went anywhere, at least not anywhere important. And, since there would be no bridge connecting Montreal Island with the mainland until 1859, one of the two did not actually lead out of the city itself, and the other did not get off the island. We have already taken note of John Molson's Champlain & St. Lawrence Railroad. Inaugurated with great pomp in 1836 by Governor Gosford and Speaker of the Assembly Papineau before they literally went to war against each other, it ran a mere sixteen miles from Laprairie, opposite Lachine on the St. Lawrence, to St. Jean on the Richelieu, and was intended to serve as a portage between the two water transportation systems, although it ended up carrying very little freight. Except during the troubles of 1837 and 1838, the line served mainly as an amusement ride and for weekend excursions. During the winter, it was not much use to anyone other than to those few who might venture to cross the ice by sleigh. Molson's Montreal and Lachine Railroad Company was another portage, this one running about eight miles from Montreal to Lachine. Commencing operations in 1847, it enabled passengers travelling to Upper Canada to bypass the Lachine Rapids by rail instead of by horse-drawn coach, as Sydney had done in 1824. Passengers still had to rely mainly on water transportation to get them to their final destination. In any event, the new Lachine Canal gave them an option of doing those first eight miles by water as well, at least when it was not covered with ice. There was a third line under construction, this one from Longueil opposite Montreal, to the Richelieu, and from there to the Vermont border, where it was to link up with its American counterpart, connecting Montreal to Atlantic shipping at Portland, Maine. The St. Lawrence and Atlantic Railroad was the first international railway anywhere when it started operations in 1853. However, from a purely Canadian perspective, there was no way to travel by rail from Montreal to Quebec or Toronto, which alternated as the capital after Montreal lost that status, or to the future capital at Ottawa, called Bytown until 1855.

The lack of a functional railway system retarded Canada's economic recovery after the severe depression of the late 1840s. The weakness of the economy prevented entrepreneurs from obtaining the enormous amounts of capital needed to build even the beginnings of a system. To break the vicious cycle, the Canadian Legislature enacted two pieces of legislation. The first, adopted in late 1849, was the *Railroad Loan Guarantee Act*, which gave developers something to bargain with in negotiating financing with lenders. The second was the adoption in 1852 of a *Municipal Loans Act*, which enabled investors to leverage off the credit of municipalities and open up a whole new source of financing. Those two pieces of legislation created a burst of activity. Dozens of charters were granted to new companies, although few of them ever actually laid any track. One of the few that did was the Montreal and Bytown Railway, which received its charter in August 1853. Its secretary and treasurer was Sydney Bellingham.

The scheme was a grand one, rivalling in scope the Grand Trunk project underway with the support of powerful political backers and government money, neither of which the Montreal and Bytown Railway ever enjoyed. The line was planned to run northward from the centre of Montreal, around the eastern flank of Mount Royal, and then continue to the North Shore after crossing Île Jésus at points where the waters could be relatively easy to ford. Once it reached the mainland, the route would turn east, running just north of St. Eustache, and continuing west through Carillon and St. Andrews to Grenville. At Grenville, it would proceed on to Bytown, either along the northern shore of the Ottawa, or crossing the river and following the southern shore. The prospectus even floated the idea of further extensions, one south to Brockville on the shore of Lake Ontario, and the other all the way to Georgian Bay on Lake Huron, the gateway to the western Great Lakes. Such further expansion would provide the shareholders with benefits from transporting not just the lumber and agricultural products of the Ottawa Valley, but also the vast mineral wealth of the West.

Sydney signed the prospectus in his capacity of secretary and treasurer. Signing as president was A. M. Delisle. Sydney probably did the drafting, in collaboration with the new company's solicitors, Badgley & Abbott, whose office was a few doors from Sydney's on the same side of Little St. James Street. The more senior solicitor, William Badgley, was an inveterate Tory. He was one of the founders of the Constitutional Association set up in Montreal in 1837 to oppose the *Patriote* party, and one of the principal spokesmen for the British Party, which advocated the union of the two Canadas and racial assimilation as a means of "redressing" the grievances of the English in Lower Canada. Badgley was attorney general for Canada East from 1847 until the Baldwin–La Fontaine Liberals defeated the Tories the following year. Later in life, he had a distinguished career as dean of McGill University's Faculty of Law and as a judge, first in the Superior Court and then in the Court of Appeal. In his political writings and even in his later court decisions, he betrayed arrogance and bigotry towards French Canadians that detract from an otherwise admirable intellect. The younger John Abbott was a natural fit with the project, having been born at St. Andrews and raised at Grenville. The collaboration between Sydney and Abbott was short-lived. In 1857, they ran against each other for election to the Assembly as the member for the County of Argenteuil.

Alexandre-Maurice Delisle, the president of the new company, was a well-connected conservative entrepreneur who had dabbled in politics and the public service. He was close enough to Sydney, and wealthy enough, to bankroll Sydney's first foray into politics later in 1854. Other shareholders included Benjamin Holmes, Jacques Viger (the former mayor of Montreal), Jean-Louis Beaudry (a wealthy former *Patriote* and future mayor of Montreal), and A. A. Dorion (a future chief justice of Quebec).

In October 1853, Sydney set out along the proposed route on a quest for supporters and rights-of-way. He knew the route well as far as St. Eustache. It was basically the same itinerary he had followed on horseback with his troop of Royal Montreal Cavalry in December 1837. He visited St. Benoît, St. Andrews, and Lachute. In November and December, he went farther up the Ottawa, all the way to Bytown and beyond. In his memoirs, he describes his visits with some of the more prominent people. Ironically, the first stop he describes was at Montebello, the newly built seigneurial manor of Louis-Joseph Papineau, on the northern bank of the Ottawa about halfway between St. Eustache and Bytown. Papineau, then on the eve of his retirement from politics, promised him a right-of-way across the seigneury and expressed his approval of the project. His younger brother, Denis-Benjamin Papineau, bought a few shares. Far more importantly, his cousin André-Benjamin Papineau, who had survived the Battle of St. Eustache and was now mayor of the County of Terrebonne, pledged £26,000 on behalf of the county as the third-largest subscriber. It appears that the former cavalry officer and the rebel members of the Papineau clan held no grudges for the events of 1837.

After leaving Montebello, Sydney continued along the northern shore of the Ottawa towards Hull, a lumber town across the river from Bytown. It was a region of dense forest with scarcely any settlement, and Sydney travelled on horseback. Twelve miles west of Montebello, he reached Major's Landing, where he found a well-stocked inn run by a man of that name. It was located at the point where the Petite Nation River flows into the Ottawa, and where the narrower channel made it easier for settlers and forestry workers to cross from Upper Canada to Lower Canada. In his younger days, Major

33. Papineau Manor, Montebello, *oil painting by Napoléon Bourassa, 1865, LAC, MIKAN 4100537*

had been a trapper and fur trader, portaging up the Petite Nation into the interior and trading with the Weskarini Algonquin. Major told Sydney about a quantity of silver ore, that an Algonquin had brought to him for smelting. For centuries, the Ottawa had been a trade route linking the Algonquin with other Aboriginal peoples farther east, and small quantities of silver had long been one of their principal items of barter. No one had ever succeeded in discovering where the silver ore came from, although there were rumours that it was as far away as the great

Lake Temiskaming at the headwaters of the Ottawa. Major told a tale about an Ottawa lumber baron who had patronized his inn, a man called Audet, who invited two Algonquin to winter with him in the vain hope of discovering the source. It was not until 1903 that workers excavating the roadbed for the Temiskaming and Northern Ontario Railway discovered the ore beds near Cobalt, Ontario, triggering the Cobalt silver rush.

Reaching Hull, Sydney stayed as a guest for two days in the home of Ruggles Wright, one of the sons of Philemon Wright, the New Englander who founded the original settlement there. Ruggles Wright was prominent in the timber trade, and Sydney's prospectus touted the advantages of the proposed new railway in delivering squared timber to the Montreal and Quebec export markets without incurring the losses and damage inherent in floating it downriver. Wright was enthusiastic about the railway and freely promised it a right-of-way. He told Sydney the story of how his father had owned 200 acres of land in what is now the centre of the city of Ottawa but had been persuaded to sell it to a man named Nicholas Sparks for £50. The equivalent of that sum today ($8,000) would barely be sufficient to pay six months' rent for a bachelor apartment on Sparks Street. Sparks, previously one of Philemon Wright's agents, and later the new husband of the widow of another of his sons, was a ruthless Anglo-Irish land speculator and moneylender.

Before heading back to Montreal, Sydney visited John Egan at his home in Aylmer, a few miles west of Hull. Egan was an Anglo-Irishman who at that time ran one of the largest timber and milling operations in North America, with more than 3,500 employees. He was elected to the Legislative Assembly in 1848, and Sydney got to know him better after he joined him there in 1854. In the Assembly, they collaborated on a project to secure government funding for a canal on the Ottawa at Chat's Falls to enable steamboats to get past Bytown and onto the upper Ottawa. Although Egan owned shipping operations on the Ottawa and was interested in other railways, he gave Sydney a subscription for £500 in the Montreal and Bytown.

Sydney's description of the manner in which Egan's timber operations were conducted suggests that, in contrast with some other big players in that industry, he was as much concerned with the welfare of his people and their communities as he was with his own prosperity. Egan initiated and financed a number of local improvements, including bridges, roads, and schools. Sydney also gives us a close-up view of life in a timber shanty.

Egan's 130 shanties were spread out along the rivers and streams that ran into the Ottawa, each one providing a base of operations over as much forest as the men could work in a day during the winter. A shanty was a large, crudely built log dormitory, where thirty men ate and slept, and dried their clothing by an open fire. A cook provided them all they could eat, the menu consisting mainly of boiled pork, boiled dried peas, and bread. The bread was made daily in a Dutch oven, which was buried in the ashes of the fire. One comfort the men did not have was alcohol. Egan was a teetotaler. But when spring came, and the rafts of logs were floated downriver, the men collected their pay and returned to civilization. There were plenty of taverns on the way. With wages of £3 to £4 a month, there was also plenty of money for booze. This, combined with rivalry between Irish-Catholic and Orange factions, made for a fair amount of rowdiness and even bloodshed. It had been worse in the 1830s, when a marauding Bytown timber baron named Peter Aylen capitalized on the frustration of unemployed Irish canal workers to intimidate and beat up *Canadien* forestry workers in an attempt to steal their jobs.

Less than two years after his visit to Aylmer, Sydney sadly witnessed the collapse of his friend John Egan's empire. Overexpansion through investments in sawmills, shipping, and other railway schemes, combined with the decrease in British demand for North American timber, led to insolvency. Egan died at Quebec in 1857.

Through his contacts at Quebec and Montreal, Sydney knew a few of the notables on the other side of the river from Hull. One of them was Lieutenant-Colonel Richard Boteler, who had succeeded Colonel John By in the supervision of the Rideau Canal. The canal, linking Bytown on the Ottawa with Kingston on Lake Ontario, had been built between 1826 and 1832. It was originally intended to provide British forces with access by boat to Lake Ontario in the event of the upper part of the St. Lawrence being cut off by the Americans. Boteler was the brother-in-law of Sydney's cousin Henrietta Bellingham. He told him of the care Colonel By had taken to prevent the construction of the canal from becoming a boondoggle, like some other British military projects undertaken in the colonies, where competent contractors were scarce and almost all of them knew one another. For the first forty miles, By ruled that no single contractor could be awarded more than ten miles of work. Four separate contractors completed those first forty miles to By's satisfaction. But when the time came to call for tenders on the remainder, no other contractor could compete with the advantage gained on the ground by the first four, who had become, according to Boteler, secret partners. These "shrewd and clever operators" were Scotsmen, and the way Sydney refers to them and other Scottish entrepreneurs who had come to make their fortunes in Canada shows a certain grudging respect for the ability of the Scots to become highly successful in business. It is somewhat surprising that he does not mention them more frequently, given they were the dominant commercial community in Montreal. He does mention the firm of Pollock, Gilmour & Company, which dominated the timber trade throughout Upper and Lower Canada, as well as in New Brunswick, until its partners retired in 1853. He comments wryly on the fate of Arthur Pollock who, instead of returning to his native Glasgow, invested much of his huge fortune in

bankrupt estates in the west of Ireland, only to learn the hard way that a Scotsman could be just as unsuccessful in collecting rents from impoverished "paddies" as their former Anglo-Irish masters had been.

Sydney knew one of the four Rideau Canal contractors personally. Thomas MacKay, after amassing a considerable fortune through the canal and his mills at Bytown, became a member of the Legislative Council at Quebec and was in Quebec when Sydney was in the Assembly. MacKay was not a dour Scot. Sydney describes him as having "a charming personality and that rare gift, an exquisite tenor voice." He also had, like many

34. Locks on the Rideau Canal, drawing by W. H. Bartlett, from Canadian Scenery, by N. P. Willis and W. H. Bartlett, 1842

of his countrymen who immigrated to Canada, a flair for building a fine home. He called it Rideau Hall, and today it is the official residence of the governor general of Canada.

The year after Sydney's trip up the Ottawa to Hull, a young Vermonter named Ezra Butler Eddy settled in Hull, drawn by the commercial incentives of the Reciprocity Treaty of 1854. Working in a shed he rented from Ruggles Wright, E. B. Eddy and his wife manufactured matches by hand. What Sydney called "his inventive genius" enabled him to develop a machine "capable of making a thousand matches at each revolution of the engine." His inexpensive matches became known around the world. Eddy then branched out into the manufacture of other products made of wood, such as buckets and clothespins. Next he expanded into lumber mills. From there he moved on to pulp and paper, developing an improved and more efficient process for the manufacture of paper. Sydney got to know him when Eddy became a member of the Quebec Assembly in 1871, representing the County of Ottawa, next to Sydney's riding of Argenteuil. Like Sydney, he bolted the Conservatives to run as an independent in 1875, but unlike Sydney, he was not returned. The political events of the 1870s are the subject of a later chapter.

After his exploratory travels up the route of the proposed railway, Sydney returned to Montreal to work with Maurice Delisle to organize construction. James Sykes, an experienced railway engineer and contractor from Sheffield, England, received the contract. The original cost estimate was £831,750, most to be financed by a bond issue that Sykes would market to English investors in collaboration with a Manchester financier, Charles de Bergue. Additional capital would be raised through stock subscriptions from the City of Montreal and the rural counties directly interested in the project, and private shareholders. Sydney and Delisle were in for £1,000 each.

Although some work started at other points, the short thirteen-mile stretch in Argenteuil County between Carillon and Grenville was the first priority. There was regular steamer service between Lachine and Carillon, and between Grenville and Hull, but the rapids of the Long Sault,[29] in between limited water transportation to much smaller vessels that could pass through the narrow and shallow military canals at Carillon, Chute-à-Blondeau, and Grenville. Over the course of construction during the summer of 1854, Sydney got to know Argenteuil County and its residents, including a few who had been at St. Eustache and St. Benoît with the St. Andrews and Carillon Volunteers in December 1837. St. Andrews, near the entrance to the canal at Carillon, was a considerable town with a population of 1,100. Grenville, at the other end of the system, had 250. A branch line was to connect the more recent settlement at Lachute, six miles north of St. Andrews.

---

29 Not to be confused with the Long Sault on the St. Lawrence between Cornwall and Prescott.

*35. Carillon & Grenville
Railway engine, c. 1895,
LAC, MIKAN 3207134*

The Carillon-Grenville stretch went into operation just before the freeze-up in December, but there was not much to cheer about. Only £930 of the private share subscriptions had actually been paid up. The City of Montreal and the County of Two Mountains had not yet delivered on their promised financing, and never would. The principals behind the Grand Trunk project announced their intention to build a competing road on the south side of the Ottawa, making it even more unlikely that Montreal and the rural municipalities would make good on their promised subscriptions. The London money market had tightened up as a result of the outbreak of the Crimean War, and financier de Bergue pulled out.

James Sykes still managed to raise £50,000, badly needed to pay the labourers and landowners. He left Liverpool in late September 1854 aboard the American paddle steamer *Arctic*, bringing with him the £50,000 in cash. On September 27, 1854, in a dense fog off the coast of Newfoundland, the *Arctic* collided with another ship and sank with the loss of 300 lives, including Syke's. Work was scheduled to resume in the spring of 1875, but nothing happened. William Sykes tried to take over operations, but the assets were seized. English bondholders followed with bankruptcy proceedings. The end result was that the line, which had cost $400,000, was auctioned off in January 1859 for a mere $21,200. The successful bidder was none other than John Abbott, the company's original solicitor.

Before this disaster occurred, and while the prospects were still reasonably good, Sydney had resigned as secretary and treasurer of the company to avoid a conflict of interest arising out of his election to the Legislative Assembly in August 1854. It was later assumed that he had sunk a lot of money into the failed project, but there is no record of his stock subscription ever having been paid, and he had received most of his salary of £600 for the first year of his work as an officer of the company. His biggest gain, however, was getting to know the people of Argenteuil, the county that would be the focus of his political life for the remainder of his years in Canada. His very real experience with the Montreal and Bytown Railway served him well in that political life, first as a member of the special committee inquiring into the affairs of the Grand Trunk, and then as a member of the Standing Committee on Railways, Canals, and Telegraph Lines. His skill as a lawyer and knowledge of railway construction and financing made him a formidable interrogator of witnesses appearing before those committees, particularly when a witness attempted to evade a question that probed into personal gains and free-riding on government subsidies of the sort that had not been available to the promoters of the Montreal and Bytown.

Having reached the end of the line on the Montreal and Bytown Railway, we can now set out on the first leg of Sydney's adventure as a member of Parliament.

CHAPTER 7

POLITICS—FIRST PERIOD

*S*YDNEY'S FIRST EXPERIMENT AS AN ELECTORAL CANDIDATE was in the general election of 1834, when at the age of twenty-six he polled a respectable 21 percent of votes for the two-member riding of Montreal's East Ward. On December 17, 1840, with the first general election for the Legislative Assembly of the new United Province on the horizon, he wrote John Neilson, a prominent moderate anti-Unionist, to request his party's nomination for Bellechasse riding. Arabella's properties in that riding and Sydney's familiarity with the inhabitants made it a logical choice, but the nomination was not forthcoming.

Sydney next set his sights on the newly created riding of Montreal, but then changed his mind. Still involved in litigation over the failure of his former partner Charles Dunlop, he let his desire for financial security win out over political ambition and decided not to run when Lord Sydenham's Tory organizers lured him away from the race. There were hints that he would get an appointment as emigration commissioner, and a salary of £800 per year, if he stepped aside in favour of Sydenham's candidate, Benjamin Holmes. It was a proposition all the easier to

accept given that Holmes was his friend and collaborator. Benjamin Holmes was the first president of the Montreal St. Patrick's Society, formed in 1837 with Sydney as a vice-president. It was not their only collaboration. Years later, after Holmes became vice-president of the Montreal Annexation Association upon its creation in 1849, Sydney reappeared as secretary *pro tem*. Holmes, a lieutenant colonel in the Montreal Light Infantry during the rebellion, was the general manager of the Bank of Montreal. The Tories had high hopes for him as a backer of Sydenham's policy of autocratic rule and assimilation. They expected he would be an important piece in the political machinery engineered by Sydenham to ensure his control of the first Union Parliament.

Sydenham's people reneged on the deal with Sydney, but they missed out on what they expected to get from Holmes. Once elected, he moved over to the Reformer side with Baldwin and La Fontaine and became a supporter of their ongoing efforts to dilute the effects of the *Act of Union*.

Benjamin Holmes, like Arabella's father, William

Holmes, was born in Dublin and may have been related to Arabella. He left Ireland for Canada with his parents at age three, but the voyage was far more eventful than Sydney's crossing twenty years later. Holmes did not arrive at Quebec until he was seven. It was the summer of 1797, when England was at war with France and Spain, but with much of the British fleet incapacitated by mutinies. A couple of days after setting sail from Dublin, a French frigate captured their unescorted passenger ship. The family was taken to Spain and spent the next four years there as civilian captives. Benjamin Holmes's younger brother, Andrew Fernando Holmes, was born in Spain. Years later, as a young physician practising in Montreal, Andrew collaborated with William Robertson to incorporate the Montreal General Hospital and set up McGill's Faculty of Medicine. We will remember Dr. Robertson as the man who dispatched Sydney to the home of Louis-Joseph Papineau in 1834, bearing his challenge to a duel.[30] Through his connections with Robertson and the Holmes brothers, Sydney was named a member of the board of the Montreal General Hospital. In 1841, Arabella and Juliet, Andrew Holme's wife, were among the incorporators of the Montreal Ladies' Benevolent Society, which gave assistance to impoverished women and children in an era when there was no state relief for the indigent or the sick. The Roman Catholic religious orders had been taking care of their own for two centuries, starting with the arrival of Jeanne

---

30 See Chapter 3.

Mance at Montreal in 1642. The Protestant communities had some catching up to do.

With his connections in the legal and medical professions, the military elite, and Montreal's high society, Sydney Bellingham was well positioned to succeed in politics. But the complex demographic of Montreal was not a good political environment for a man with his cavalry officer's baggage. Success at the polls would have to wait until he found a better fit. He seems to have come to that realization slowly, flirting one more time with the prospect of winning Montreal.

Benjamin Holmes resigned his seat on February 1, 1844, during the political battles between supporters of La Fontaine and Sydenham's successor, Governor Metcalfe. Both camps viewed the ensuing by-election as a test of strength that would influence the outcome of the next general election, just a few months away. Having resigned as editor of the *Times*, Sydney immediately announced his intention to run in the by-election as a pro-Metcalfe candidate, but then withdrew in favour of a unilingual Tory candidate, William Molson. Sydney's decision was probably triggered by the realization that La Fontaine's candidate, Lewis Thomas Drummond, would be the likely winner. Drummond was a bilingual Irish Catholic lawyer who had made a name for himself defending *Patriotes*. He could be expected to garner most of the Irish vote and had a much better chance of attracting *Canadien* voters than a former captain in the Royal Montreal Cavalry, especially one who was now being attacked in the press as a traitor to the Reformer cause.

However, before Sydney withdrew from the electoral contest with Drummond, their exchanges of vitriol from the podium and in the papers came close to ending in a more deadly competition. Sydney took offence at Drummond's use of a metaphoric reference to a "cloven hoof," the implication being that Sydney Bellingham was the Devil. A letter followed from Sydney, delivered to Drummond by a friend, which might be construed as a challenge to a duel, with the friend acting as his second. The matter was defused when Drummond served up to Sydney the same story that Papineau had used to avoid a duel with Dr. Robertson ten years earlier: he had only meant to target Sydney's recent change in his political opinions and had not intended to injure him as an individual, nor have his words interpreted as applying to his character as a gentleman.

The by-election held in April was a violent one, with Irish Catholic and *Canadien* dock and canal workers forging an unlikely alliance against Protestant Orangemen. Drummond was declared the winner, but six months later the general election ended in an overall majority for the Tories.

It would be another decade before Sydney stood again for election, but he did not cease to be impassioned by Canadian politics. After his return from abroad in 1847, he made his views known in opposition to the *Rebellion Losses Bill* and in support of the annexation movement. But that ardour faded, along with the annexation movement itself. By 1853, his focus was on building a railway, and although the railway project was, for the most part, a failure, it got him out of Montreal and into the countryside. It was in Argenteuil County, rather than the grimy corridors straddling St. James Street, that Sydney would fight his next political battles. And it was in Argenteuil that he would accomplish for himself what Thomas Stewart had set out to do with the settlement of Douro Township in the 1820s.[31] Before we can understand the parallel, we need to know a bit about Argenteuil.

The County of Argenteuil was first set up in 1854, creating a new seat in the Union Parliament and a new opportunity for anyone seeking to be its first representative.[32] It had been split off from the County of Two Mountains. The new configuration was probably driven by demographic considerations, with Argenteuil consisting of areas settled mainly by English-speaking newcomers, with what remained of Two Mountains retaining the older areas of *Canadien* settlement. The new opportunity was thus one of obvious appeal to Sydney, made even more tempting by the significant number of Scots-Irish and Anglo-Irish settlers among the more recent arrivals.

The new county took its name from the Seigneury of Argenteuil, which had been created on the north

---

31 See Chapter 2.
32 *Parliamentary Representation Act*, 16 Victoria, c. 152, s. 33.

bank of the Ottawa in 1682. The old seigneury occupied the southeastern corner of the county, where the town of St. Andrews was located, along with its new rival, Lachute. The much larger area to the west and north was originally made up of eleven townships, each of them as large or larger than the old seigneury: Chatham and Grenville fronting on the Ottawa west of the seigneury; Gore, Wentworth, and Harrington in the second tier; then Howard, Montcalm, and Arundel in a third row; and finally De Salaberry, Wolfe, and Grandison in the northern extremity.[33] Grenville had been named in honour of George Grenville, father of the author of the *Constitutional Act of* 1791, William Wyndham Grenville. Chatham had been named for the Earl of Chatham, the father of the prime minister who presented the bill, Grenville's cousin William Pitt the Younger.

The County of Argenteuil, which has a width of about twenty-eight miles, fronts on the Ottawa. As originally constituted in 1854, Argenteuil had a depth inland of some fifty miles as far back as its northwestern corner. The front part of the county consists mostly of a band of fertile land inherited some 7,000 years ago from the receding waters of the Champlain Sea. An escarpment marks where the sea met the land, and the terrain is hilly beyond that, dotted with lakes, and, even today, still heavily forested. Here and there in the backcountry there are pockets of arable land, but in the 1850s these served only to partially

sustain a small population, which unlike their neighbours below the escarpment, depended mainly on forestry for their livelihood. The western side of the county is bisected by the Rouge River, one of the principal tributaries of the Ottawa, which runs almost directly from north to south. The lumbermen and occasional trappers who ventured up the Rouge in the 1840s and early 1850s brought back with them reports of a broad stretch of fertile land straddling the river in the northwestern townships of Arundel and De Salaberry, uninhabited except for a small band of Algonquin.

After more than a year's involvement in meeting the citizens of Argenteuil County to gain their support for the Montreal and Bytown Railway, Sydney decided to run in the general election in July 1854 as their member in the Legislative Assembly. He had the financial backing of Alexandre Delisle, his mentor in the railway project. English-speaking immigrants occupied most of the new riding, except the extreme eastern portion, which was mainly French-speaking. Sydney, as a former cavalry officer during the turmoil at nearby St. Eustache and St. Benoît was obviously not a popular candidate in the two French-speaking parishes of St. Hermas and St. Placide. Nor was he the favourite among the older American and Scottish families in the St. Andrews area, who saw him as an outsider. Others suspected his election was part of the railway's strategy to overcome the refusal of some of the local establishment to support it.

---

33 De Salaberry, Wolfe, and Grandison were later split off and added to the County of Terrebonne.

Sydney's real backing came from the Irish canal workers at Grenville and the Scots-Irish and Anglo-Irish of the newer settlements farther back from the Ottawa. These were people who felt squeezed by the owners of the stores at St. Andrews and Grenville where they bought tools, clothing, and seed supplies on credit, and brought their grain for milling. A Grenville storekeeper, George Kains, in a letter to his brother, condescendingly described the backcountry voters as "Dowdies." Less dowdy were the opinion leaders in the new upstart town of Lachute, which had begun to rival St. Andrews as the county town of the future. Lachute was particularly grateful to Sydney for seeing to it that a spur line linking it to the new railway was included in the company's plans. The railway would have enabled the people in the Lachute area to bypass the merchants at St. Andrews and obtain what they needed directly from the Montreal market. They would have to wait another two decades for that to happen, but when it did, the town boomed.

Sydney could not have embarked on a political career in Argenteuil without influential local sponsors to support his campaign. His scouting for the railway helped to build those connections, but some of them had their roots in his brief adventures in the area of St. Eustache in 1837. His best introduction to the county was through Charles Forbes, who had served in the British Army as deputy commissary general, first in England and then with the British forces in Canada. Forbes had been responsible for procurement during the building of the

three canals along the Long Sault and had acquired a substantial property near the canal entrance at Carillon, where he erected a large stone building in the Georgian style. Originally a warehouse, the building became a barracks for the troops stationed at Carillon to protect the canal. Today it is the Argenteuil Regional Museum.

In 1837, at General Colborne's urging, Forbes raised 800 militia volunteers in just two weeks to reinforce the regular troops during the Battle of St. Eustache. The St. Andrews Carillon Volunteers arrived late on the scene, but not too late to join in the looting and destruction at St. Benoît. After the end of hostilities, Forbes settled permanently at Carillon as the local squire. In 1842, he was elected to the Legislative Assembly. He knew the election process better than anyone else in Sydney's camp.

Another military acquaintance was Joseph Barron, the largest landowner at Lachute, who had been colonel of a battalion of the Two Mountains Militia in the 1837 conflict. Not all of the storekeepers of the front townships were against Sydney. Three of his supporters were merchants who had prospered from the building of the canals on the Long Sault. One was Thomas Meikle, the postmaster at St. Andrews. That association was short-lived. Three years later, he and his elderly father were among the 264 passengers who perished in a fire aboard the steamer *Montreal*, twelve miles upriver from Quebec. At the other end of the Long Sault, Sydney could rely on Edwin Pridham, a merchant and the postmaster at

Grenville. Pridham, an English emigrant, was the captain of the Grenville Volunteers in 1837.

The third local merchant was another Forbes, James, the son of a Jacobite who had come to Canada to avoid arrest in Scotland. He owned a shoe-and-boot store at Carillon and operated a stage line between there and Grenville until the railway came. Forbes had made himself conspicuous as a dispatch rider between Carillon and Montreal during the troubles of 1837. Among the local professionals, Sydney could count on Gaspard de Laroche, the notary at St. Andrews, and Thomas Christie, the first physician to set up practice at Lachute. After Sydney retired from the Legislative Assembly of Quebec in 1878, Christie was one of his successors as the sitting member for Argenteuil.

The election process for the Fifth Parliament of the Province of Canada in 1854 was a modest improvement over the rules that enabled Sydenham to engineer the results in 1841. New legislation adopted in 1849 required a poll to be held in each township or seigneurial parish of a rural county, and for the polling station to be centrally located. It was now the county registrar for land titles, and not the governor general, who picked the locations and appointed the local deputy returning officers. There were new rules specifically banning bribery, intimidation, and multiple voting, but they made scarcely any difference. There were still no voters' lists or identification papers, and anyone claiming to be eligible to vote simply showed up at the nearest polling station, or often at more than one polling station, to declare that he held the necessary property qualifications. There was no secret ballot, with the result that a candidate's agents who huddled around the poll could know in each case whether their bribes or threats had worked. There was no effective police presence to enforce the new rules. There were, however, Orange lodges throughout the county whose many members made their physical presence felt. George Kains, in his letter to his brother, accused Sydney of "inciting the passions of the Irish Orangemen," but he would have been at a loss to find any election riding in Canada where there were dispassionate Orangemen. As we will see, it was also a case of the pot calling the kettle black.

The process in Argenteuil started off with a call by the returning officer for nominations, which was done by open outcry at a gathering in St. Andrews on July 24.

Sydney was laid up with dysentery in Grenville, but his backers saw to it that his nomination was accepted on his behalf. The St. Andrews notables had drafted Robert Simpson, a harness-maker from St. Andrews who was popular with both the local establishment and the French-speaking voters. Sydney's correspondence with Alexandre Delisle shows that Sydney had toyed with the idea of offering the inarticulate "Bob" Simpson £50 to retire from the ring. In the election that took place only a few days later, two of the polling stations were located in the opposing "establishment" strongholds of St. Andrews, in the southeast corner of the county, and neighbouring

Chatham. People from the back areas who wanted to vote for Sydney had to travel several miles through the bush to get to their polling station. For some of them, the trip was made easier when Delisle hired every stagecoach he could find to get them there, at least part of the way, in style. In addition to the two establishment strongholds, there were two polls, one at St. Hermas and the other at St. Placide, in the French-speaking part of the county, close to St. Benoît in the neighbouring county of Two Mountains. Simpson's supporters ensured that every voter in that area knew that the former Captain Bellingham had been with General Colborne when St. Eustache and St. Benoît were sacked and burned in December 1837. On the other hand, Sydney was counting on Delisle to lend him a hand with French-speaking voters, and Delisle did more than just that.

Although the deck had seemed very much stacked against him, a solid majority declared Sydney the winner on August 4. His opponents moved to unseat him. The petition signed by Simpson alleged fifteen grounds for declaring the election void. Some of these were stock accusations that appear to have been routinely included in electoral contestations, such as the assertion that Sydney lacked the necessary property qualifications, or that he had paid for "entertainments" near the polling stations, or offered bribes and promises of employment. But some of the accusations were serious. There were allegations that residents of Mille-Isles, an English-speaking community that was not even then a part of the County of Argenteuil,

had voted at the poll in the Township of Gore. There were complaints that gangs of outsiders working on the railway between Carillon and Grenville had driven French-speaking voters away from the polling stations at St. Hermas and St. Placide, and that the local deputy returning officers were complicit in closing the polls earlier than required by law. If this was true, as seems to be the case, it was likely the work of the railway's president, Alexandre Delisle. This all sounded very much like the events in Terrebonne twelve years earlier when Sydenham's gangs of Orangemen drove away La Fontaine's supporters. Given Sydney's connections with Delisle and the railway, it would not be a stretch to imagine that he was complicit in the intimidation.

Oddly, there was also an assertion that the election was void because polls had not been set up in the mostly uninhabited townships at the north end of the county. The venerable county registrar and chief returning officer, Colonel Daniel de Hertel, appeared unaware that this was one of the new requirements adopted to reform the electoral rules. A committee of the Assembly convened at Quebec, and on November 29, 1854, it voided the election on the ground that no polling stations had been set up in the northern townships, including Arundel and De Salaberry. This might have been called a "technicality," but it would be better described as an absurdity. Neither of these townships had been surveyed at that time, there were no inhabitants possessing the necessary property qualifications, and there was no public place to hold a poll in any event. Sydney was exonerated of any wrongdoing, but the Assembly sentenced the deputy returning officer at St. Hermas, a local notary, to a day in jail for closing the poll prematurely.

It seems Sydney had become a popular member of the House during the first three months of the session, and the committee's rather picky ruling outraged several of his colleagues. Fifty of them held a dinner in his honour to finance a second campaign. Among his supporters were notables such as Francis Hincks, Allan MacNab, Augustin-Norbert Morin, and John A. Macdonald— all of whom at one time or another were co-premiers.

During his three months as the sitting member for Argenteuil in 1854, Sydney convinced Co-Premier Morin to propose a bill gerrymandering the riding by transferring the two French-speaking parishes to the County of Two Mountains in return for an additional English-speaking township in Argenteuil, which not surprisingly was Mille-Isles.[34] Morin, who had previously been the member of the Assembly for his native Bellechasse, was then representing Terrebonne.

The way for Sydney's re-election seemed well paved. In the ensuing by-election, Sydney's opponents chose wealthy local merchant Lemuel Cushing to run against him, but on January 5, 1855, Sydney was declared the winner for a second time, by a margin of 1,113 votes to 777. He took his seat again when the session resumed at Quebec on February 23, 1855, and held on to it until the session adjourned on May 30. Sydney's memoirs intimate that many voters were turned off by Cushing's attempts to buy their votes. Be that as it may, his opponents again moved to unseat him and again were successful, the by-election being declared void on April 3, 1856. By this time, the capital of the United Province had moved from Quebec to Toronto. Cushing's petition alleged that 728 of the votes cast for Sydney were invalid mainly on grounds that the voters lacked the necessary property qualification, or that they had voted more than once. There were also aspersions of corruption and intimidation, and although the committee absolved Sydney of the accusations of bribery, it was on findings of intimidation by Sydney's "friends and partizans" that the committee upheld Cushing's petition. The committee's decision was based on a judicial inquiry conducted by Justice William McCord of the Superior Court for Lower Canada. Philip VanKoughnet, a Montreal lawyer whom Sydney greatly admired, represented him in those proceedings.

By the third round, Sydney's opponents threw in the towel, and he was quickly returned by acclamation. On May 15, 1856, in Toronto, George-Étienne Cartier and John A. Macdonald escorted Sydney to his seat. He remained active in the House until the Fifth Parliament was dissolved on June 10, 1857.

It is unlikely that there is any other Canadian politician who can claim to have been elected three times in the same riding to the same session of Parliament. But

---

34 "Mille-Isles" sounds very much like the name of a predominantly French-speaking township, but it is a corruption of "Mile Hill."

the problem seems to have been with the way things were done in Argenteuil, and not so much with Sydney Bellingham the candidate. The repeated drama over elections in Argenteuil prompted the future minister of justice, Antoine-Aimé Dorion, to table a bill "to secure the freedom of Election at the next Election for the County of Argenteuil." Unfortunately, the bill was later withdrawn.

Had it been allowed to pass, Argenteuil electors might have been spared even more frequent trips to the polls following the annulment of the elections of three of Sydney's eventual successors.

On the eve of his second attempt to win in Argenteuil, another of Sydney's physician friends, the Dublin-born Dr. Robert MacDonnell, approached him with a proposition. MacDonnell hinted that if Sydney withdrew from the contest for health reasons and took a trip to Europe, he would find a sum of £1,000 "under his pillow." Sydney declined the offer. Years later, information came his way to suggest that the deal had not been proposed on behalf of Cushing, but rather to enable John Rose, a prosperous Montreal lawyer and collaborator of John A. Macdonald, to obtain an uncontested seat. It was one of a number of reasons why Sydney came to view Macdonald as duplicitous.

The Fifth Parliament lasted nearly three years, and despite the interruptions, Sydney made a meaningful contribution to its accomplishments. The list gives us some insight into both the needs of the day and his active role in addressing them. He sat on or chaired committees on the regulation of the militia, the adoption of a system for transcribing debates in the House, the deepening of the shipping channel between Montreal and Quebec, the investigation into the fires at Montreal and Quebec, an inquiry into the affairs of the Grand Trunk Railway, and improvements to the judicial system, including judges' salaries and the construction of new courthouses. He was a member of the prestigious Standing Committee on Railways, Canals, and Telegraph Lines. In the area of social legislation, he proposed measures to alleviate the hardships suffered by immigrants through overcrowding of vessels, for the protection of family homesteads and farming equipment from seizure, for the prohibition of canal labour on Sundays, and to permit the solemnization of marriages by Methodist clergy (a move vigorously opposed by the Anglican establishment, which held a monopoly on Protestant weddings). In 1858, Sydney was one of the sponsors of a bill to launch a canal project linking Ottawa to Georgian Bay. The same year, he was one of the founders of the Montreal Mountain Boulevard Company, which planned to build a ring road around Mount Royal and provide public access to what would later become Mount Royal Park. He co-sponsored the charter of a railway in the Peterborough region and the revival of the old Marmora ironworks, which he had visited during one of his forest treks in 1826, as well as the merger of the Champlain & St. Lawrence Railroad with the Montreal and Lachine Railroad, and legislation to render operative the Carillon-to-Grenville section of the failed Montreal and Bytown Railway. To encourage new investment, Sydney sponsored legislation to improve the registration requirements for mortgages, to encourage the construction of macadamized roads, and to permit mining companies to build spur lines connecting them to railways or waterways. In support of local interests, he presented bills to establish Argenteuil as a municipal corporation separate from the County of Two Mountains, to provide financial support to the Académie de St. André d'Argenteuil, and to incorporate Lachute College. In the midst of all this, he secured for himself in March 1856 an appointment as the lieutenant-colonel of the 1st Battalion of the Argenteuil Militia. The previous year, in response to the gradual withdrawal of British regular forces from Canada, a *Militia Act* had been passed making all males between the ages of eighteen and sixty automatically members of the militia—at least on paper.

It all—or nearly all—constituted an enlightened and progressive contribution. The one exception was a most peculiar piece of legislation setting up the northern part of the Township of Chatham in Argenteuil as a separate township. The settlers in the hilly northern part, including what is now the town of Brownsburg, were at odds with the older communities along the Ottawa, so the bill made sense demographically and geographically and was actually passed. What made it peculiar was that the new township was to be named "Bellingham." Sydney was not, it seems, a humble man. Although the bill became law, it was eventually allowed to lapse.

Like every politician, Sydney also had detractors in the House. The most famous was the former rebel leader from Upper Canada, William Lyon Mackenzie. Mackenzie was one of the exiled rebels who benefited from the Baldwin–La Fontaine amnesty of 1849. He returned to Toronto from exile in the United States and was elected to the Assembly in 1851. He continued to publish his own newspaper, the *Weekly Message*, attacking everyone and anyone with Tory connections, past or present. It says something about Mackenzie that he would write something so clearly unfounded as to assert that the new member from Argenteuil was the son of the Bellingham who had murdered British Prime Minister Spencer Perceval in 1812. According to Sydney's later recollection, Mackenzie (the same Mackenzie who had condoned the killing of Colonel Moodie at Montgomery's Tavern) accused him of being "imbued with all the bloody instincts of his father." It was one thing for the snooty collector of customs at Quebec to make that mistake in 1826,[35] but quite another for a fellow member of Parliament to turn it into an insult. In his memoirs, Sydney indicates that he bore no resentment towards Mackenzie, probably because by that time Mackenzie had alienated practically everyone in the House through his persistent personal attacks.

Let us pause to reflect on what it must have been like to represent the County of Argenteuil over a three-year period during which the Parliament was located

---

35 See Chapter 3.

first at Quebec and then at Toronto. By the end of 1854, it was possible to get most of the way from Montreal to Quebec by train, but the traveller had to first cross the St. Lawrence by boat from Montreal to Longueil and then back again from Lévis to Quebec. Train service between Montreal and Toronto did not begin until October 1856 and took fourteen hours. Until then, travel by steamer was the only relatively comfortable option during the seasons when the water was free of ice. The trip was a bit simpler than it had first been for Sydney in 1824, as a result of the opening of the Beauharnois Canal in 1843. The canal enabled steamboats from Montreal to travel from Lake St. Louis, past the rapids at Pointe des Cascades, and onto the calmer waters of Lake St. Francis to Cornwall and then, passing through the locks at Cornwall, to Kingston and the open waters of Lake Ontario. Getting from the Legislature at Quebec or Toronto to his riding in Argenteuil was another challenge. Lachute was not connected by rail to Montreal until 1876. Until then, Sydney had to travel by steamer between Lachine and Carillon and by coach the remaining ten miles to Lachute. Despite these difficulties, his correspondence with Alexandre Delisle shows that a letter took no more than a day to reach Montreal from St. Andrews, less than half the time it would take today. It also shows that Sydney and Delisle were coordinating their efforts through the telegraph at St. Andrews. Later dubbed "the instantaneous highway of thought," personal use of the telegraph had caught on fast after the incorporation of Hugh Allan's Montreal Telegraph

Company in 1847—faster than it took for e-mail to catch on after the introduction of the personal computer—although in most cases it involved a trek to the nearest railway station.

Another logistical reality that challenges the imagination is the difficulty Sydney faced in getting about within his riding, both in the mad rush to get out the vote during what were then very short election periods and in visiting his constituents during calmer times. There was a road good enough for travel by coach along the front of the county between St. Andrews, in the eastern part of the riding, to Grenville, closer to the southwestern corner. Bypassing the rapids of the Long Sault, this was the road that the Montreal and Bytown Railway had sought to replace for travel between Montreal and Ottawa. There were lesser roads branching northward. One was to become known, in deference to the origins of the first settlers who relied on it, as the Scotch Road. It ran a few miles inland from Grenville in the general direction of Harrington, becoming a dirt track before it reached that point. Another road connected St. Andrews to Lachute and a few points a bit farther on. Until Sydney saw to the extension of the Scotch Road as far as Arundel in 1858, the northern half of the county could be reached through the bush only on horseback. Wheeled vehicles were out of the question, but provisions could be dragged through the bush on a sort of sled called a "jumper." The only other option was an expedition by canoe, with portage up the Rouge River from a point west of Grenville, something no sensible person would do without first arranging for a party of Algonquin guides and carriers. If the settlers in the backcountry were hoping for someone to actively represent them in Parliament, it would have to be a man experienced in the rougher forms of travel then available to politicians, and Sydney Bellingham was remarkably qualified in that respect. However, something more than his affable personality and bushwhacking skills has to explain why he received so many votes from the backcountry settlers—more votes, in fact, than there were eligible voters.

When the Fifth Parliament was dissolved in the summer of 1857, Sydney might have been hoping for a smoother return to the Sixth, but that was not what happened. The Tory establishment of the front townships picked one of their own to challenge him in the election that fall. It was John Joseph Caldwell Abbott, formerly the junior partner in the firm of Badgley & Abbott, which Sydney and Alexandre Delisle had retained when they incorporated the Montreal and Bytown Railway in 1853.[36] That had not stopped Abbott from secretly working against Sydney in his contests with Robert Simpson and Lemuel Cushing in 1854, when Abbott was still the company solicitor and Delisle was campaigning for Sydney. One of Abbott's chief organizers was the Grenville shopkeeper George Kains, who had worked for Simpson and Cushing in their campaigns.

Sydney won, again with a suspiciously wide margin.

In many respects the contest was a repeat of the one waged by Lemuel Cushing, but this time with the added sideshow of the sort of acrimonious and protracted legal proceedings that only two lawyer-adversaries could provide. Abbott became so obsessed with the saga that, at his own expense, he arranged for the printing of some 400 pages of materials relating to the case, as if to say to the general public, "If you want to see what I had to go through to unseat Sydney Bellingham, read it for yourself!"

The opening salvo was Abbott's petition on January 16, 1858, to have the election declared void on the usual grounds. Sydney responded with a gigantic barrage of procedural attacks that kept prominent and expensive lawyers on both sides busy for months. Abbott's lead counsel was Edward Brock Carter, a distinguished Montreal barrister.

The five-member committee appointed to hear the case initially included Alexander Tilloch Galt, whom Sydney had grilled during the inquiry into the Grand Trunk four years earlier. Galt had to resign when he became a cabinet minister, but before leaving he told one of the members, Donald Alexander Macdonald, that the committee had to get rid of "that damned fellow Bellingham." Sydney's counsel, the Irish-born Charles Joseph Alleyn, picked every procedural nit that could be found. Alleyn's own election in 1857 as member for Quebec was itself annulled, and he knew every angle in the process. The Parliamentary Committee appointed

---

36 See Chapter 6.

Abbott's former partner, William Badgley, by then a Superior Court judge, as judge commissioner to hear the evidence. Sydney challenged Badgley's impartiality in a bold letter delivered to the man personally on the steps of the courthouse by Sydney's other attorney, William E. Holmes. Infuriated, Badgley refused to recuse himself and fined Sydney £10 for contempt. Then one of Sydney's technical arguments hit home when the committee found that Badgley had not adhered to the procedural timetable required by the statute. They annulled the proceedings before Badgley, and the whole process began again under another Superior Court judge, Jean Casimir Bruneau. All this time, Sydney continued to occupy his seat in Parliament, while a furious Abbott waited in the wings.

During the wait, Abbott consoled himself by acquiring his former client, the Montreal and Bytown Railway, and flipping it at a handsome profit.[37]

The evidence in the end was that Sydney's majority had been gained by the votes of backcountry settlers and squatters who lacked the proper property qualifications for voting. Abbott's principal witness was George Kains, wearing his hat as Crown Land agent at Grenville. His carefully scripted evidence impugned the property qualifications of several Bellingham supporters. However, in cross-examination, some of the witnesses admitted that they had each been paid a dollar to vote for Abbott. It also came out that they had collected payment at George Kains's store, and it would not be unreasonable to assume

that Kains had previously handled similar campaign "disbursements" for Simpson and Cushing. It is in that context that we should perhaps be a bit circumspect about Kains's criticisms of Sydney's election practices.

On March 12, 1860, more than two years after Sydney had taken his seat, the committee finally ruled in Abbott's favour. The vote was two to two, but the chairman, Angus Morrison, another man with railway subsidy interests, used his tie-breaking vote. Walking down Toronto's King Street later in the day, Sydney bumped into Edmund Murney, a former conservative member of the House who had been elevated to the Legislative Council. Murney had heard the news, and when Sydney expressed surprise at Morrison's actions, Murney explained that Morrison was "one of John A. Macdonald's jackals." To Sydney, the outcome suddenly appeared to have been a stab in the back by Macdonald, with whom he had always been on friendly terms.

He never forgave Macdonald. Fourteen years later, on the eve of his departure for a sojourn of several months in England and Ireland, Sydney dropped in on Hector Langevin, until recently his colleague in the Quebec Assembly, to say *au revoir*. Langevin had been one of the two committee members who had voted against the motion to unseat him in 1860. He may not have been Macdonald's lackey then, but in 1873 he succeeded George-Étienne Cartier as Macdonald's Quebec lieutenant following Cartier's death.

Langevin had held seats simultaneously in both the

---

37 See Chapter 6.

federal Parliament and provincial Assembly and was a frequent conduit of information on anything that could affect Macdonald's interests. On June 6, 1874, Langevin wrote Macdonald from Quebec to report on a number of matters, including the meeting he had with Sydney the previous Friday:

> He seemed to be under the impression that you had not treated him well in the matter of the County of Argenteuil and of Abbott. I have tried to change his mind and to have him to think otherwise. He will be [in Ireland] about 4 or 5 months. I have no doubt that one of your John A. shakes of the hand and a few words at the proper time will put him all right again.

We do not know if Sydney ever met up with Macdonald again, but if there were any such "shakes of the hand," they did not work in the way Langevin had hoped they would. Long after Sydney had retired permanently to Ireland, even as late as 1897, his correspondence reveals that he had still not forgiven Macdonald.

The six years of Sydney's first period as a parliamentarian were eventful ones for the United Province and particularly for what had been Lower Canada. In 1854, the seigneurial system of land tenure was abolished. In 1857, the first step was taken towards the codification of Lower Canada's Civil Law. The years 1857 and 1858 brought economic depression and increased emigration to the United States. There was pressure on members of the Assembly to stem the tide. Sydney held firmly to the idea that economic development, with increased employment opportunities and increased wages, was the proper solution. He was a strong sponsor and supporter of legislation enabling the construction of roads, bridges, railways, and canals, but legislation was not enough. It was not until the government was willing to provide financial assistance, in the form of subsidies, that entrepreneurs were prepared to take risks in a difficult capital market. Sydney's support for railway development stalled when the politicians started doling out taxpayers' money to pay for it, and when greed replaced risk avoidance as the principal financial objective of the promoters. On the broader economic scene, the dollar became the official monetary unit in 1858, signalling the shift towards a North American, as opposed to Imperial trade. Commercial relations with the United States began to thaw, but the political and territorial relations were heating up. Those events will be touched on later in this chapter, but first we should pause to have a close look at some of the people in Sydney's world in the middle of the century.

During his time in the Union Parliament, Sydney got to know a lot of interesting personalities, not all of them politicians. Some, like John Egan and Thomas MacKay, we have already met. Another was Sir William Logan, the geologist and cartographer who for many years was the director of the Geological Survey of Canada. His *Report of Progress* published in 1863 ran to nearly 1,000 pages, with illustrations and maps detailing the geological makeup of most of the territory of Canada as it then existed. By 1870, Logan's work had become so well-known that one of the highest peaks in Lower Canada, located in the Gaspé Peninsula, was named after him. After his death, topographers elevated him from the mere 3,700 feet of Mont Logan, to the nearly 20,000 feet of Yukon's Mount Logan, Canada's tallest peak.

Surveying the surface of the land is one thing, but tracing and inventorying what lies beneath it is quite another, particularly with only the tools of the mid-nineteenth century. Logan exhibited extraordinary physical stamina and self-discipline in accomplishing what he did over such a vast and varied wilderness. His scientific interests were also wide-ranging. In 1846, his investigation of the ice jams that had caused flooding and structural damage to buildings in Montreal was used in the design of Victoria Bridge. One of the regions he painstakingly explored was the part of the Laurentian Mountains that runs through the northern half of the County of Argenteuil. He hoped to find there the mineral wealth he succeeded in unearthing in other parts of Canada, such as coal in Nova Scotia and copper in the Eastern Townships of Lower Canada and in the rocks of the Canadian Shield north of Lake Huron. The prospects for iron in Argenteuil seemed reasonable, given the very visible redness of the rocky cliffs overlooking Harrington

Township, and the name of the Rouge River itself, with the faintly distinguishable reddish hue of its waters. In the end, the marketable mineral wealth of the county was limited to magnesite deposits at Kilmar, a few miles north of Grenville. Logan's earlier work in the area around Grenville was the basis for a scientific rock classification he named the Grenville Series, which defines a vast geological area of northeastern North America called the Grenville Province.

Sydney repeats a tale told by one of his constituents in Dalesville, the wife of a relatively prosperous farmer by the name of Archibald McArthur. The hamlet of Dalesville is located northwest of Lachute in a pocket of arable land just above the escarpment. Mrs. McArthur told him how one summer afternoon a shabbily dressed and red-bearded vagabond, carrying a backpack and a pickaxe, called at their door and asked for some bread and milk. Speaking in their Scottish Gaelic so that their visitor would not understand, Archibald berated his wife for putting up with such a lowlife, with his cracked spectacles and his hair matted with spruce gum. They did not learn until later that the vagabond was none other than the first Canadian-born Fellow of the Royal Society and the third Canadian to have been knighted by Queen Victoria. More to their chagrin, they learned that he was fluent in Gaelic. Sydney first got to know Logan from Little St. James Street, where Logan lived abstemiously above his laboratory and sample room. In 1856, upon his return to Montreal from the knighthood ceremony in London,

Logan proudly showed Sydney the gold medal he had received there from the Geological Society, and the cross of the Legion of Honour given to him the previous year by Napoleon III of France. That a man of such modesty and accomplishment would share these moments with Sydney tells us something about the respect Logan had for him. In his *Geological Atlas of Canada* published in 1866, Logan labelled the northern part of the Township of Chatham as "Bellingham," in line with Sydney's failed attempt to make that the official designation in 1856. In 1875, shortly before Logan's death, Sydney visited him in London, where the ailing Sir William had gone to seek medical treatment.

Sydney's work on the Standing Committee on Railways, Canals, and Telegraph Lines brought him into contact with Walter Shanly, a civil engineer who built hundreds of miles of railway track and designed or built canals and tunnels in Canada and the United States. Shanly was an Anglo-Irishman whose first experience as an engineer was gained through the construction of canals on the St. Lawrence at Beauharnois, on the Richelieu, and bypassing Niagara Falls at Welland. In 1858, at the age of forty, he became chief engineer of the Grand Trunk Railway. He gained broader recognition in 1875, doing what others had failed to accomplish, as the engineer who completed the Hoosac Tunnel through the Green Mountains in northwest Massachusetts. It would remain, for the next forty years, the longest tunnel in North America. Late in his career, Shanly was consulted on the feasibility of a tunnel under the St. Lawrence at Montreal and another one under Northumberland Strait between New Brunswick and Prince Edward Island. Sydney described his fellow countryman as being recognized as much for his probity as for his engineering skills, but unpopular with government officials "because he would not lend himself to any intrigues or corrupt practices." He recounts how the engineering skills were demonstrated in excavating the Hoosac Tunnel, through nearly five miles of rock at an average depth of 1,400 feet, starting at both ends and ending up with only half an inch's difference in the middle.

Another engineer—albeit also a lawyer—whom Sydney met through the work of the select committee was Casimir Gzowski, (later "Sir"), a rebel refugee from the Czarist domination of his native Poland who amassed considerable wealth and prestige through his wheeling and dealing in Canadian railway construction contracts. Sydney's admiration for Shanly stands in contrast with his contempt for Gzowski, and it is revealing that writing nearly half a century later, he remembered Gzowski not for what he built (which included the International Bridge linking Fort Erie, Ontario, and Buffalo, New York), but for how much he bilked. Sydney mentions one incident in particular, where Gzowski and his political cronies, including Alexander Tilloch Galt (likewise later "Sir"), made a huge personal profit through the sale of 600 acres of prime land at the important railway hub of Sarnia. The

land had previously been held as a military reserve. Sydney was familiar with the incident because he knew Colonel W. R. Orde of the British Royal Engineers, who had been instructed to dispose of the land on behalf of the imperial government. Orde told him that he had been led to believe that the sale at the token sum of £200 was intended to be a subsidy to the Grand Trunk, but the deed had been crafted in such a way that Gzowski and his cronies were able to acquire it for themselves and flip it to the Grand Trunk for £20,000.

It was Sydney, with his probing questions to Galt and others during the hearings of the special committee

36. Sir William Logan, F.R.S., photograph by William Notman, 1869, McCord Museum 1-42425, with permission

appointed to inquire into the affairs of the Grand Trunk, who frequently led the charge in trying to get at the facts. When the committee chairman, George Brown, put a question to a witness, it was often Sydney who followed up with an even more hard-hitting one. The transcript shows that when he pressed for a proper answer because the witness was being evasive, Macdonald's majority members would vote that the answer already given was sufficient. Almost all of the shareholders of the Grand Trunk were British, and Sydney was incensed that deals like the one at Sarnia could be engineered through the complicity of Canadian politicians who had been appointed to the board of directors by the Macdonald-Cartier government. His old ally Benjamin Holmes was a member of the board in his capacity as vice-president of the St. Lawrence and Atlantic Railroad Company, which had been merged with the Grand Trunk. Holmes had also been critical of the disregard for the interests of shareholders and was likely the source of much of the information brought out at the committee hearings. Sydney made a lot of friends when he was in the Parliament of the United Province, but he also made powerful enemies among members, like John Ross, Alexander Tilloch Galt, Francis Hincks, and Luther Holton, whose interests were merged with those of the railway developers and who, in his words, "had gorged themselves with the plunder of the Grand Trunk Railway of Canada." He was not a loner, but neither was he a team player when the team was driven as much by personal greed as the interests of their electors. Had he been more of a team player, he probably would not have lost his seat in 1860, and he might have received a cabinet appointment.

Alexandre-Édouard Kierzkowski was a compatriot of Gzowski, with a similar revolutionary and engineering background in his youth, who came to Canada at about the same time. Unlike Gzowski, however, Kierzkowski was someone whom Sydney admired for his integrity, and considered a friend. In 1845, Kierzkowski married a daughter of Pierre-Dominique Debartzch, the seigneur whose manor house at St. Charles had become Thomas Storrow Brown's short-lived headquarters in November 1837. A progressive thinker who would have succeeded as an economist if such a profession had existed in mid-nineteenth-century Canada, Kierzkowski advocated for a system of land credit that would enable tenant farmers to extricate themselves from the constituted rents that had survived the formal abolition of the seigneurial system. In line with those proposals, he published a pamphlet in 1852 calling for reforms to the civil law of hypothecs (mortgages), in order to make farm credit more attractive to lenders. It advocated a system making it possible for lenders to check whether some other creditor ranked ahead of them on their security, without which banks could not be expected to lend money to farmers at affordable interest rates. In March 1857, Sydney introduced a "Bill to Encourage the Introduction of Foreign Capital into Lower Canada, by Better

Securing the Rights of Mortgages." Inspired by his friend Kierzkowski's proposals, Sydney sought to outlaw hidden mortgages but failed to get the Assembly's support until provisions to the same effect were incorporated in the new Civil Code adopted in 1866. In 1867, Kierzkowski was elected to the first Canadian Parliament.

One of the highly successful Scots who had established themselves in Montreal was John Boston. A prominent lawyer, and, for a time, the head of the Montreal bar, Boston was also the sheriff of Montreal, a position that came with a huge salary and expense allowance. Boston owned two seigneuries and was a shareholder in banks and railways. He balanced his financial interests with intellectual pursuits and was one of the founders in 1843 of the High School of Montreal. Boston was one of Sydney's frequent contacts in the St. James Street legal community, and his next-door neighbour at Dunany Cottage.

We have already taken note of some of the medical men Sydney knew well, both in their professional lives and as prominent players on the political stage, but there was one intriguing character he saw at work who practised on the fringes of medical science. All we know was that he was an American "biologist" who came to Montreal to give a "lecture" at the Théâtre Royal. It was more of a show than a lecture, and the topic was hypnosis. Sydney was one of about a hundred spectators who watched as their entertainer pulled a dozen young boys from the audience and made them unconsciously

dance a jig or believe they were drowning. It was not just show business. At a time when the use of ether and chloroform as anesthetics was only beginning to gain acceptance, hypnosis, in the cases where it worked, was the only effective way of managing the pain of the brutal surgical techniques of the day.

Among the politicians Sydney admired was Allan MacNab. MacNab, whose earlier military career started at the age of fourteen during the War of 1812, was joint premier from 1854 to 1856, first with Augustin-Norbert Morin and then with Étienne-Paschal Taché. In his memoirs, Sydney recalls sitting beside him when an attack of gout forced MacNab to address the House sitting down. He recalls the brutality with which MacNab was deposed and replaced in 1856 by John A. Macdonald. He similarly witnessed the long-standing animosity between Macdonald and George Brown, which made their later alliance in bringing about Confederation all the more remarkable. In Sydney's words, Macdonald hated Brown "as cordially as the devil hates holy water." Sydney supported the efforts of Brown to root out corruption when he was a member of the special committee that Brown chaired on the affairs of the Grand Trunk.

Sydney recalled with admiration Augustin-Norbert Morin and George-Étienne Cartier, each of whom, despite their participation in events of 1837 for which they had been arrested, became a joint premier many years later. Morin had been one of the principal drafters of the Ninety-Two Resolutions in 1834. Like Sydney, he was both a lawyer and a journalist. In 1826, he founded a newspaper called *La Minerve*, which initially advocated for the *Patriote* cause and was banned during the rebellion. Morin may also have been one of the inspirations behind Sydney's efforts in the settlement of the northern part of Argenteuil County. As commissioner for Crown Lands, Morin had helped settle parts of neighbouring Terrebonne. The villages of Val-Morin and Morin Heights were named after him. The village of Sainte-Adèle was named after his wife. Known for his legal intellect, he was one of the founders of Laval University in 1852 and was later the first dean of its Faculty of Law. For health reasons, he resigned from the government, which he co-led with MacNab in early 1855, and after being appointed a justice of the Superior Court, became one of the commissioners entrusted with the monumental task of codifying the Civil Law of Lower Canada. As we have seen, it was Morin who presented the bill that redefined the Counties of Two Mountains and Argenteuil along clearer demographic lines.

Sydney had first known George-Étienne Cartier as a fellow member of the bar of Montreal in the 1840s. He stood out from the crowd by his vivaciousness, and one image that remained in Sydney's mind was the small gold figure of Napoleon that Cartier always sported. He would occasionally encounter the young Cartier hanging around the corner of St. Vincent and Notre Dame Streets, where the imposing Parisian-style bookstore of another former

Patriote, Édouard-Raymond Fabre, was located. In 1846, Cartier married Fabre's daughter Hortense. A decade later, Sydney got to know Cartier the politician, when they were both in the Legislative Assembly. In Sydney's mind, it was to Cartier that John A. Macdonald owed his political success, both then and after Confederation. For the sake of completeness, we need to add Cartier to the roster of people Sydney knew who fell prey to the impulse of the duel. In Cartier's case, it happened twice. The first one ended without shots being fired when Cartier's opponent delivered an abject letter of apology. The second duel, involving the editor of *L'Avenir*, Joseph Doutre, ended when both protagonists fired but missed. They had earlier appeared genuinely determined to go at each other, since the duel took place at a second location after their planned encounter the previous day had been interrupted by the police. Doutre's paper had accused Cartier of cowardice at the Battle of St. Denis.

Sydney's biggest political regret was in being manipulated by Macdonald into voting in support of his Grand Trunk subsidy bill on May 1, 1857. He describes Macdonald's ability to convince as practically hypnotic. On the night of the vote on the bill, Cartier approached Sydney in the House and whispered to him that Macdonald wished to speak with him privately. With the galleries packed with anxious onlookers, Sydney left his seat and joined Macdonald in a room behind the speaker's chair:

He said: "Bellingham, we have counted noses, and the division will be so close that if you vote against us, the ministry will be compelled to resign. Now you have always been a friend of our party, and I want to know what measures on our part will satisfy you." I said: "I object to any member of the government being a director of the Grand Trunk company." He asked me if that would satisfy me. I answered: "I have never asked for, nor received any benefit from the Government, and if you turn out the members of the government who are directors of the Grand Trunk, I should be satisfied."

As it turned out, the bill passed second reading by a comfortable margin of fifty-eight to forty-seven, and Sydney was "rewarded with a roar of scorn and derision from the opposition." His memoirs record the shame he felt for having been duped into supporting Macdonald through the assurance that his vote was essential to prevent the fall of the government. Worse, he had not realized that the bill already provided for dispensing with government directors, the big concession he thought he had won in exchange for supporting the subsidy.[38] "I felt that I had been guilty of an act of unpardonable stupidity."

Sydney's resentment towards Macdonald was matched only by his contempt for Galt and the personal

profits Galt made in arranging for the Grand Trunk to take over the St. Lawrence and Atlantic Railroad. In his memoirs, Sydney gave Galt none of the credit others have given him for starting the discussion on uniting the British North American colonies, which eventually led to Confederation. He probably felt that if it was Galt who proposed it, Galt saw in it a way of making money. Sydney hardly mentions Confederation at all in his memoirs, but we can tell from his correspondence that he was as much opposed to it as he had been to the Union.

Having digressed, we return now to the period following the success of Abbott's campaign to unseat Sydney. With some significant interruptions, Abbott would hold on to Argenteuil, first in the Union Parliament and then in the post-Confederation Canadian Parliament, until 1887, when he was appointed to the Senate. Abbott's comments on Sydney Bellingham in his account of "The Argenteuil Case" betray a certain sanctimonious self-righteousness in regard to matters of electoral morality, but he himself was unseated twice on grounds of bribery. One has to pity the electors of Argenteuil, who may well hold the Canadian record for trips to the polls in the second half of the nineteenth century.

Sydney had considered running federally against Abbott in the elections of 1872 but bowed out as a result of pressure on his constituents from the all-powerful shipping and railway baron Hugh Allan. John Abbott was the legal adviser to Sir Hugh, who had an interest in the Montreal Northern Colonization Railway, of

---

38 20 Victoria, c. 11

which he was president. The plan at that time called for the Montreal Northern Colonization to run northward from Montreal, with a branch from St. Jérome running westward through Argenteuil to Ottawa. Allan let it be known to Sydney's backers at Lachute that if they allowed Sydney to be elected instead of Abbott, the new railway would run through St. Andrews and not Lachute. Abbott was elected by acclamation, but in a sense he had won through a most egregious form of bribery and intimidation.

The Second Canadian Parliament lasted only a few months. The Montreal newspaper *The True Witness and Catholic Chronicle* reported on January 9, 1874, that Sydney was going to resign his seat in the provincial Assembly and run as a Liberal against Abbott in the federal election later that month, but it was only a rumour. Lemuel Cushing Jr., the son of the Lemuel Cushing who had run against Sydney in 1855, challenged Abbott. Abbott won, but Cushing petitioned for his removal on grounds of bribery, and Justice Francis Godschall Johnson of the Superior Court found against Abbott in November 1874. Cushing's victory was short-lived, his own election being annulled a year later. Sydney's friend, the Lachute physician Dr. Thomas Christie, won the seat in the ensuing by-election on December 31, 1875, and again in the general election in September 1878, but that election was overturned and Abbott recaptured the seat from Christie for a brief period in a by-election held in early 1880. Then that

by-election was annulled, again on the basis of bribery allegations. Finally, in a by-election held in August 1881, Abbott was re-elected unopposed. The electors of Argenteuil had had enough.

Abbott often claimed to hate politics and elections, but even after he was appointed to the Senate, he sought and won two one-year terms as mayor of Montreal. Then, in 1897 he became Canada's third prime minister, a position he held for seventeen months before retiring for health reasons.

The interests of the County of Argenteuil never ranked very highly in John Abbott's list of priorities. Montreal society, government appointments, a highly lucrative law practice, the big business of railways, and politics on a grander scale would consume most of his energies in the years to come. Sydney does not have much to say about Abbott and appears to have borne him no ill will. On the other hand, Sydney does not spare Abbott's family. His memoirs contain some unflattering vignettes about certain clergymen—Protestant and Catholic alike—and he has one to tell about Abbott's father and uncle, both High Church of England clergymen. The Abbott brothers disdained fellow Protestant souls who were either "dissenters," like the Presbyterian Scots and Scots-Irish, and the "latitudinarian" Anglo-Irish who refused to follow the High-Church rituals. Sydney recites the terms with which the uncle, the Reverend William Abbott, rejected a request for funds to assist in the building of a church in the backcountry Township of

Gore, stating that he would rather subscribe to a fund for building them a jail. In the end, it was their MP, Sydney Bellingham, who succeeded in raising the money for the new Gore church, which still stands today as one of the cultural landmarks of Argenteuil County.

John Abbott's father, Joseph, had briefly been the rector at St. Andrews before his brother William took over. Later on, after removing himself to the Eastern Townships following some sort of unrecorded "strife," Joseph returned to Argenteuil and became the rector at Grenville. He ceased to tend to his flock in Grenville in 1843. The published histories and biographies explain that he was then appointed registrar and bursar of McGill University by the acting principal, his good friend the Reverend John Bethune. John Bethune was the brother of James Gray Bethune, the merchant Sydney had met at Cobourg when he first came to Upper Canada. The new registrar and bursar retained as his deputy his son John, then a young McGill law student, to do whatever work this sinecure involved. John married Bethune's daughter a few years later. The double nepotism may not have been in the institution's best interests given that an audit in 1844 disclosed irregularities and inaccuracies in the bookkeeping.

Sydney sheds some light on the real reason why Joseph left Grenville for Montreal. William Ermatinger, the brother of Sydney's old Royal Montreal Cavalry friend Charles Ermatinger, had become the Montreal police commissioner in 1842. At some point he was instructed to proceed to Grenville to investigate a woman's complaint of attempted criminal assault by Joseph Abbott in the vestry of the church at Grenville. According to Sydney, whose source appears most credible, the result was that the Reverend Joseph was defrocked and deprived of his Anglican church income.

Unlike many of the Montreal anglophone gentry, particularly other members of the bar, Sydney was no snob. He was cordial in his dealings with constituents, no matter where they ranked in the social scale, preferring to meet them in person rather than rely on local backers or agents to do the door-to-door. One example was an impoverished, elderly man he had heard about from the McArthurs. The man lived with his daughter and grandchild in a twelve-foot-square shanty about four miles into the bush from Dalesville. The family managed to survive off a small patch of cleared land on which they grew potatoes and oats, supplemented by the charity of a few neighbours, who must have been moved by the plight of the daughter and her fatherless child. The old man told Sydney that he had been an officer in the British army and had served in what is now southern Ontario. Somehow the story came out that twenty years earlier he had lent the sum of £300 to a fellow British officer to help him settle in the area, but the debt had not been repaid before he himself left to settle in Argenteuil. Despite sitting on opposite sides of the House and often voting at cross-purposes, Sydney had struck up a friendship with the member for the riding of London, a lawyer known as "Honest John" Wilson. He prevailed upon Wilson to track down the borrower in his riding and secure repayment of the debt. Through Wilson's efforts, the sum was recovered, and Sydney was able to deliver to the old man more money than he had seen in two decades.

Many years earlier, when he was a twenty-three-year-old law student, Honest John had become entangled in an argument over a young lady with another law student, whose name was Robert Lyon. A fistfight ensued, but the dispute remained unresolved. The lawyer Wilson had articled with goaded him to challenge Lyon to a duel. The men both missed with their first shots, but then Lyon's second persuaded Wilson to agree to a second round. In the second round, Wilson's aim was true, and Lyon was killed. Like Robert Sweeney, who killed Sydney's friend John Warde nearly a decade later, Wilson was tried and acquitted on a charge of murder, likely because the fatal shot was at the urging of the victim's agent. Wilson and the young lady were married two years later. He went on to become a successful barrister known for defending some of the same rebels he had helped round up as a militia captain during Mackenzie's rebellion. Later, he became a judge.

In the decade following Confederation, the people of Argenteuil continued to have hands-on representation from Sydney, their member in the Quebec Assembly, while the lawyers and judges who had been entangled in the "Argenteuil Case" went on to other files. Abbott's lawyer, Edward Carter, would later team up with Levi Ruggles Church and the future premier of Quebec, Joseph-Adolphe Chapleau, to set up the law firm known a century later as Ogilvy Renault. Charles Alleyn became provincial secretary in the Cartier-Macdonald government. Philip VanKoughnet became minister of agriculture and then a distinguished Toronto judge. William Badgley's prestigious legal career peaked in 1866 when he was elevated to the Quebec Court of Appeal presided over by Chief Justice Jean-François Duval, the same Duval who many years before had been Sydney's lawyer in the Freer case.[39] Badgley resigned in 1874 after the Montreal bar went on strike to protest the incompetence of four of the five members of the Duval court, including Badgley, who was by then deaf as a post and known for the frequent heated exchange of insults with his colleague on the bench, his former political adversary Lewis Thomas Drummond—the same Drummond who won the election for the Montreal riding that Sydney had stepped back from in 1844.

After his removal from the Assembly in March of 1860, Sydney maintained his connection with Argenteuil through his properties in Arundel but absented himself for several months in England. The early 1860s were a relatively quiet period in his life, but a frenetic one in the history of Montreal and Canada generally. With his focus on his farm in Arundel and his other properties in that township and in Bellechasse, Sydney was more of an observer of political events than an active participant. But

---

39 See Chapter 3.

there was a lot going on. On the positive side, the early 1860s brought increased economic activity and relative prosperity. Ocean-shipping tonnage in the harbour at Montreal in 1862 was nearly three times what it had been in 1854. The St. James Street banks were gaining a reputation for stability that came to characterize the Canadian banking system, in contrast with American banks. Warehouses and factories were sprouting along the eastern end of the Lachine Canal, and there was a building spree in the centre of town. A horse-drawn tramway service began operating in 1861 and quickly expanded to handle the bustling downtown pedestrian traffic. By the middle of the decade, Montreal would have a population of nearly 100,000, four times what it had been when Sydney first arrived in the city in 1824.

On a less positive note, the Civil War in the United States, and events there before and after the war, created a mood of uncertainty for Canadians and for Montrealers in particular. Before the war, the attitude of Canadians towards slavery had been a source of displeasure for some American statesmen. For years, Montreal had been an important outlet for the Underground Railroad, which provided an escape route for American slaves. In 1849, critics of the annexation movement warned that Canadians would thereby "degrade themselves to the level of slaveholders." In 1861, a public rally took place in Montreal at which prominent citizens, including Sydney's old ally Benjamin Holmes, spoke out against returning escaped slaves to comply with

American demands. Ironically, after the outbreak of the Civil War later that year, Montreal became a refuge for Confederate sympathizers and agents. Despite its stand against slavery, Britain was known to be somewhat supportive of the Southern cause, largely inspired by its dependence on cotton to feed its textile industry. The seizure of two Confederate agents aboard the British steamer *Trent* nearly led to war and sparked an increase in the number of British regular troops garrisoned in Canada and the Maritimes. A previously slimmed-down Montreal garrison suddenly took on new life with 3,400 newcomers whose arrival provided a greater feeling of security, and more concretely, a big boost to the city's economy. Soldiers were posted at the vital new Victoria Bridge to ward off possible saboteurs. The Cartier-Macdonald government fell in the spring of 1862 over the adoption of a conscription bill.

In October 1864, Confederate soldiers used Montreal as the base for a raid on three Vermont banks. The "St. Albans Raiders" were arrested upon their return, but their release on jurisdictional grounds created an uproar in the border states. One of their lawyers was John Abbott. The American authorities hired Bernard Devlin as prosecuting attorney—the same Bernard Devlin who fifteen years earlier had been trying to drum up support for Irish independence. In the aftermath, the American government initiated a requirement for passports for entry into the United States. Towards the end of 1864, the Irish-American Fenian Movement began its raids into

Canada in the rather forlorn hope of using it as a hostage in bargaining for the freedom of Ireland. The Fenian nuisance would last until 1871. The impact of the Fenian raids was felt as far north as Sydney's Argenteuil County, where the Argenteuil Rangers—including men from Arundel—were called out to garrison Ottawa while the Ottawa militia were away protecting the border. By mid-1866, 20,000 militiamen were on active service in Canada. Growing U.S. militarism was perceived as a much greater threat than Irish Fenians and was becoming a powerful incentive towards Confederation. In 1866, the Reciprocity Treaty came to an end, providing another incentive.

One of the characters Sydney got to know during these frenetic years was James Diament Westcott. Westcott had been one of the first two senators for the new State of Florida when it was admitted to the Union in 1845. Before that, President Andrew Jackson had appointed him secretary of the territory, and he was the acting governor when the governor was away. Since 1862, Westcott had become a permanent resident of the St. Lawrence Hall Hotel on St. James Street, two blocks from Sydney's office.

The hotel belonged to Sydney's friend Henry Hogan. The reason given by Sydney for Westcott's presence in Montreal was that "being a southern man of pronounced opinions, he sought safety in flight from the attentions of the Washington government." Another reason was that he was a Confederate spy. Whatever benefits came with the job expired with General Robert E. Lee's surrender in 1865. Having forfeited his property in the United States, Westcott was penniless, and he looked it. "At the best he was very careless how he dressed, and I often wished that he had more use of a nail brush for his nails, and a comb for his head." Hogan gave him free room and board, and Sydney would "take the hint" when Westcott mentioned that his purse was empty. After the war, Westcott liked to entertain patrons of the St. Lawrence with stories of how he would relay messages from Montreal to Richmond by writing them in cipher on tissue paper, which was then rolled up inside a quill stem and hidden in a courier's boot.

Westcott had other stories from before the war, when he had been secretary and acting governor of the Florida territory. He talked about the first Seminole War, which he described as costing $100,000 and a hundred soldiers' lives for every Seminole killed in the Everglades. He talked of convening a large palaver in 1834 to explain the terms of peace dictated by the United States, under which the Seminoles would migrate to new land in the West. In keeping with the solemnity of the event, a Methodist minister had prevailed upon Westcott to let him read a few passages from the Book of Genesis. In response, a Seminole chief rose to give his people's version of the creation myth. He said that the great Manitou "had given a hoe and an axe to the black man, as his life was to be one of labour. To the red man he gave a rifle and a tomahawk, as he was a hunter and a warrior. To the white man he gave a bible and a bottle of whiskey;

with the one he enslaved the black man, and with the other he robbed the Indian."

Westcott was not the only Confederate agent to lodge at St. Lawrence Hall, or dine next door at Dolly's Chop House. For a couple of weeks in 1864, American actor John Wilkes Booth accompanied him. Hogan later described Booth as a rather genial individual. Booth joined Westcott and other Confederate agents in schemes to kidnap Abraham Lincoln.

St. Lawrence Hall quickly became known to Americans as "the only hotel in Canada to serve mint juleps." During the trial of the St. Albans Raiders, the hotel was so crowded with Americans that Hogan had to resort to putting three or four guests in a single room. Presumably, he was sensitive enough to separate the Confederate agents from the Union officials and lawyers. Hogan knew how to handle overbooking, as he had done in 1860 when the Prince of Wales and his retinue arrived to officially open Victoria Bridge. He also knew how to keep sworn enemies on separate floors, as on the several occasions when John A. Macdonald and George Brown arrived in town at the same time.

Another visitor to Montreal in the 1860s who failed to escape Sydney's eye for the unusual was Dr. James Barry. Sydney described the doctor as "a small-sized gentleman, with a sallow face and no beard." Born in Dublin, Barry had been in the British Army medical service since the age of eighteen. Wealth and friends in high places compensated for a rather scrappy personality.

Often in conflict with colleagues, Barry had been transferred from one part of the empire to another: Cape Colony, Mauritius, Jamaica, St. Helena, Trinidad, Malta, and, during the Crimean War, Corfu. Good with patients and caring about the living conditions that affected their health, the doctor was irascible with peers. Florence Nightingale wrote that Barry was "the most hardened creature I ever met." At one point, Barry had been arrested for duelling and sent back to England under arrest. In 1857, Barry came to Montreal as inspector general of military hospitals for British North America. It was a position similar to the one Arabella's father had held at Quebec half a century earlier. Barry maintained a luxurious new home on Dorchester Street equipped with a retinue of servants, a handsome carriage, and six small tan terriers. Sydney and Arabella visited there for dinner on more than one occasion. They tried their hand at matchmaking, linking Barry up with the daughter of an artillery colonel, but the effort failed. Forced by an illness to return to England two years later, Barry died there in 1865. Based on the claims of the charwoman who clothed the body, rumours circulated in the press about Barry's true gender. If they were true, they give us some idea of the courage and guile that Barry displayed throughout a career in the army and in a profession that was still exclusively a male domain.

After a few years on the sidelines, Sydney's interest in politics was revived through journalism when his friend John Lovell asked him to become editor of the

Daily News and the *Montreal Weekly Transcript*. Over his long career as a printer and publisher, John Lovell applied his talents to practically every kind of publication: newspapers, literary magazines, books of fiction and non-fiction, city directories, religious papers, sheet music, political pamphlets, school textbooks, and so on.

One of his most stable sources of income in this varied and sometimes risky portfolio was his contracts with government, beginning with a ten-year deal signed in 1850 for the publication of the proceedings of Parliament. With the capital shifting between Montreal, Quebec, and Toronto, this demanding undertaking re-quired

Sydney to establish premises and presses in all three cities. Sydney recounts how John A. Macdonald yanked the contract when Lovell declined to launch a partisan journal in support of his ministry.

One of Lovell's most remarkable achievements was the publication in 1851 of *The Canada Directory*, edited by a Montreal librarian and compiler of statistical information, Robert W. S. Mackay. The nearly 700-page compendium of businesses and professionals in practically every village and town in Upper and Lower Canada involved huge expenditures in recruiting and managing the agents who gathered the data, some of it in remote parts of the colony. Twenty years later, Lovell would embark on an even more ambitious project, leading to the publication in 1871 of his *Canadian Dominion Directory*, with 2,635 pages covering the new country in its entirety, along with Newfoundland. Aided this time by railways and the telegraph, Lovell's fifty travelling agents collected data on the residents, as well as the businesses, of nearly 5,000 places. Undertaken with assurances of financial support from Hugh Allan, the massive undertaking resulted in a loss to Lovell of $80,000, which according to Sydney, Allan advanced on the condition that Lovell pay him interest of 9 percent and agree to work off the debt by doing the printing for his telegraph and steamboat companies for free. In the preface to the *Canadian Dominion Directory*, Lovell thanked Sydney and others, including William Logan, for their support, but mentioned Allan only in passing.

Before we turn to the second period in the political career of Sydney Bellingham, we need to return to the mid-1850s and travel with Sydney and a land surveyor, George Albright, to the northwest corner of Argenteuil County.

38. Advertisement for the St. Lawrence Hall Hotel, The Canada Directory, *1851*, archive.org

39. The FitzAlan farm today, photograph by the author

CHAPTER 8

THE SETTLEMENT OF ARUNDEL

B Y THE MID-1850S, THERE HAD BEEN MUCH GRANDER settlement schemes in what was then the Province of Canada, but there is something more personal, and possibly more endearing, about Sydney Bellingham's Arundel project. Of all the things he helped create during his fifty-four years in Canada, the village of Arundel and the beautiful valley farms that surround it are the most enduring. The stately brick mansion on the north slope of Montreal's Mount Royal is gone. So are the ties and rails of the Carillon & Grenville Railway. The street named after him in Outremont is now called something else.[40] But the large and elegant house overlooking the village of Arundel still stands where he built it in the late 1850s, and descendants of some of the first families he encouraged to settle in the valley continue to live there.

The thought of some day settling a small piece of the Laurentian hinterland may have been in the back of Sydney's mind ever since arriving at Quebec from Ireland

at the age of fifteen and listening to his future father-in-law's prediction that the mountainous, densely forested lands distant from the St. Lawrence River would never be brought into civilization. His work the following year for Colonel Peter Robinson in Douro Township had taught him that the land needed to be surveyed before it could be settled. Robinson also served as a model for settlement promotion driven by altruistic, or at least constructive, motives rather than personal gain, in contrast with the people behind other Canadian colonization schemes.

At about the same time as Robinson was supporting colonization of the Peterborough area, the shareholders of the Canada Company were reaping profits from the 2.5 million acres of land—half of it Indian land— that the company had acquired at minimal cost in the western part of Upper Canada. Through mismanagement and corruption, the Canada Company, one of the symbols of the Family Compact, had become a target of William Lyon Mackenzie's rebellion in 1837. Another large colonization scheme was the British American Land Company in Lower Canada's Eastern Townships, created by John

---

40 Bellingham Avenue shows up for the first time in the John Lovell's Montreal Directory for 1911. It became Avenue Vincent d'Indy in 1972.

Galt, the founder of the Canada Company, after being dismissed from his position as the Canada Company's superintendent. The Sherbrooke scheme nearly collapsed until Galt's son, Sydney's political nemesis, Alexander Tilloch Galt, took over its administration and revitalized it through railway subsidies.

Sydney's project was minuscule by comparison. With grants totalling less than 7,000 acres, he might have hoped to make a small profit or at least break even. His real motivation seems to have been the satisfaction of creating a small agricultural community in which he would be an active member. This is reflected in the lead-in to his few paragraphs on the Arundel project: "In 1859 I commenced farming operations in the then unsurveyed wild lands in the northern section of the county of Argenteuil where I had acquired land." He was no absentee landowner. He accompanied the survey crew for two weeks in the summer of 1856. Two years later, he led a crew of bushwhackers to scout out a route through the forest for a road from Dalesville to Arundel and beyond. He describes in his memoirs being caught one night in a furious windstorm on the hill between Beaven Lake and Round Lake and taking shelter as best he could from falling trees. During the same period, he supervised the construction of his large frame house, near which the village of Arundel would take its present form. To put this endeavour in context, we should remember that while he was travelling to and from Arundel between 1856 and 1858, the Legislative Assembly of which he was a member was holding its sessions in Toronto, a journey of 400 miles on horseback, by river steamer, and by rail. During the same period, Sydney dealt with more than a hundred leases of properties in Buckland Township, nearly 200 miles in the opposite direction.

Through his involvement in the commercial and political affairs of Argenteuil County in the early 1850s, Sydney would have heard about the township that was the second farthest from the St. Andrews county seat. The Township of Arundel existed only on paper, having first appeared on government maps in 1795. Along with its five original sister townships in what would later become the County of Argenteuil, Arundel was mentioned in the statute books of 1829 as part of what was then the County of York. The surveyor-general, Joseph Bouchette, mentioned Arundel in his remarkable two-volume gazetteer covering all of King George IV's possessions in North America, published in 1832.

Although it was in the farthest corner of Argenteuil County, beyond the hilly and rocky forests above the escarpment, there must have been talk in the older settlements that some parts of Arundel were far from barren. Fur traders and lumbermen who ventured up the Rouge in the early nineteenth century knew that members of an Indian band cultivated small patches of ground in the area where the Rouge Valley opens up into a sort of rolling plain. Sydney would later credit the underlying bed of limestone with keeping the soil "eternally fertile," no matter how badly it was used. The legendary Curé

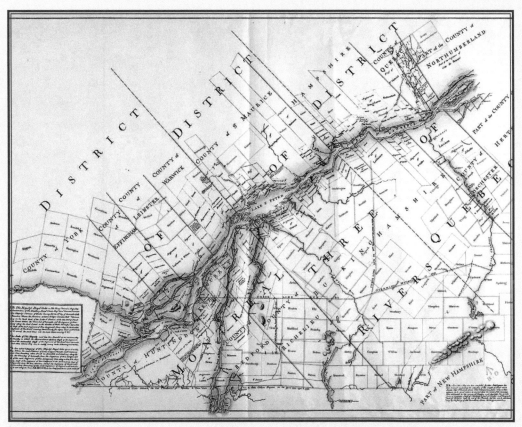

Antoine Labelle, who later settled the lands north of Arundel, called it "the garden of the north." The larger township immediately to the south, Harrington, had been surveyed and partially settled as early as 1834. After that date, there was a large influx of settlers, refugees from famine, dispossession, and poverty, mainly from Ireland and Scotland. Many of the more recent arrivals had been left with the rocky, hardscrabble back lots of the second tier of townships that lay in a band ten to twenty miles north of the Ottawa and that consisted of the eastern part of Harrington, along with Wentworth and Gore. It would not have taken much to convince them to seek

16. Plan of part of the Province of Lower Canada, 1795, by Samuel Gale and John B. Duberger, LAC, MIKAN 4143456

greener pastures in the relatively fertile and level lands of the Arundel Valley. Many of those newcomers were squatters, or had not yet obtained patents for the Crown Land they farmed. Several were supporters of Sydney Bellingham in his campaigns to gain, and regain, a seat in the Canadian Parliament in 1854, 1855, and 1856.

The settlement of Arundel that Sydney promoted provides us with an example of how the myriad of townships established throughout Canada in the nineteenth century came into being. The land belonged to the Crown, and the Crown could grant or sell it with the stroke of a pen, but it was pointless to do so until settlers could know exactly where their new lots were located and be able to find the boundary lines that would keep them in relative peace with their neighbours. The surveyor was a key player in the creation of new communities, both in their legal framework, and, literally, on the ground.

While there were a few people, like the fur trader Stephen Jakes Beaven and members of the Algonquin nation, who had lived off and on for years in the Arundel Valley, there could be no formal grant or sale of Crown Land until the township had been properly surveyed on instructions from the commissioner of Crown Lands. Rules for the surveying of Crown Lands had been on the books since 1785. A government employee, usually one with a military background, did an official survey, in much the same way as seigneurial lands had been surveyed under the French regime. In 1849, land surveyors became independent professionals required to meet certain standards of education and apprenticeship, and just like lawyers, notaries, and physicians, had to pass an examination. The surveyor was required to be proficient in geometry, trigonometry, map drawing, astronomy, and geology. As a member of what unquestionably has always been, at least in times of peace, the least sedentary of the professions, a man bearing the title of provincial land surveyor also had to be a leader, and he had to have considerable physical stamina.

By the mid-1850s, the surveying of Crown Lands had become a fairly well-defined procedure. The process involved first marking out the boundaries of the township that had not already been fixed through the surveys of neighbouring townships. The commissioner of Crown Lands sketched out the parameters in formal instructions to the surveyor. The commissioner was a member of the Legislative Council (the governor general's "cabinet") and the equivalent of what today would be called a minister of natural resources. He was a man of considerable power and influence, overseeing everything relating to land grants, forestry, mining, and fishing. In the years 1855 to 1857, the commissioner happened to be the very powerful and influential Joseph-Édouard Cauchon, someone Sydney looked upon as a friend at the time. In regard to settlement programs, the commissioner collaborated with the minister of agriculture, and in 1857 that position was held by another friend, Philip VanKoughnet, the lawyer who had represented Sydney in the first round of his contested election proceedings.

Usually from about eight to twelve miles square, the territory of a township was to be divided into ranges or concessions, each about a mile deep. Then the lots in each range, as many as thirty or forty, of various shapes and sizes but averaging a hundred acres, had to be staked. The resulting grid was mostly asymmetrical and scrambled, rather than rectangular and uniform, bending and accommodating to the dictates of nature's lack of neatness. Once the survey had been completed on the ground, it was time to prepare an official plan. This was not something arbitrarily or notionally sketched out on paper, as had been the case with the earliest colonial maps. What was shown on the plan had to be supported by the surveyor's diary and field notes, which together constituted a painstaking record of every measurement and marker on the ground.

The first survey in virgin territory like Arundel was both intellectually and physically challenging. To begin with, it involved the technical skill of measuring a straight line, several miles long and on a perfectly horizontal plane, over uneven ground interspersed with hills, gullies, cliffs, swamps, lakes, and rivers. The terrain included portions where the line of sight was interrupted every step of the way by trees and brush that had to be cleared by the surveyor's axemen. With four boundary lines, two interior "centre" lines, and seven or eight range lines, the concept required the survey crew to trudge back and forth several times over a network in excess of a hundred miles in length. The process could involve months of work on the ground, with no food, shelter, or equipment other than what the survey team could bring with it or cobble together on its own. And then there was the weather, not to mention the insects.

The man who conducted the first survey of Arundel was George Nelson Albright, born at St. Andrews in 1819 of Anglo-Irish parents. He received his appointment as a provincial land surveyor in 1848 and was entitled to a *per diem* salary and allowance of 22 shillings, 6 pence, or about $190 in today's currency, for each day of survey work. He was thirty-seven years old when, in 1856, he was instructed to conduct a survey of the arable lands in the Township of Arundel. The previous year, he had been retained to do the survey of the neighbouring Township of Montcalm. There is no doubt that he got both jobs through the influence of his member of Parliament, Sydney Bellingham. Albright was Sydney's agent during the voting in 1857 and cast a vote for him in Harrington, where he was not a qualified elector. All this came out during the evidence before Justice Bruneau in the inquiry leading to the eventual annulment in 1860 of Sydney's election to Parliament. What also became clear was that, once John J. C. Abbott took the seat away from Sydney, Albright could not count on any further government work. His prospects may have improved again when Sydney was elected to the Quebec Legislative Assembly in 1867, but by 1872, Albright was practising his profession in Manitoba, where settlers could buy 270 acres of land for

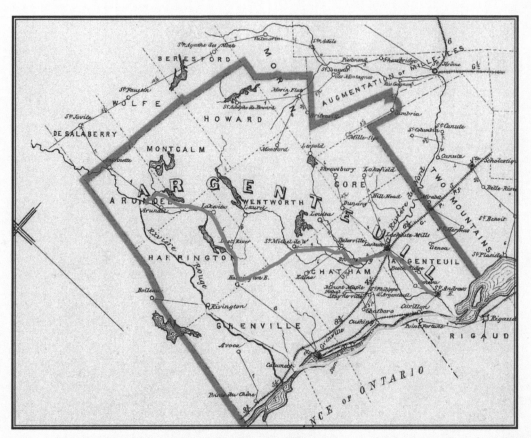

17. Albright's routes from St. Andrews to Arundel, based on an extract from the Electoral Atlas of the Dominion of Canada, 1904, LAC, MIKAN 196055

$10. In a big new country like the Dominion of Canada, there was plenty of work for land surveyors.

Despite its businesslike, rather routine entries, Albright's diary of the Arundel survey tells a story of remarkable perseverance. In a way, it is perhaps our best window on the physical reality faced not just by Albright and his crew, but also by the first settlers who followed in their footsteps.

Albright started out from St. Andrews early in the morning of August 26, 1856. He had decided to take the longer route, by river and portage, on account of the quantity of supplies and the lack of anything better

than a rough trail through the bush past the lower part of Harrington. His experience the previous year, travelling to and from Montcalm over forest trails unsuited to wheeled vehicles, probably influenced this decision. The Rouge River, which joins the Ottawa some twenty miles west of St. Andrews, runs through stretches of rapids or gorges, but at that time of year the waters in between are as calm as a lake. Albright's team included two chain bearers, four axemen, and a cook.

They left St. Andrews in two large birchbark canoes at 7:00 a.m., travelling down the North River three easy miles to where it joins the mighty Ottawa. Paddling upstream on the Ottawa against the current and strong westerly winds, they arrived at midnight, exhausted, near the mouth of the Rouge. They spent the first night of the journey in the shelter of wigwams as guests of a group of Indians encamped at Calumet. For the next two days, they ferried and portaged their supplies ten

40. A broad stretch of the Rouge River viewed from the southern end of Arundel Township, photograph by the author

miles up the Rouge to Bell Falls. Part of the supplies were carted by road from St. Andrews to Calumet, and from Calumet to Bell Falls, but from that point on there was no road other than the portage trails. With some horses hired on the spot and the assistance of five Indians, they dragged their supplies and canoes on jumper sleds up the steep ridge at Bell Falls to where they could rejoin calmer waters and pitch their tents for the night. The next day was a Sunday, and like every other Sunday until the completion of the survey, they rested.

At 6:00 a.m. on Monday, September 1, Albright and his crew set out again in three heavily laden birchbark canoes and arrived at 11:00 p.m., near where the villages of Arundel and Huberdeau straddle the Rouge today. The last leg of the journey up the river, some sixteen winding miles, involved carrying everything they had with them over two long portages and dragging the canoes by rope through lesser rapids where that could be done. It would not have been possible without the Indians, who were let go the following day, having received 7 shillings, 6 pence (about $60 in today's money) per day for their labour and guidance.

The spot Albright chose for his base camp for the next six months was in the centre of the southern half of the township at the point where a creek flows into the Rouge from a large lake three miles east of the river. Even then, both the creek and the lake bore the name of the

trapper and trader, Stephen Jakes Beaven who had made Arundel his base of operations since 1821.

The entire crew spent the next five days building a log cabin, which they called a "shanty." It would be their home away from home for the next six months. We do not know its dimensions, but it had to have been large enough to accommodate at least eight men and three large canoe loads of provisions. We do know that it had a firepit in the middle of the floor and a roof of rough boards, or "scoops" made by splitting logs, with an opening for the smoke from the firepit. The walls were not of squared timber, but of notched logs with the cracks between them stuffed with moss. It was, in effect, a smaller version of John Egan's lumber shanties that Sydney had visited in 1853. That all this could be done in the space of five days is remarkable. The decision to immediately undertake the construction of a shanty must have been driven by another experience from the Montcalm survey of the previous year: the loss of supplies to bears while the crew was working away from camp, and going without food for two days as a result.

It appears that at least occasionally Sundays were visiting days at the shanty. Albright records in his diary the visit of a group of Indians on the first such Sunday in Arundel. The Indians told him of the land their band was cultivating towards the northern limits of the township. Albright offered to survey the land for them, but they declined. What Albright was offering was the sort of accommodation a surveyor might make in a new township whose only inhabitants were squatters. Until 1859, squatters could obtain title to Crown Land if they could show they had improved it and were living on it. The surveyor might even depart from his planned grid of lots to adjust the boundaries to fit with the squatters' occupancy. The refusal of the offer in this instance suggests either that the Indians had no plans to become permanent settlers or that they did not want to lend themselves to the white man's ways of privatizing the land. Just who they were is uncertain. Some anecdotal references to Indians in the Rouge River region mention Mohawk Iroquois, and there are falls and rapids on the Rouge named after them, but the people who visited Albright's shanty were more likely the descendants of the Weskarini ("People of the Deer") Algonquin, ancient enemies of the Iroquois. In the 1881 census of Canada, twenty-four persons of Algonquin origin were shown as living in the sixth and seventh ranges of Arundel. By 1901, however, there was only one family of six. In his memoirs, Sydney mentions the site of an Algonquin burial ground on the east bank of the Rouge, just below the point where the Diable, or Devil's River, joins it. The local legend was that many of those who were buried there had been killed in the last violent clash between the Algonquin and the Iroquois.

The following Sunday, more Indians came to visit, but four settlers from Harrington also dropped in, at Sydney's urging, to see if they might find better land in Arundel. It might well be more fertile, but it would also be cheaper. We know that in 1863, the commissioner of Crown Lands offered land in Arundel at 30 cents an acre, or $36 for an average lot, which was half of what lots were selling for in the more accessible townships to the south.

Albright's diary tells us that Sydney joined them on September 8. Although by then forty-eight years old and residing with Arabella in a comfortable mansion in what is now the Montreal borough of Outremont, he had not become averse to travelling the nearly forty miles from St. Andrews through the bush on horseback. Nor was he opposed to sharing the shanty with its eight other occupants for the next two weeks. During those two weeks, he scouted the best land on the east bank of the Rouge, as well as the land straddling Beaven Creek and Beaven Lake.

The first week of the Arundel survey work was easiest, consisting of a few trips from the shanty to clean up the boundary line with Harrington, which had been surveyed fifteen years earlier but had become overgrown. Work on the western boundary was more difficult, but was made easier because it also constituted the existing county line between Argenteuil and its western neighbour, the County of Ottawa. That neighbouring county would eventually come to bear the name of Louis-Joseph Papineau, in what is now the largest of a myriad of toponymical rehabilitations of the former rebel chieftain. After being delayed by a few days of overcast weather that prevented Albright from taking the necessary astronomical readings, he moved with his crew and several days' provisions to the southwest corner of the township. The men spent the next twelve days marking the western boundary over a distance of about nine miles before returning to the shanty. Albright's diary mentions that the men were exhausted, but he, it seems, was not one to complain about his own condition, at least not in writing.

Another Sunday passed, with another visit from Indians, these having a couple of acres under cultivation on the eastern bank of the Rouge in the seventh range. Then began the most difficult part of the survey, marking out the northern line of Arundel from the post Albright had left at the northwest corner of Montcalm on March 21 of the same year. The northern line had never been cleared, and there was nothing to go by except the accuracy of Albright's compass readings and instrument sightings. After another eight days and six miles of cutting and hauling through the forest, they reached the western boundary, arriving to their dismay at a point thirty chains (660 yards) south of where, ten days earlier, they had marked the northern end of the western boundary. It all had to be done a second time. Striking out again from the northwest corner of Montcalm, Albright found his error, and after another eight days, this time in the first heavy snow, they finally came out where they should be and set a post marking the northwest corner of Arundel Township.

At this point, after three arduous months, they had confirmed or completed the four boundary lines of the township. On November 9, they returned to the shanty and the following day set out for St. Andrews to rest and retrieve the supplies and winter clothing they would need for the second part of the survey.

One month later, on December 10, Albright and his team set out again for Arundel, this time by a dirt track that got them as far as Beaven Lake from Dalesville, where Sydney had come to know the McArthurs. Two years later, Sydney opened a more passable road beyond Dalesville as far as the Diable, north of Arundel, although what already existed was good enough to allow the passage of three horse-drawn sleds loaded with equipment and provisions. Just past Lachute on the way to Dalesville, one of Albright's new men suffered a massive stroke and died on the spot. Albright's diary describes how they were obliged to return immediately to St. Andrews with the body, whereupon the county registrar, Colonel Daniel de Hertel, presided over a quick inquest. It resulted in a verdict of "sudden death by the visitation of God on the road to the township of Arundel." The men resumed their trek the following day, picking up a replacement for the dead axeman in Harrington.

During the next four weeks, with days off as usual on Sunday, and holidays on Christmas and New Year's Day, Albright and his crew staked out the east centre line of the township, running from north to south a third of the way west of the Montcalm line. Each time they reached the point where a range line should intersect the east centre line, they ran the range line westward as far as the banks of the Rouge, and to the east to the Montcalm line, or at least as far in that direction as they found arable land. Then they repeated the process by staking out the west centre line so that the township would be effectively divided into three parts, with the fertile lots in the valley straddling the Rouge laid perpendicular to the river, east to west, and the lots in the other two-thirds running north to south. The north-south configuration of the lots away from the river would enable at least the best ones to be farmed, with the farthest lots left to the lumbermen. This general layout also enabled almost all of the good arable land to have frontage on either the Rouge River or Beaven Creek.

All of this work had to be done in the worst months of the year in terms of the weather, and much of it was done too far away from the shanty to return there for the night. On January 15, Albright made the task a bit easier by procuring eight pairs of snowshoes from the Indians at a cost of a dollar per pair. It is interesting to note that at this point in his diary Albright starts recording expenditures in terms of dollars, rather than shillings and pence, although the new Canadian dollar coin did not come into circulation until 1858. On January 23, while running the line along the eastern shore of Otter Lake, some of the crew suffered severe frostbite.

On January 30, 1857, Albright and his crew completed the main part of the survey when they reached the point where the west centre line met the boundary with Harrington. On that sunny, mild day, they cleared the line that is today the southernmost stretch of Gray Valley Road. For the rest of their sojourn in Arundel Township, Albright and his crew had the easier task, aided by the winter ice, of measuring and sketching the shores of Otter Lake and Caribou Lake as well as the width of the Rouge at various points. They spent February 12 packing and procuring transport from one of the farmers in Harrington. Then, on February 13, 1857, they set out by horse-drawn sled to St. Andrews, which they reached at the end of the next day. Albright tidied up his field notes and diary and submitted them to the commissioner. In July, a government decree established the Township of Arundel as an official territorial unit in the land-registry system, making it possible, for the first time, to grant letters patent to interested settlers. The first applicant was Sydney Bellingham, acting through his brother William as agent. The Fifth Parliament had been dissolved in June. An election was looming in December, and when the time came to submit the application, Sydney was campaigning against John Abbott in the hustings of Argenteuil.

In October, Sydney received a grant of 4,793 acres, covering forty-nine lots, in the first letters patent for the newly surveyed township issued by the commissioner. His choice of lots was almost certainly influenced by discussions with Albright and his own scouting the previous fall. Following Albright's completion of the earlier survey of neighbouring Montcalm in 1856, Sydney had acquired a patent for eight adjoining lots (875 acres) on the shores of the part of Beaven Lake that lies in that township, and he probably would have acquired more

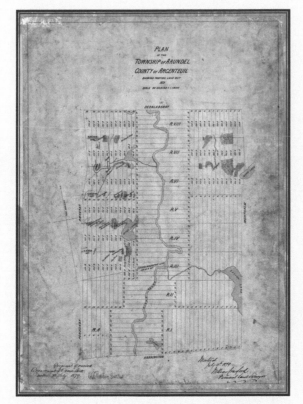

18. Plan of the Township of Arundel, by William A. Crawford, 1879, BAnQ, Fonds Ministère des Terres et Forêts, E21, S555, SS1, PA.17A

the Rouge. How much, if anything, Sydney paid for all this is a matter of conjecture. There is some speculation that he received it in exchange for assuming the cost of Albright's surveys.

By the early 1860s, the extension of the Scotch Road that had been opened at Sydney's initiative reached the Diable at a point where the traveller could get a splendid view of Mont Tremblant, the highest spot in southern Quebec. In his memoirs dictated in 1895, Sydney mused that someday the great mountain would become a favourite destination for "visitors." Indeed it has, but Sydney surely would not have imagined that many of those visitors would be downhill skiers or casino patrons.

The first settlers to arrive in the Arundel Valley at Sydney's urging were William Thomson, a schoolteacher from the Lachute-Brownsburg area, and his family. At Albright's suggestion, they reached the shanty in March 1857 and found shelter there until they had built a cabin of their own. They were greeted on their arrival by a small party of workers hired by Sydney to clear the land and start construction of a fine house on the high ground above where Beaven Creek joins the Rouge. It was every settler's dream to someday replace his or her log cabin with an elegant frame house of sawn timber, but Sydney had the wherewithal to go with the frame house from the outset. It had fifteen rooms. The lumber, window frames, and chimney bricks that Sydney's men carted over a road still being broken in must have been a source of amazement to his first neighbours. Sydney

if Albright had not found most of the rest of Montcalm to be unfit for cultivation. Then, in early 1859, following Albright's survey of De Salaberry Township, which borders Arundel to the north, Sydney acquired another fourteen lots (1,272 acres) to extend his holdings along the fertile eastern banks of the Rouge as far as Brébeuf, and on both sides of the Diable where it converges with

called his house and farm "FitzAlan" (Son of Alan) and explained in his memoirs that this was in honour of his father, Alan Bellingham, whose father's name was also Alan. It could just as easily have been in his own honour, in a roundabout way of achieving what he had hoped to accomplish when he tried to set up the northern portion of Chatham as a separate "Township of Bellingham."[41]

Some authors have projected onto Sydney the same sort of missionary zeal that drove Curé Antoine Labelle to settle the northern Laurentians in later years. It is indeed arguable that part of the Labelle initiative was a drive to outflank the advance of English-speaking Protestants north of Arundel and De Salaberry before it got as far as St. Jovite, but that is as far as the argument deserves to go. The founder of Arundel has even been described as a "career soldier" and the man who "vanquished" the *Patriotes* at St. Charles, implying that the Arundel project was a kind of quasi-military manoeuvre. Another author links Sydney's land grants in Arundel and De Salaberry directly to Lord Durham's goal of submerging the Québécois population in a sea of British immigrants. These are good examples of history being written on the basis of stereotypical assumptions rather than research. There is nothing in the written record Sydney left behind that supports either theory of religious or strategic motivation. Eleven months of militia duty do not make one a career soldier, any more than running messages on horseback makes one a conquering hero, particularly

when the messenger has yet to don a uniform. Sydney was an open-minded man and anything but a religious or racial zealot. He prided himself on his good relations with the *Canadiens*, and the ones who had arrived in Argenteuil by 1856 were just as likely to be targeted by his recruiting as the Irish, English, and Scots. He confirms as much in the way he describes the Arundel project in his memoirs. His detractors in the Abbott camp went as far as to suggest that he occasionally passed himself off as a Roman Catholic when it suited him politically. His principal political backers for the project in the Assembly were Joseph-Édouard Cauchon and Auguste-Norbert Morin. His agent in his later land sales was a French-speaking Roman Catholic who collaborated closely with Antoine Labelle, and Sydney was instrumental in setting up that relationship through his own correspondence with Labelle. He had been an outspoken critic of the *Act of Union* and its goal of cultural assimilation from the outset, and a similar concern for the preservation of French-Canadian language and institutions would later lead him to oppose Confederation. All this to say, that Sydney Bellingham was about as far away from the militant anti-French-Catholic stereotype as anyone could have been.

With the formal opening of the Township of Arundel in July 1857, the prospects for the new community were good enough for Sydney to secure an appointment for William Thomson as postmaster later that year. More settlers trickled in so that by the census of 1861 the

---

41 See Chapter 7.

population included six families. The pace of arrivals picked up after that, and aided by natural increase, the township had a population of 1,098 by 1901, divided equally between French and English.[42] Of the 480 adults, 118 males listed their occupation as farmer.

A few of the original settlers obtained direct grants of Crown Land lots that Sydney had not cornered from the outset, but most acquired their land from him. Over the next several years, he sold—some today would say flipped— all of his seventy-seven lots in Arundel, Montcalm, and De Salaberry, except for the five surrounding his house. As for those five lots, he mentions in his memoirs that he "transferred" them to a certain Auguste Filion in 1869. Filion also acted as his agent, under power of attorney, in the sale of some of his lots. More about Filion later. Speculation as to why Sydney would "transfer" such a valuable property to a twenty-six-year-old makes for an interesting story.[43]

Unlike some other land developers, Sydney could not have made much of a windfall out of his properties. As late as 1901, a settler could still get a grant of good Crown Land in Arundel Township at 30 cents an acre.[44] With this yardstick, Sydney's 7,000 acres might have yielded $2,000 in 1869 (about $35,000 in today's money), plus the value of any timber harvested before selling the land. However,

as he remarked in his memoirs, much of the best timber had been cut along the banks of the Rouge before he got there. The forests of Argenteuil County had long been part of the fiefdom of two generations of the Hamilton family (not to be confused with Sydney's old boss, James Hamilton). By 1856, the firm of Hamilton Brothers had moved its operations farther north. If Sydney ever made much money from the timber trade, it was rather from the forests of Bellechasse County, not Argenteuil.

Even before land in the Arundel Valley had been cleared, the forests of pine, hemlock, oak, and maple could not conceal that there was something remarkable about the township. After trudging for miles over hilly, rocky terrain, the early newcomers would find themselves on gently rolling, sometimes even level ground. On some lots, the absence of rocks would require them to retrieve stones for their hearths and chimneys elsewhere. The few horses or oxen they brought with them would have an easier life hauling logs or pulling a plough.

Many of the first settlers were Anglo-Irish families whose previous generation had settled in Gore, the easternmost township north of Lachute. One of these families descended from a James Bennett, who had come to Canada around 1820 and worked on the construction of the Carillon and Grenville Canals. There were Scots-Irish and Anglo-Irish, like the Craig, Graham, Morrison, Rathwell, and Swail families who came to Arundel around 1865, likewise in search of greener pastures

---

42 Not including the 225 children lodged in the Orphelinat Agricole Notre-Dame-de-la-Merci
43 See Postscript.
44 Grant to Henry Gray of Lots 31 and 32 in the First Range, May 20, 1901.

compared to the hardscrabble, rocky fields of Gore and Mille-Isles.

Robert and Mary Gray were Anglo-Irish immigrants who settled first in Chatham and then moved to the southwestern corner of Arundel Township, an area now called Gray Valley. Another Anglo-Irish settler was Joseph Boyd Jr., whose father came to Canada alone at the age of fourteen. The elder Joseph did not, however, travel in relative style as Sydney had done. He was a stowaway, fleeing an abusive father. Joseph Boyd Jr. and his wife moved from Grenville to Arundel around 1865. Like others, they were not original grantees but purchased

41. A farm in the Township of Gore, photograph by the author

their land from Sydney. Well after he had returned to Ireland, Sydney was still selling land in Arundel. In 1884 and 1889, the Boyds acquired additional land from him through Auguste Filion as his agent.

Among the Scots-Irish, the Loughrans, from County Tyrone, came to Arundel from Grenville in the late 1850s. The McGrandles arrived in 1858 from Lachute. John Scott, originally from County Armagh, was married to Ann McNeely, whose father was related to Arabella Bellingham.

A few of the early English-speaking settlers were not Irish. The first family, the Thomsons, arrived at Montreal from Glasgow in 1831 and settled first near Lachute. The Staniforths came to Canada from Yorkshire in 1845 and reached Arundel in 1858. Coral Cooke, a descendant of one of the original Plymouth pilgrims and the son of a refugee from the American Revolutionary War, arrived from Grenville with his family in 1859. He had first met Sydney in 1837, when he was with the St. Andrews Militia at St. Eustache. He obtained a grant of three of the few remaining lots that had not been snapped up by Sydney.

One afternoon in 1875, Cooke's son Samuel received a visit from his neighbour Jean-Baptiste Narbonne, who asked if he could borrow his shotgun for a day. He returned it the following day, with some bruising showing on the stock. He explained that he had dropped it. Five years later, it was revealed that Jean-Baptiste and his elderly father and stepmother had conspired to murder Jean-Baptiste's brother Daniel, who had returned from work in the lumber shanties with an enviable supply of cash. Daniel was shot, then clubbed to death by Jean-Baptiste while the two other conspirators waited in the adjoining room. All three died in prison. Like all sweeping generalizations, Sydney's perception of *Canadiens* as non-violent would have suffered an exception if word of this incident had ever reached him during his retirement at Castlebellingham.

Like Coral Cooke, two of the other early settlers who came to Arundel in 1862 also had a connection with St. Eustache, but on the other side of the conflict of 1837.

The father of Jean-Baptiste and Pierre Dubeau had been imprisoned for treason until the amnesty of 1849. Another Pierre Dubeau, their uncle, was among the *Patriotes* killed during the siege at the church. In one of Quebec history's peculiar ironies, the entire family was excommunicated by the Roman Catholic Church for disloyalty to the king of England and defender of the (other) faith. Thus the Dubeaus, who could trace their Quebec roots as far back as 1665, became Protestant. Being Protestant, many of their descendants became English-speaking.

In addition to the Dubeaus, and of course, the Filions, other *Canadien* family names recorded in the 1881 census of Arundel included Aubry, Champagne, Jolette, Labelle, Labrosse, Labrie, Larose, Laurin, Major, Mayer, Millette, Samson, St-Pierre, and Trudel. Many others would follow in the last two decades of the nineteenth century.

Sydney's Arundel project, in contrast with the Montreal and Bytown Railway, was a success. Forty years after Sydney visited George Albright in the surveyors' shanty, Arundel had four churches, two schools, and a railway station. There were two sawmills and a gristmill. The railway opened up the Montreal market for wheat, dairy products, and lumber. There were two butter and cheese factories, a blacksmith's shop, a butcher's shop, and two general stores. The railway brought more newcomers, some of them city dwellers vacationing on the farms or by the lakes. Dry goods and farm implements could now be procured locally from travelling salesmen, instead of from distant merchants in Lachute or Grenville. Winter visitors re-baptized a boarding house sanctimoniously called "Temperance Hall" as "The Iceberg." A bridge spanned the Rouge in front of the Bellingham-Filion property, and a large orphanage had been established on the other side of the river in what is now the village of Huberdeau.[45] The farm Sydney had begun to clear in 1857 now had nearly 300 acres of hay, wheat, and oats and more than a hundred head of cattle,

horses, and sheep managed by Arthur Filion, Auguste's second son. Auguste and his wife, Margaret, retired there around 1900 when their eldest son, Sydney, replaced Auguste as Crown Land agent at Grenville, a position Sydney Bellingham had obtained for Auguste in 1874.

We can speculate—and indeed in the Postscript to this book that is exactly what we will do—as to what motivated Sydney to transfer his Arundel homestead to Filion in 1869. In the next chapter, we will learn that in 1867 he resumed his political career and was elected to the first provincial Assembly at Quebec City. He also returned to journalism with John Lovell at Montreal. Sydney may simply have found that he could not be in three places at once, particularly since one of them was still only accessible by a complicated and uncomfortable journey by steamboat and horse-drawn cart for only six months of the year. Or it may be that it had always been Sydney's intention that someday this young man called Auguste Filion would inherit what he had built.

---

45 Huberdeau, on the west bank of the Rouge, was split off from Arundel Township in 1926.

CHAPTER 9

POLITICS—SECOND PERIOD

*T*HE YEARS LEADING UP TO CONFEDERATION IN **1867** were a gold mine for journalists of all stripes. The debate touched upon every aspect of life in Canada. In what had been Lower Canada, talk focused on the prospect of the formal dissolution of the Union, with Quebec becoming a separate province once again, but this time as part of a single dominion made up of all the British colonies in North America. Would the French-Canadian majority in Lower Canada be better able to preserve its language and institutions by keeping the status quo, relying on the double-majority convention of the United Province, or as a separate province with its own Assembly but in a larger federation in which its overall importance would be diluted? Would the English-speaking minority in a new province be able to keep the privileged position it had enjoyed under the Union? We learn from Sydney's correspondence from Ireland in the late 1870s that he was all for the dissolution of the Union of Lower and Upper Canada but against a new arrangement that would prevent Lower Canada from regaining the relative autonomy it had enjoyed

as a separate colony. The former cavalry officer in the Rebellions of 1837 and 1838 was more concerned about the survival of *Canadien* language and institutions than he was about the prosperous anglophone minority. His friend John Lovell did not share Sydney's opposition to Confederation, but the friendship endured nonetheless. One of Lovell's publications that stands out for its support for Confederation—erroneously attributed to Sydney as editor of the *Daily News*—was a pamphlet written by journalist George Henry Macaulay in response to an attempt by editor Edward Goff Penny of the *Montreal Herald* to dissuade the British Parliament from approving the deal. The *Daily News* had the gall to accuse Penny and his friends of being "a small rump of a quasi-annexation party," a reference to Penny's work two decades earlier as assistant secretary of the Montreal Annexation Association. What made it particularly galling was that the *pro tem* secretary of the association in its early days had been Sydney Bellingham.

In 1867, Confederation brought with it the creation of a Quebec Legislative Assembly, and Sydney's supporters in Argenteuil prevailed upon him to run in the first election, which he won by acclamation. In 1871, Abbott's supporters put forward a candidate, a physician named Bernard, but Sydney won easily. He would be elected by acclamation once again in the 1875 election. Although he never held a cabinet post, Sydney was regarded as one of the more influential members of the Conservative majority under the premierships of Pierre-Joseph-Olivier Chauveau (1867–73) and Gédéon Ouimet (1873–74). By 1874, however, he had begun to move towards the Liberal side under the leadership of Henri-Gustave Joly de Lotbinière. Sydney admired Wilfrid Laurier, the future Liberal leader who prefaced his career in the Canadian Parliament with a brief stint in the Quebec Assembly. He supported Laurier's proposal to make members of the federal Parliament ineligible to sit in the provincial Assembly. Nearly a third of the Assembly's first members were also members of Parliament, sitting one week in Ottawa and the next in Quebec City. The dual mandate enabled those who were so inclined to coordinate their activities along party lines, something that many others viewed as detracting from the independence of the Assembly. Sydney recalled being so impressed with Laurier's first speech in 1871 that he crossed the floor and congratulated him. In 1875, Sydney ran as a Liberal, having earlier broken ranks with the Conservatives under the redundantly named Charles Boucher de Boucherville. He did not run in the election held on May 1, 1878, because he had returned permanently to Ireland.

Sydney's drift to the Liberal side of the Assembly was worrisome to Conservatives, not just in the Assembly, but in Ottawa as well. In 1874, John A. Macdonald and his Quebec lieutenant, Hector Langevin, found themselves sitting on the Opposition benches of the federal Parliament following their defeat over the Canadian Pacific Scandal. But up until January, Langevin had also been a member of the Quebec Assembly, where the de Boucherville government was under siege. Langevin had been forced to resign his seat in the Assembly after the abolition of the dual mandate but continued to act as Macdonald's eyes and ears from his nearby law office. Through Langevin's letters, Macdonald kept informed, practically on a daily basis, of what was happening in Quebec. As we have seen,[46] Langevin wrote Macdonald on June 6, 1874, to report on Sydney's expressions of resentment, suggesting that he could be brought back into the fold by a few friendly words and a handshake. This is a good example of what the opponents of the dual mandate had been concerned about when they argued it undermined the independence of the provincial Assembly.

It is during this period that Sydney's political philosophy becomes clearer. Writing in 1875, towards the end of his political career, he describes himself as belonging to the conservatives, but "not that spawn that robbed and sullied the name of conservatism and plundered the country with impunity, but conservatives in

46 See Chapter 7.

the true acceptation of the word; defenders of the rights and liberties of the electors and guardians of the public purse." The description, of course, is intended to set himself apart from the ministries of John A. Macdonald in Ottawa and de Boucherville in Quebec City. Sydney was a political conservative, not a social conservative. He chastised the government for privatizing the care of the mentally ill and young offenders, which he believed should remain the government's responsibility. He was both practical and frugal, preferring to spend taxpayers' money on more efficient land-registry offices than on a grandiose new Parliament Building. He distained those who failed to keep religion and politics separate at a time when the Conservative Party and the powerful Bishop Ignace Bourget were hand in glove to the point where, in 1871, Bourget's priests were telling their parishioners to vote only for Conservatives. He denounced hypocrisy and political expediency and praised the actions of even political foes when he saw that they were motivated by principle rather than self-interest. In his personal dealings, Sydney was a generous man and egalitarian. He viewed political office as a duty, not an entitlement:

> The elector of the present day will not be satisfied with platitudes. He means business. He wants to know the why and the wherefore. The days when the long purse could command a majority at the polls cannot be restored. The battles of the future must be fought with pen or on the platform, and those who have been under fire must be prepared to prove they performed their duty.[47]

In 1871, journalist M. A. Achintre published a handbook on the first Quebec Assembly, with a short sketch of each of its members. He described Sydney as tenacious in his opinions, eloquent, practical, open-minded, of rare intelligence, refined, very aware of the political environment, a flawless writer, and well researched. As to his political orientation, Achintre describes him as conservative, committed to constitutional stability, freedom, and economic progress. He praised Sydney as one of the best journalists in the province, both past and present, one who could rise above his party affiliation in his role as editor, putting principle ahead of party. Sydney was said to speak frequently in the House, with an easygoing and dignified style in the British tradition, his motives or intentions never in doubt. Of course, Conservatives who later felt betrayed by his criticisms called him an opportunist.

There is one peculiarity that transcended party alliances in Sydney's political thinking—an abiding attachment to Lower Canada, particularly to its French-speaking majority. That in part helps explain his opposition to Confederation. He felt genuinely concerned for the preservation of French-Canadian language and

---

47 Sydney Bellingham, *Reasons Why British Conservatism Voted Against the Boucherville Ministry* (Rouses Point, NY: Lovell, 1875), 18.

institutions. As we shall see, even after he had retired to Ireland, his outrage over Macdonald's interference in Quebec politics would bring him close to advocating the withdrawal of Quebec from Confederation.

The First Parliament of the new Legislative Assembly of the Province of Quebec began very much as a work in progress. More than half of its members were new to political life. A whole new bureaucracy had to be created to take over the administration of matters that were now within provincial, as opposed to federal, jurisdiction. These included education, courts, agriculture, Crown Lands, and those railways not interprovincial in their operations. There were anxieties to be sorted out with the English-speaking minority, particularly with regard to education.

One of the events during this period that Sydney recalled in his memoirs was falling out with his friend Joseph-Édouard Cauchon over the Beauport Lunatic Asylum. Cauchon, a wealthy newspaper proprietor with railway interests and a former mayor of Quebec, was both an influential member of the Assembly and a federal senator. Sydney's friendship with Cauchon had proven invaluable when Cauchon held the cabinet post of commissioner of Crown Lands in 1856 and 1857. It was during that period that Sydney acquired his extensive land grants in the northern part of Argenteuil. A political cartoon in the 1870s depicted Cauchon as a pig, aided by the fact that his name was pronounced exactly the same as the French word for that animal. Sydney recalled that earlier, when they sat together in the Legislative Assembly of the United Province, an unfriendly Scottish member from Upper Canada (likely Allan MacNab) would grunt like a pig every time Cauchon spoke. Sydney admired Cauchon for his erudition and eloquence. In the Quebec Assembly, Cauchon was a powerful figure, and as Sydney put it, "more feared than loved." In 1867, the lieutenant governor had asked him to form the first provincial cabinet, and he would have been the first premier of Quebec had it not been for his inability to put together a compatible and representative group of ministers. Due to his opposition to legislation protecting English schools, not a single English-speaking member would join his administration.

The asylum, a large and imposing installation, had recently opened just north of Quebec City. Cauchon had concealed his personal interest in the ownership of the facility, which was subsidized through government funds. Under the management of his nominees, its population was greatly expanded through the inclusion of people not seriously mentally ill. Sydney's concerns regarding the management of Beauport, the welfare of its inhabitants, and the drain it caused on the public purse were rooted in the work of his father-in-law. Dr. William Holmes had been a commissioner for the care of the insane at Quebec and had advocated for the establishment of an asylum devoted exclusively to them. Although two physicians nominally owned the asylum, the real owner was Cauchon. The subsidy was payable on the basis of so much per inmate; the more inmates there were, the more money the asylum made. The population of the new institution rapidly expanded. A letter from a parish priest was all that was required to round up and confine a new patient, occasionally for reasons that confused morality with mental health. The less spent on food, clothing, and attendants, the greater the profits. Independent of the scandal that arose over Cauchon's ownership and conflict of interest, there was a debate over whether the government should be relying on private enterprise to care for the mentally ill. Sydney supported the charge led by the Liberal leader, Joly de Lotbinière. The uproar created over Beauport eventually led to Cauchon's resignation in 1872. The man who had been one of the most influential politicians and businessmen in Quebec was shunted to Winnipeg as lieutenant governor of Manitoba. He consoled himself there by amassing a huge fortune through land speculation, but lost it all in the crash of 1882.

In 1875, Sydney denounced another arrangement similar to the Beauport Lunatic Asylum scandal. This one involved a contract awarded in 1869, at the behest of Bishop Bourget, to a Belgian order of friars, the *Frères de la Charité*, enabling them to immigrate to Quebec to manage a reform school for 200 young offenders and street urchins. He called it an "insidious form of white slavery" and an "abandonment by the government of its duty," with the friars reaping not only a yearly subsidy from the government, but profiting from the sale of

MORES PORCI.

boots, shoes, and cigars that they forced their charges to manufacture. Whereas the cost of a college education with room and board was then about $120 per year, the government paid the Belgian friars $180 (nearly $4,000 today) for each inmate. In Sydney's words, it was "minus education, except that education which is derived from manufacturing cigars and boots and shoes, the profits whereof fall into the pockets of the Belgians."[48] Sydney calculated the yearly profit at $36,000, equivalent to $800,000 today. Productivity and quality control were assured by "the power of the lash if the boot or cigar making be shirked or carelessly done."

Ignace Bourget's presence was felt constantly throughout the first decade of the Quebec Assembly. He deserves a few words at this point in our overview

48 *Bellingham, 13.*

42. A political cartoon satirizing Joseph Cauchon, from archive.org

of that period. Although not the highest-ranking cleric in the province, he wielded tremendous power. His reign as bishop of Montreal ran from 1840 to 1876 and was defined by his ultramontane conviction that the state should be subservient to Rome. His attachment to Rome was such that in 1868–70 he sponsored the recruitment of a battalion of French-Canadian fighters and sent them off to Rome with great pomp to assist the pope in his war with the newly united Kingdom of Italy. They were called "Zouaves," although it is hard to understand why the name given by the French Army to its traditional Algerian Berber mercenaries should have been the inspiration. After the pope's final defeat, many of Bourget's Zouaves were fortunate in that their status as subjects of the British Crown entitled them to seek sanctuary in the British embassy in the eternal city. Bourget had first drawn attention to himself when he oversaw the completion in 1825 of Saint-Jacques Cathedral and the Bishop's Palace at the corner of St. Laurent and St. Denis Streets. We gain some insight into his wisdom and equanimity through his pronouncement following the destruction of both buildings in the great fire that occurred on that hot and windy day in July 1852: "it is God who blew, who blew a breath of anger on the flames which the hand of man could not extinguish… God saved those [buildings] that he wished to save, and destroyed those that he wished to destroy." Bourget was a master at putting the fear of the wrath of God into the hearts and minds of his faithful, and he was also

probably a bit angry at the bungling of the volunteer fire department, which allowed his great project to be destroyed.

Sydney describes how the members of the Assembly fell under the grip of railway fever, and how the province, which had no debt when it entered Confederation, soon became burdened with the cost of railway subsidies. He describes how the first provincial governments fell prey to the profiteering of a London financial firm, Morton, Rose & Company. Sydney became part of a vociferous minority who denounced the flurry of subsidies and borrowing, with words like, "a spirit of wild, reckless railway speculation invades the land, and that spirit was fostered and stimulated by the action of the Deboucherville [sic] cabinet last session."[49] One thing that moved Sydney to do this was his belief that a large segment of the population, particularly in the agricultural areas, had no idea what was going on and the impact it had on the financial situation of the province. His great fear was that soon the province would have to resort to direct taxation to support its burden of debt. His experience with railways in the Parliament of the United Province had left him wary of the pitfalls of government participation in railway financing. His earlier involvement with the bankruptcy of the Montreal and Bytown Railway, which had occurred before the practice of government subsidies became so paramount, added a feeling of unfairness.

---

49 *Bellingham, 7.*

One of his principal targets both in the Assembly and in his writings was Joseph Gibb Robertson, who was provincial treasurer (today's minister of finance) in both the Ouimet and de Boucherville ministries. Robertson, a wealthy land speculator from Sherbrooke, doled out government subsidies to railways, including ones with which he had a personal connection. One of the "insane railway schemes hatched into vitality" by Robertson's subsidy program was a second line built between Sherbrooke and Lévis, in competition with the Grand Trunk, prompting Sydney to write: "where one railway lost money it must have been supposed that two would pay." What he described as the "obscure and needless" Sherbrooke, Eastern Townships, and Kennebec Railway, later known as the Quebec Central, had Robertson as its president and Robertson's brother-in-law as principal contractor. A fine example of Bellingham political sarcasm can be found in the following extract:

> This line illustrates what engineering genius can achieve under the stimulating influence of Government subsidies. It traverses at one place a ravine built on stilts elevated sixty feet in the air. Natural decay ensures the certain destruction of this crib work within eight years, unless a brush fire or incendiarism destroys it.[50]

It was not just that the railway was redundant and poorly built that irked him, but also that the bond issue that financed the subsidy was sold for much less than what could have been raised through competitive bidding on the London market. Instead, Robertson fell prey to the charms of the wily John Rose, previously John A. Macdonald's first finance minister, whom Robertson had known before Rose left Canada for London in 1869. Rose sent a telegram to Robertson warning him that his ability to market the bonds in London would be hampered if Sydney were allowed to continue his attacks on the deal. Within a matter of months, the Quebec bonds were being quoted on the London market at 8 percent more than what Robertson had sold them for to Morton, Rose & Company.

Sydney's opposition to the railway subsidy fever did not mean that he had given up on railways. He was one of the few members of the Assembly who had experience in building railways, and he knew what he was speaking about. The folly of wooden trestles was one thing, but the idea of using wooden, instead of iron, rails really got him going. In late 1870, he renewed his interest in the prospects for a line through his riding and courted the support of the influential Curé Antoine Labelle of St. Jérome. Labelle chose instead to endorse Hugh Allan's Montreal Northern Colonization Railway. As we have seen, Sydney backed away from running against Abbott in the federal election of 1872 when Allan threatened to have the new line to Ottawa run through St. Andrews

---

50 *Bellingham, 8.*

instead of Lachute. By 1876, the line had reached only as far as St. Jerome, thirty-six miles north of Montreal. It reached St. Jovite in 1892, giving the people of Arundel their first rail access to Montreal until the more direct Montfort line reached them in 1895.

Towards the end of his time in the House, Sydney became the personal adversary of the young and fast-rising Joseph-Adolphe Chapleau, the member for the neighbouring riding of Terrebonne. Chapleau became Ouimet's solicitor general at the age of thirty-three in 1873, provincial secretary in 1876, and, after Sydney's departure for Ireland, premier of the province in 1879. In 1874, Sydney accused Chapleau of disclosing cabinet information that enabled his cronies to profit from a land swap, creating the scandal known as the Tanneries Affair, which led to Ouimet's resignation as premier. In his memoirs, Sydney describes Chapleau as a long-haired opportunist "who acted the part of the devoted patriot." In 1877, in one of his last appearances in the Assembly, Sydney questioned Chapleau's eligibility to continue to sit in light of his interest in the Laurentian Railway Company. Chapleau claimed to have agreed to be on the railway's board solely because the railway would run through Terrebonne, and when it was disclosed that he received shares in the company, he professed his ignorance of the gift. Chapleau was the law partner of Edward Carter, who had been John Abbott's lead counsel in the bitterly fought proceedings over Sydney's election in 1858. A third partner was Levi Ruggles Church, who was de

Boucherville's attorney general, and who later replaced Robertson as provincial treasurer. The successors to the firm of Carter, Church & Chapleau, who today number more than 400 in Montreal, Toronto, Ottawa, and Quebec City, would not be enchanted were they to plumb the thoughts of Sydney Bellingham in regard to their much-revered founding trinity.

In all these matters, Sydney made his arguments known not only through his eloquence in the Assembly, but also with articles in John Lovell's *Daily News*. In 1875, after the *Daily News* had gone out of business, he published a pamphlet entitled *Reasons Why British Conservatives Voted Against the Boucherville Ministry*, which is a cutting and forceful summary of his position.

The eleven years of Sydney's second period as a parliamentarian were eventful for the new Dominion of Canada. In 1868, an Irish-born Fenian sympathizer became the last person to be publicly executed, his crime having been the assassination of Thomas D'Arcy McGee. The power of the Roman Catholic Church, which had become more firmly established in Quebec than ever before, was brought to bear on liberal or freethinking movements such as the *Institut Canadien*. It was not until 1877 that priests were instructed not to preach that it was a sin to vote for the Liberals. That year the huge regions of Rupert's Land and the North-West Territories were wrested from the Hudson's Bay Company and became part of the dominion. Louis Riel's first rebellion and the admission of Manitoba into Confederation took place

in 1870. That summer a force that included 400 British regulars, 700 Canadian militia, and a number of civilian support workers made the rather remarkable 1,400-mile journey by land and water all the way from Montreal to Fort Garry to suppress Riel's provisional government. Lieutenant-Colonel Garnet Wolseley led the expedition.

Wolseley, yet another Anglo-Irish officer whose military career had brought him to Canada, was the deputy quartermaster general of the British forces in Canada. Earlier in 1870, when talk of a Red River Expedition began, Wolseley walked into Sydney's office at the *Daily News* and showed him a copy of his *The Soldier's Pocket-Book for*

43. Joseph-Adolphe Chapleau, photograph by William Notman, 1869, McCord Museum 1-37191, with permission

Field Service, a little guide he had published the previous year. He hinted that if Sydney printed a favourable review of the book, it might attract the attention of the politicians and military brass deliberating on the choice of a man to lead the expedition. Wolseley did get the job, and the success of the expedition boosted his career. It bears mentioning, however, that he arrived at Fort Garry only to find it abandoned by Riel, and that, as Sydney points out, the "only shots fired were to obtain a supply of game." The real accomplishment was in just getting to the destination. Their passage by steamer on the Great Lakes was interrupted at Sault Ste. Marie, where the canal was on the U.S. side, guarded by a small American force at Fort Brady, Michigan. An advance party under Lieutenant-Colonel Bolton opened up a portage on the Canadian side to bypass American obstruction as well as to head off the threat of attack from Fenian sympathizers. When the expedition returned, Sydney wrote about it in the *Daily News*, getting the inside scoop from Bolton himself. Wolseley later became a field marshal, a Viscount, and commander-in-chief of the British Army, but was best remembered for his failed expedition up the Nile River to rescue General Charles George Gordon at Khartoum and for being Gilbert and Sullivan's inspiration for the "model major-general." Indeed, Sydney mused in his memoirs that the Red River Expedition could have rivalled HMS *Pinafore* in popularity as a burlesque.

There was another rather coincidental connection between Sydney and the Red River Expedition. In 1866, a young man whose name was Félix Chénier was admitted to the notarial profession and became Lachute's first notary. It was he who, in July 1869, drew up the marriage contract between Auguste Filion and Margaret Milway, who shortly thereafter married and moved into the FitzAlan house that Sydney had built in Arundel. In 1870, Chénier enlisted in the militia to take part in the Wolseley adventure. He was the nephew of the martyred Dr. Jean-Olivier Chénier of St. Eustache. His father, also named Félix, was a notary at St. Eustache and had been imprisoned in January 1838 for his participation in his brother's rebellion. Ironically, the nephew of one famous rebel martyr enlisted to fight another. When the first Riel Rebellion fizzled out, Félix stayed in Manitoba and eventually became a member of the provincial Assembly. The following year, 1871, British Columbia joined Confederation, and the last British troops, except for a small contingent at Halifax were withdrawn from Canada.

John A. Macdonald and his government were forced to resign in late 1873 over allegations that Macdonald, Cartier, and Langevin had received bribes from Hugh Allan and his cronies in return for the contract for construction of the Canadian Pacific Railway. The year after that, the Liberals under Alexander Mackenzie passed the *Dominion Elections Act*, requiring voting by secret ballot and the closing of bars on Election Day. The year 1873 also marked the start of a severe economic depression that lasted until 1881. In 1876, the last link in

the Intercolonial Railway between Montreal and Halifax was completed, and Alexander Graham Bell made the first long-distance telephone call to his home in Brantford, Ontario. In September 1878, Macdonald returned as prime minister, remaining there until his death in 1891. Throughout those years and beyond, Sydney vented his

resentment of Macdonald in his correspondence with Quebec political leaders.

In 1874 in Montreal, the provincial Assembly incorporated the Montreal Stock Exchange. In 1875, the first organized indoor hockey game was held in the Victoria Skating Rink. By 1876, a seat on the exchange

44. Arabella Bellingham, 1871, photograph by William Notman, McCord Museum, 1-64474.1, with permission

cost $2,500, or $55,000 in today's money. In 1875, 1,000 militia troops were called out to prevent rioting when the body of a deceased member of the *Institut Canadien*, who had been excommunicated by Bishop Bourget, was buried in Côte-des-Neiges Cemetery (the "Guibord Affair"). In 1876, as well, Mount Royal Park was officially opened, tracing its roots back to the Montreal Mountain Boulevard project of which Sydney had been a founder in 1858. In 1877, there was mob violence between Orangemen and Roman Catholics. That year the Montreal Harbour Commission began using electricity to light the waterfront.

Quebec City was plagued by fires in the 1870s, including a disastrous one in 1871 that left 5,000 people homeless in the St. Roch district. Four years earlier, a fire in the same area had destroyed the homes of 2,000 people. In 1875, a terrible fire razed the women's section of the Beauport Lunatic Asylum, costing twenty-six lives. On a happier note that year, Governor General Lord Dufferin presciently urged the municipal government to preserve the city's fortifications for their potential value as a future tourist attraction. In 1878, the iconic St. Louis Gate was added, likely for no other reason than to embellish what has become a tourist magnet. Work on the new Hôtel du Parlement, which Sydney had argued against as a waste of good money, began in 1877. The following year, the military, called in to break up a strike, shot two construction workers on the site.

The *Daily News* and the *Weekly Transcript* lasted until October 1872. With the losses incurred in the publication of the mammoth *Canadian Dominion Directory*, Lovell could not afford to sustain them. Sydney lost whatever income could be squeezed out of journalism, with the newspapers' demise, and he cast about for other employment. In 1873, at the start of the Long Depression, things must have been bad enough for him to swallow his pride and write to John A. Macdonald in the hope of getting whatever patronage appointment Macdonald could spare. Nothing came of it, but Sydney's fortunes improved when he was able to cash in on his substantial real-estate holdings.

Throughout the period of his career in the Legislative Assembly, Sydney and Arabella continued to reside at Dunany Cottage. In 1871, like practically everyone else in polite Montreal society, Arabella had her photograph taken by the legendary William Notman. Her portrait shows her in the standard attire of the era, modelled on Queen Victoria's mourning dress, which the monarch still wore no less than ten years after the death of Prince Albert.

CHAPTER 10

RETURN TO IRELAND

*S*YDNEY WRITES IN HIS MEMOIRS THAT HE TOOK UP residence in Ireland in 1874, and that he returned to Quebec to take up his seat when the Legislative Assembly was in session. He had sailed for Londonderry with Arabella on June 29, 1874, aboard the Allan Line's *Polynesian*, but came back a few months later. He was elected by acclamation in the Quebec general election of July 1875 and held the seat until Liberal-leaning Lieutenant Governor Luc Letellier de Saint-Just dissolved the Assembly in March 1878 following a raging political debate over railways, and political interference by Letellier de Saint-Just, which the Conservatives described as a *coup d'état*. Curiously, Sydney had written to the speaker of the House from Castlebellingham in November 1876 to resign his seat, but then followed up with a cablegram withdrawing his resignation. The short-lived resignation may have been prompted by the speaker's refusal to reimburse Sydney's travel expenses, followed by sober second thoughts. The *Courier du Canada* reported on December 20, 1877, that Sydney had returned to Quebec the previous day after an absence

of eight months. A political storm was brewing, and Premier Joly's Liberals needed every man on deck. That Sydney chose to spend the winter in Canada, rather than Ireland, suggests his support for the Liberal Party was more than just a passing whim. In January 1878, he gave a rousing speech in Lachute to promote the establishment of industry in the new town, which had finally become accessible by rail via the Quebec government's Quebec, Montreal, Ottawa & Occidental Railroad. It sounded very much like a pre-election speech. Sydney was active that same month in the Assembly, on the Liberal side, in the debate leading up to the lieutenant governor's *coup d'état*. On February 21, 1878, he rose in the Assembly to challenge Joseph-Adolphe Chapleau's eligibility to sit on grounds of conflict of interest. He did not run in the provincial election held in May. By March 27, he had returned to Castlebellingham whereupon the *Journal de Québec* reported there was uncertainty as to whether he would run again, given that he was now living abroad. Robert Greenshields Meikle, a Lachute merchant, ran in his place in Argenteuil and won the seat for the Liberals.

On August 24, Sydney wrote Joly from Castlebellingham in response to an earlier cablegram. Joly was doing what he could to prop up his federal Liberal counterpart, Alexander Mackenzie, in the upcoming federal election. Mackenzie had taken over as prime minister in 1873 when Macdonald resigned as a result of the Canadian Pacific Scandal. Sydney mentioned that he would have been happy to put in a few appearances in support of the federal Liberal candidate, Dr. Christie, but that he was unable to leave Ireland, where he had been told that his presence was "indispensable." He revealed that he had declined an invitation by the "St. Andrews notables" to run for the Conservatives instead of Abbott, whom he referred to as Macdonald's "alter ego." He mentioned his respect for Mackenzie, but that he could not support the Liberal leader's free-trade policy, which he felt was benefiting New York at the expense of Quebec. Not wanting to miss a chance to express his feelings towards Macdonald, Sydney described him as "treacherous and without moral fibre," conceding that his dislike for him was "personal and permanent." He appeared anxious to convince Joly that, although he was not prepared to endorse Mackenzie, it was not out of loyalty to Macdonald.

During the spring of 1879, when Macdonald was back in power and manoeuvring towards the dismissal of Letellier de Saint-Just, Sydney wrote Joly to offer the assistance of his contacts in the British Parliament in the debate over the power of the Canadian prime minister to dismiss Queen Victoria's representative in Quebec. One of those contacts was John Bright, an influential Liberal; another was Spencer Cavendish, the Marquess of Hartington. Bright at least had the candour to tell Sydney that the Letellier Affair, which was viewed as a major constitutional crisis in Canada, was simply not of any real interest to anyone in England. Macdonald, spurred on by Chapleau, finally sacked Letellier de Saint-Just in July. Sydney was incensed by what he saw as a federal incursion into provincial affairs. He wrote Joly twice in August, urging him to mount a campaign calling for the preservation of Quebec autonomy. Recalling his earlier opposition to both the Union and Confederation, he expressed fear that the latter was evolving in a way that threatened the preservation of the language and institutions of the French-speaking majority. He voiced the same concerns in a letter to the *Argenteuil Advertiser*, which was picked up in other newspapers as far afield as Winnipeg. In substance, it was a call for the resurgence of French-Canadian nationalism and the withdrawal of Quebec from Confederation, the ultimate goal being a return to what Lower Canada had been before the Union, free of the debt of the other colonies that now dominated the federal Parliament.

In October, Joly's minority government fell on a vote of confidence, and Chapleau became premier of Quebec at the age of only thirty-eight. We have no clear record explaining why Sydney decided to retire to Castlebellingham, never to return to Canada after the winter of 1878, but the shift in the political climate, added to milder weather in Ireland, may have been factors.

The oral legend that took root in Arundel, and which has been repeated elsewhere, was that Sydney had inherited a castle. It may have been assumed that, since he had returned to Castlebellingham, he had acquired a castle, but Castlebellingham is a village, not a castle. It is certain at least that he did not inherit the manor called Bellingham Castle House and its 4,500-acre estate. He did acquire, but probably not through inheritance, substantial property in the village. When Montreal author Margaret Dixon McDougall visited him on her tour of Ireland in 1881, he was living in South Gate House, which she described as "one of the houses that tempts one to breach the tenth commandment." His engraved stationery shows South Gate House as his address. It was a large house with well-tended gardens and a conservatory. He most likely either purchased it or had it built. None of his close male relatives had died in the decade preceding his return to Ireland, and his older brother, Sir Alan Edward, was still very much alive and would remain so until 1889. The childhood reminiscences of Sir Alan Edward's grandson, the British author Evelyn Wrench, paint a picture of a man in his eighties who was still doing the daily rounds of his large estate on horseback. Alan Edward had inherited the property upon the death of their father in 1827 and raised his seven children at Bellingham Castle House. The estate, with its fertile farms and a salmon fishery on the coast at Dunany, appears to have prospered during his tenure, and the family connections in Irish and English society were enhanced through the marriages of each of his five daughters. Evelyn Wrench wrote that when his mother, Charlotte Bellingham, talked of her childhood at Castlebellingham in the 1850s, he found himself "back again in the pages of a Jane Austen novel."

The will Sydney signed on December 17, 1898, gives us some clues as to his situation not long before his death on March 9, 1900. It appears from the will that he had enough resources of his own to acquire other properties at Castlebellingham, including another cottage he had built and premises in the village, which he had rebuilt and leased to the Ulster Bank. The will also discloses that Sir Alan Henry, his nephew and trustee, owed him £1,800 ($350,000 in today's money). He was wealthy enough to leave the equivalent of about $50,000 in today's money as a scholarship endowment to the Lachute College in Argenteuil and $25,000 for the maintenance of his father's grave in France. The money likely came from the sale of his properties, not just in Argenteuil, but also in Buckland Township and in Montreal, and it appears that he had substantial investments in Canadian stocks. The support for this conclusion can be found in Hector Langevin's letter of June 6, 1874, in which he reported to John A. Macdonald that Sydney had told him that he had "sold some of his property to great advantage and that he is now comfortable in life."[51]

---

51 See Chapter 7.

As we saw in Chapter 3, Sir William Bellingham, the first baronet, acquired the "Castle" in about 1824 from Monique Bâby Bellingham, the widow of Sydney's cousin Alan. The acquisition followed a period of litigation between Monique and Sir William, who claimed that the estate had become his, as oldest surviving male relative, upon the early death in 1822 of Monique's only son, also named William. Monique's claim was likely based on the good fortune of having been married in community of property under the Custom of Paris.[52] Sir William's widow, Lady Hester,

52 See Chapter 1.

was living at the Castle when Sydney and Arabella visited her in 1831. So was the third baronet, Sydney's older brother, Sir Alan Edward. In his will, Sir William had made Hester the life tenant of the Castle, but the ownership had devolved to Alan Edward. When Alan Edward died in 1889, Bellingham Castle House and the estate passed to his son, Alan Henry. It never belonged to Sydney.

In his will, Sydney left South Gate House to his grandniece Ida, who was Alan Henry's daughter.[53] Ida and her sister Augusta were to receive the interest on the £1,800 Sydney had loaned to their father. He need not have worried about Augusta. In 1905, she married the 4th Marquess of Bute, one of the richest men in Britain, in a lavish wedding held at the Castle. It was one of the first weddings to be filmed, and the footage contains views of the Castle that can be seen online at *https://scotlandonscreen.org.uk*. Augusta's brother Sir Edward was the last baronet to live in the Castle. He was a veteran of the Boer War and the First World War and served in the Royal Air Force in the Second World War. Without Sir Edward's foresight, this book would not have been written. It was he who sent the manuscript of Sydney's memoirs to the dominion archivist at Ottawa in 1955, the year before he died.

Sydney left another cottage, the one he had built, to his niece Alice, the daughter of his younger brother, William. His residual heir was Alan, William's grandson.

53 See the genealogical tables at the back of this book.

As the residual heir, Alan inherited everything that had not been specifically bequeathed under the will, including the remaining real estate in Canada and the investments. It was all to be held in trust until Alan reached the age of thirty, and the trustees named in the will were his uncle Sir Alan Henry and Sydney's Quebec City notary, Edward Graves Meredith, the son of a former chief justice. William's daughters, Alice and Dora, were to receive the income from one-half of the residue until Alan reached the age of thirty, with Alan receiving the income from the other half. Alan was only twelve when his father, Colonel Sydney Edwin, met an early death in the Punjab in 1893, leaving the young Alan without support.

In all probability, Sydney inherited nothing at Castlebellingham and simply decided to retire there. Since coming to Canada, he had made several trips back by sail and by steam to revisit Ireland, England, and his father's grave in France. The prospect of another election in 1878 may not have been as inviting as it had been in his younger years, particularly given his dislike of Chapleau and Chapleau's spectacular gains in political power. Sydney had turned over the Arundel farm to Auguste Filion in 1869, and the *Daily News* had folded in 1872. The revenues and proceeds from his properties in Canada would not have been huge, but they were at least sufficient to finance a comfortable retirement. Arabella was his only family in Canada, and she accompanied him back to Ireland. That William, his younger brother, had returned to Castlebellingham may have influenced the decision; Sydney and William had always been close. William named his first son, Sydney Edwin after him. The inability to leave Ireland, which Sydney mentions in his letter of August 24, 1878, to Quebec Premier Joly, may well be a reference to pressing family matters. In addition to the strong family connection, another explanation for Sydney's return to the place of his birth was an attachment to Ireland itself. Few of his Anglo-Irish contemporaries, such as Francis Hincks and Benjamin Holmes, made as many return visits after coming to Canada. His sympathies for the Irish Repealers in 1848 show that, despite his great interest in Canadian politics, he had never lost touch with what was happening in the country of his birth.

The return to Ireland did not mean that Sydney severed all ties with Canada. He still had properties there to manage, and he relied on Auguste Filion to do that for him. He kept abreast of Canadian affairs through his correspondence with Filion, and Filion visited him at Castlebellingham at least once, in 1896. He retained his association with John Lovell, who had given him the presidency of the Lovell Publishing Company in 1877. In Lovell's annual *Montreal Directory*, from 1878 to 1883, Sydney is listed as living in Castlebellingham but still having an office at 23 St. Nicholas Street, the Lovell Building, and he continued to support his old friend's business interests from a distance. In April 1878, Sydney wrote Premier Joly to intercede for Lovell, who had been replaced as official printer for the clerk's office at the Superior Court at Montreal.

Arabella died at Castlebellingham in January 1887, by which time, Sydney had become involved in the community's affairs. A local newspaper's list of attendees at a big County Louth social function in August 1889 referred to him as the "deservedly esteemed and highly popular Sydney Bellingham." He was active even in his eighties as the chair of committees on sanitation, teachers' rights, and the local railway. In 1897, at the age of eighty-nine, he chaired a committee of local notables that raised funds for the support of the families of six fishermen from the coastal village of Annagason who had drowned on March 16, 1897, when their small boat foundered in a squall off Dundalk Bay. The speech quoted in the Dublin *Evening Herald* shows that Sydney still had the mental acuity and oratorical skills he had begun to hone in the Canadian Parliament four decades earlier. He remarked, with approval, on the ability of Catholics and Protestants to come together on the occasion, and with disapproval, on the failure of the government to provide decent port facilities enabling fishermen to support their families in larger, safer boats. These newspaper accounts reveal that the Sydney Bellingham who dictated his memoirs around this time was still an active, independent, and engaged personality and probably remained so until close to the end of his life.

46. *Sydney Bellingham in later life, photograph, LAC Ref. No. R7618-0-1-E*

RUMOUR, MYTH, LEGEND, AND HISTORICAL FACT

*L*ITIGATION LAWYERS ARE INCLINED TO BE STICKLERS FOR factual accuracy. Researching this book has taught me that historical source materials, even primary ones, can be inaccurate. Sydney Bellingham's memoirs are a case in point, but the inaccuracies are relatively unimportant. They relate mostly to the precise timing or sequence of events and are to be expected in a manuscript dictated by someone in his late eighties whose failing eyesight prevented him from checking his facts. Even competent compilers of secondary sources can make mistakes. As an example, the Alan Bellingham who was at Quebec from 1799 to 1801 has been mistaken for Sydney's father, when in fact he was his cousin, Monique Bâby's husband. But, of all the sources a writer needs to be wary of, the least reliable is local or family tradition. I learned that long ago when I discovered that, contrary to the assurances passed down to me by my mother, my first Quebec ancestor was not among the founders of Montreal in 1642. According to a more credible legend, Joseph Massé-Gravel did indeed come to Canada on the same ship as de Maisonneuve in 1641, but he settled near Quebec and let de Maisonneuve

and his other followers proceed up the St. Lawrence the following year. Like others who had come over with de Maisonneuve, he was likely dissuaded by the gossip at Quebec about the Iroquois menace farther upriver.

As I mentioned in the Preface, it was the Arundel centennial family histories that spurred my interest in Sydney Bellingham. As we saw in Chapter 8, it was indeed Sydney, as local legend has it, who can take credit for the settlement of Arundel; but contrary to the local legend, it was not Sydney who named it. Even the Quebec government website for official place names has that wrong. It claims that he named the new community Arundel in honour of the town in West Sussex that bears that name, because his family owned land there. The local legend goes further than a mere property connection, suggesting that he was the illegitimate son of the Duke of Norfolk, the Earl of Arundel. I latched onto that theory with a passion, because it made for a really interesting story. When I learned that the family name of the Dukes of Norfolk was Howard, and seeing that one of the townships bordering Arundel is called Howard, the legend seemed to make a lot of sense.

The 12th Duke of Norfolk was Bernard Edward Howard, who was born in 1765 and died in 1842. He held the title from 1815 to 1842 and would have been the right age (forty-two) to sire Sydney. Bernard Howard was sadly bereft of conjugal oversight following the scandalous elopement of his wife, the very young Lady Elizabeth Belasyse, with her first love, Richard Bingham, the son of the Earl of Lucan.[54] Being a Catholic, Bernard could not remarry and must have been rather lonely. The legend appeared to be getting closer and closer to historical fact. It seemed clinched when I discovered that the name of the first post office in Arundel Township was FitzAlan, and that Sydney named his farm FitzAlan. The family name sometimes used by the Dukes of Norfolk was FitzAlan-Howard.

Then the legend fell apart. I found the Dale & Duberger map of 1795, published thirteen years before Sydney was born, with the outline of the Arundel and Howard Townships printed on it. The map published around 1798 by Samuel Holland, the surveyor-general, corroborated this. I saw the same two townships mentioned in *Bouchette's Gazetteer* published in 1832 and in the *Act 9 George IV, chapter 73*, adopted in 1829, well before Sydney was in a position to give an official name to anything. In 1854, when Sydney's first election was annulled, Arundel was one of the un-polled townships mentioned in the Legislative Committee's findings. It existed, at least on paper, for election purposes, despite not being formally set up as a territorial division for the purposes of land tenure, and even though no one living there could claim the necessary property qualifications to vote.

Then, when I found Sydney's memoirs, I learned that he had named the post office and the farm in honour of his late father. "FitzAlan," he explains, means "son of Alan." There is absolutely nothing in his memoirs or correspondence that suggests any sort of connection with the Duke of Norfolk, nor even with the town of Arundel in England. Sydney speaks repeatedly and affectionately of his father, Alan Bellingham. True, in those days it was not in a young man's interest to claim to be anyone's illegitimate son, particularly if he stood to inherit, through legitimacy, from some other father. But near the end of his life, Sydney included in his will an endowment for the upkeep of Alan's grave in the Protestant cemetery at Châtillon-sur-Loire. If Alan Bellingham was not his father, Sydney either thought he was or wished it to be so.

Nor could I find any connection between the County of Louth in Ireland and the English County of West Sussex, where Arundel Castle is located. If there is any part of England that can be closely linked to Ireland, it is the northwest coast on the other side of the Irish Sea, between Liverpool and Blackpool. Arundel is near the southeast coast, in the diagonally opposite corner of

---

54 Lady Elizabeth, very pregnant at the trial that preceded the divorce in 1794, was represented by the famous William Garrow.

the country. Sydney's mother, Elizabeth Walls, was from Boothby Hall in Lincolnshire, 200 miles north of Arundel.

There is one little detail, however, that prevents us from totally dismissing the rumours of Sydney's illegitimacy. We know that Alan Bellingham's regiment was the 5th (Northumberland) Regiment of Foot. From 1781 to 1787, the "Fighting Fifth" was in Ireland. From 1787 to 1797, it was in North America. After 1797 until December 1807, it was in other parts of the world fighting the French and their allies. From early December 1807 to July 1808, it returned briefly to Ireland (Cork).[55] Sydney was born on August 2, 1808. For Sydney to be the son of Alan Bellingham, one of three possibilities must have occurred: (1) Sydney was born at least four weeks prematurely, or (2) Alan had either left the regiment or was on leave in Ireland during the month of November 1807, or (3) Sydney's mother, Elizabeth, had travelled abroad to be with her husband.

The local legend did not stop with Sydney when it came to rumours of illegitimacy. Today, the concept of legitimacy has all but disappeared in Quebec, which has the distinction of having moved rapidly, in the space of one decade (the 1960s), from being the most religious society in North America to the most secular. It means next to nothing today, but in the 1850s and 1860s, illegitimacy was hushed up as much as it could

be. It might be one thing to romantically imagine the late Sydney Bellingham to be the bastard son of some distant English duke, but quite another to confidently state that a prominent current member of the Arundel community was Sydney's illegitimate son. That, in any event, is the connection that local legend makes between Sydney Bellingham and A. B. Filion. In this case, though, it is a conclusion not devoid of substance. The legend has a lot of circumstantial evidence to support it. Here are the facts.

We do not know where, or exactly when, Auguste (aka "Augustus") Bernard Filion was born. It is odd that no trace can be found of his birth in church records. In the mid-nineteenth century, that is something that might occur if the child were illegitimate. The declaration of transmission of his real estate following his death in 1908 says that he died on November 5, 1908. October 12, 1843, is given as his date of birth in the 1901 census, but according to the 1871 census he was born in 1845 and the 1891 census suggests 1844. His mother was Mathilde Filion, who was interred at Grenville at the age of seventy-eight in 1899. The act of burial shows that Auguste was present, and he is described as her son. She appears to have married a Pierre Rolland late in life. Prior to that, the 1871 Census shows Mathilde living with Auguste and his young wife in Arundel. A Mathilde Filion, the daughter of a carpenter, was born in Montreal on December 27, 1824, and baptized the following day at Notre Dame Church.

We know that Auguste married Margaret Milway

---

55 In 1814, after the first defeat of Napoleon, it returned briefly to Lower Canada and launched an unsuccessful attack on the Americans at Plattsburgh in Upper New York State. That defeat eventually led to the departure of Governor Prévost, the unhappy patron of the inn mentioned in Chapter 4.

47. A. B. Filion, photograph by
William James Topley, 1890,
LAC, MIKAN 345856

sometime after July 19, 1869, which is the date of the
marriage contract executed before notary Félix Chénier
at Lachute.[56] This was the same year in which Sydney
"transferred" his Arundel farm to Auguste. Margaret
was from Grenville. The first of their ten children was
baptized at Grenville in July of the following year. They

56 See Chapter 9.

named him Sydney Augustus Filion. "Sydney" was not a
name that French-Canadian fathers were in the habit of
bestowing upon their children in those days.

In Cyrus Thomas's *History of Argenteuil* published in
1896, Filion is described as "one of the prominent public
men in Grenville," that he came to that town in 1872, and
that two years later "was appointed Justice of the Peace,

Forest Ranger of Argenteuil and parts of two adjoining counties, and secretary-treasurer of the township and augmentation of Grenville." By Forest Ranger, Thomas must have been referring to Filion's appointment as Crown Land agent, his occupation as shown in later census reports. Sydney was sitting in the Quebec Legislative Assembly as the member for Argenteuil in the year of Filion's various appointments in 1874, at the age of only thirty-one. In December 1872, in his correspondence relating to railways with Antoine Labelle, Sydney had lobbied for Auguste's appointment as Crown Land agent at Grenville, and in his correspondence with Premier Félix-Gabriel Marchand a quarter-century later, he mentions having got him the appointment. There is

48. The Bellingham-Filion House in Arundel, photograph by the author.

some irony in that the position had been previously held by George Kains and after him, Kains's brother-in-law. Kains, we should remember, had devoted his energies, and some of his money, to the campaigns of Sydney's political opponents in the 1850s.

Thomas says nothing about Filion's background, other than that he had come from "Western Ontario" to Arundel in 1866, where he took up 600 acres of land. Thomas is referring to the five lots Sydney had partially cleared and built a large house on, and which he then "transferred" to Auguste in 1869. There is no mention by Thomas of how a young man of twenty-three, newly arrived in Argenteuil, could afford to "take up" 600 acres of land and a large house. Fluently bilingual, he had obviously spent part of his youth gaining the education he would need in order to qualify for the kind of appointments obtained for him by Sydney. Given his election to the Quebec Assembly in 1867, Sydney may have decided that the time had come to spend less time in Arundel, but he offers no explanation in his memoirs for why he would transfer the valuable FitzAlan house and farm to a twenty-six-year-old, who had no local connections and who had arrived in the area only three years earlier. Nor does Thomas offer any insight into how a young man newly arrived at Grenville in 1872 could leapfrog over the sons of well-established Argenteuil families in gaining appointments of such local importance. According to the 1871 census, there were no Filions already living in Grenville.

Perhaps the most significant piece of circumstantial evidence is in the census of 1891, where "Ireland" shows up as the place of birth of Auguste's father. Filion is not an Irish name. But then this could have been just a census taker's error. The census taker might have spoken only to Margaret, who would have given Ireland as her father's birthplace, and the same entry for Auguste could have been based on the census taker's assumption that it was the same for him. But that is only a possibility. It is more likely that the census taker would not have placed the birth of the father of someone named Auguste Filion in Ireland unless that is what he had been told.

The census of 1901 shows that Filion and his large family had moved up from Grenville and were living full-time in Arundel. The big house we first heard of in Chapter 8 had by then become known locally as the "Bellingham- Filion house." After it was damaged by fire in 1907, a tower was added to one corner, the dormers were removed, and the shingled roof was replaced with tin, but the distinctive wrought-iron fence remained.

In letters he dictated in 1897 at the age of eighty-nine, addressed to Premier Félix-Gabriel Marchand, Sydney mentions Filion as his "active & useful agent," for whom he had obtained the appointment as Crown Land agent at Grenville twenty-five years earlier. He mentions in one of the letters that Filion had taken a leave of absence to visit him in Ireland in September 1896. In the third and final letter, he lobbies Marchand to appoint Filion as chief Crown Land agent for the entire

province. Nearly twenty years earlier, he had made the same pitch for him in his correspondence with Premier Joly. Clearly, there is an abiding attachment of loyalty and concern for Filion's welfare that transcends a purely business relationship.

Premier Marchand is another example of how the people, places, and events in Sydney's life in Canada were interconnected. Marchand was related to Sydney by marriage. His mother, Mary Macnider, was Arabella's aunt. In his letters to Marchand, Sydney reminisces about his visits in the 1830s to the home of Marchand's father, Gabriel, at St. Jean and to a visit there after Félix-Gabriel had inherited it. As we saw in Chapter 4, his familiarity with the road from the Longueuil ferry to St. Jean had

49. Auguste Bernard Filion, at left, with Curé Labelle in 1889, photograph, LAC, MIKAN 3217897

launched his brief military career in November 1837.

Auguste Filion never did get the top post in the hierarchy of provincial Crown Land agents, but he appears to have become responsible, as an inspector, for a large area of which Argenteuil County was only a part. He dealt extensively with Antoine Labelle in the acquisition of Crown Land for Labelle's settlement program in the upper reaches of the Rouge, and in 1889 he accompanied Labelle and his party at La Chute aux Iroquois, where the town of Labelle now stands. In the group photograph on the previous page, he appears to have been of above average height for that period, like Sydney Bellingham.

Auguste's correspondence with Labelle includes an expression of thanks for helping him obtain a salary increase. He was able to travel to Ireland to visit Sydney in 1896, and if local legend is again true, to Arundel Castle to visit the Duke of Norfolk. According to the legend, the duke asked Auguste what Sydney looked like, to which he replied, "He looks like you, sir." Could Auguste have been the source of the rumour that Sydney was the illegitimate son of the duke's predecessor? Could it have been just a romantic fantasy? Or had he gone to Arundel Castle simply out of a desire to see what the original Arundel looked like, leaving the folks back home in the much newer Arundel to embellish the story later?

Rickson Albert Outhet (1876–1951) was a Montreal-born landscape architect and town planner. He trained with the firm of Frederick Law Olmsted, the much more famous designer of Montreal's Mount Royal Park and of Central Park in New York City. Like many of his wealthy clients, Outhet lived in the posh Montreal enclave of Westmount, but he had a passion for the Laurentian hinterland and owned a log cabin on Lac Tremblant. Lac Tremblant is the large lake at the base of Mont Tremblant and the source of the Rouge River's main tributary, the Diable. Following the dual calamities of his wife's untimely death in 1929 and the Great Depression, Outhet retired from city life and spent his last two decades at Lac Tremblant. He left behind a brief account of his understanding of the history of the Rouge Valley. It reveals that he knew Auguste Filion in his capacity as Crown Land agent, and that he had actually accompanied him in 1902 on an inspection by canoe of an island in Lac Tremblant. At the time, the young Outhet had only a small shanty on a smaller neighbouring lake, closer to the railway linking the town of Labelle with Montreal. It was his excursion with Filion that resulted in his acquisition of land on the shores of Lac Tremblant itself.

Outhet briefly mentions the settlement of Arundel, which he attributes to "Sir" Sydney Bellingham and refers to Auguste as Sydney's son by his housekeeper, Mrs. Filion. His source for this information was most likely not Filion, who was by then a prominent county official unlikely to proclaim his illegitimacy. The source appears to have been Edward J. Graham, whose notes were appended to Outhet's brief history. Graham, known as "E. J.," was the grandson of one of the original Arundel settlers, John Graham. E. J.'s father, William Dawson Graham Jr., owned the village store and served as mayor of Arundel. E. J. was born and raised in Arundel before becoming a lumber-company manager and acquiring a cottage on Lac Tremblant. He would have been well versed in the local Arundel gossip.

The claim that Mathilde was Sydney's housekeeper is entirely believable. In the early 1840s, when Auguste was conceived and born, Sydney was working on St. James Street as the managing editor of Walker's daily newspaper, the *Times and Commercial Advertiser*. He could not have being doing that while commuting every weekday by carriage or sleigh to his large house on the other side of Mount Royal. He likely continued to rent a *pied-à-terre* on St. James Street, as we know he had done in the 1830s. We can even entertain the possibility that, at some point, Mathilde and young Auguste lived under the same roof as Arabella, with Mathilde performing the duties of housekeeper at Dunany Cottage. In Sydney's memoirs, he mentions living at Dunany Cottage with his "family." He refers to both Dr. William Robertson and Dr. Robert MacDonnell as his "family physician." A "family" usually means more than two people. Young William would have stayed with them briefly, when not away at school in Toronto, from 1832 to 1837. William Robertson was, as we have seen, a big part of the Montreal scene during those years, but MacDonnell was still studying medicine at Dublin's Trinity College. He could not have been Sydney's "family physician" until after William

Bellingham joined the British Army.

E. J. Graham's very brief notes, which were appended to Outhet's account, are a good example of how family and local history can be distorted. He states that his father had come to Canada with others from "Lord Bellingham's estate." There was, of course, no such Lord Bellingham. The Bellingham baronets of County Louth were not lords, and John Graham came over from the neighbouring County Monahan, where there was no Bellingham estate. "Sir" Sydney, who is described as "Lord" Bellingham's son, is said to have become Earl of Arundel Castle, which fits well with the legend that he was the illegitimate son of the Duke of Norfolk, except that an illegitimate son cannot inherit the title. According to Outhet, Sydney signed over all his properties to Filion during a meeting in Paris, of all places, when he "returned to Sussex castle."[57] The myth had become a legend, and the legend, with its confused geography, is simply not credible.

Well-meaning, inconsequential mistakes by lay writers are understandable. It is another matter when historians perpetuate false assumptions, particularly if those assumptions work against ethnic or linguistic harmony. A case in point is the claim that the Arundel settlement was spearheaded by a zealous career soldier and that the land grants he received were inspired by Lord Durham's goal of Anglo-Protestant demographic

---

57 "Rickson Outhet, "Lac Tremblant History to 1902." In Vieux Temps Stories—Lac-Tremblant-Nord, 1915–1990 (Municipalité de Lac-Tremblant-Nord, 1990), 4–9.

dominance.[58] On the other hand, the rumours of Auguste Filion's pedigree appear much closer to historical fact, and the story is a happy one. If he could have read the letters that Sydney Bellingham sent Premier Marchand, Auguste would have known that Sydney was very proud of him. He was, indeed, an accomplished and respected figure in Argenteuil County.

When Auguste died, he owned land in six other townships in addition to Arundel. He had also been able to provide an education to his numerous children. One of them (Sydney) had succeeded him as Crown Land agent at Grenville. Arthur became a mine manager in Sault Ste. Marie. Thomas became a physician in Montreal, and John went on to become the highest-ranking member of the Jesuit Order in Canada.

Today, there are two streets that intersect each other in the town of Lachute. One is Bellingham, and the other is Filion. On that note, Dear Reader, I leave it to you to tie up whatever loose ends may remain.

---

58 See Chapter 8.

GENEALOGICAL TABLES

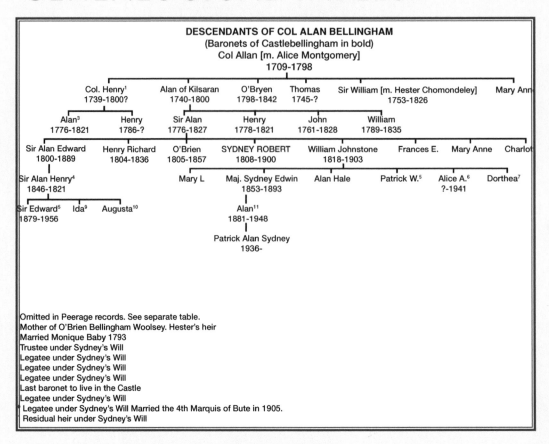

DESCENDANTS OF COL ALAN BELLINGHAM
(Baronets of Castlebellingham in bold)
Col Allan [m. Alice Montgomery]
1709-1798

Col. Henry[1] 1739-1800? — Alan of Kilsaran 1740-1800 — O'Bryen 1798-1842 — Thomas 1745-? — Sir William [m. Hester Chomondeley] 1753-1826 — Mary Ann

Alan[3] 1776-1821 — Henry 1786-? — Sir Alan 1776-1827 — Henry 1778-1821 — John 1761-1828 — William 1789-1835

Sir Alan Edward 1800-1889 — Henry Richard 1804-1836 — O'Brien 1805-1857 — SYDNEY ROBERT 1808-1900 — William Johnstone 1818-1903 — Frances E. — Mary Anne — Charlot

Sir Alan Henry[4] 1846-1821 — Mary L — Maj. Sydney Edwin 1853-1893 — Alan Hale — Patrick W.[5] — Alice A.[6] ?-1941 — Dorthea[7]

Sir Edward[5] 1879-1956 — Ida[9] — Augusta[10] — Alan[11] 1881-1948

Patrick Alan Sydney 1936-

Omitted in Peerage records. See separate table.
Mother of O'Brien Bellingham Woolsey. Hester's heir
Married Monique Baby 1793
Trustee under Sydney's Will
Legatee under Sydney's Will
Legatee under Sydney's Will
Legatee under Sydney's Will
Last baronet to live in the Castle
Legatee under Sydney's Will
Legatee under Sydney's Will Married the 4th Marquis of Bute in 1905.
Residual heir under Sydney's Will

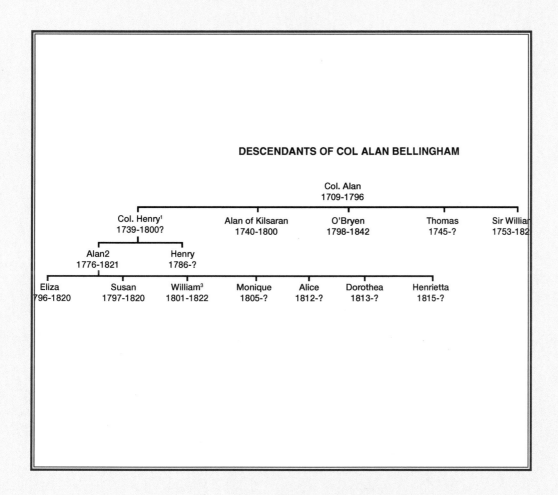

DESCENDANTS OF COL ALAN BELLINGHAM

Col. Alan
1709-1796

Col. Henry[1]
1739-1800?

Alan of Kilsaran
1740-1800

O'Bryen
1798-1842

Thomas
1745-?

Sir William
1753-182

Alan2
1776-1821

Henry
1786-?

Eliza
1796-1820

Susan
1797-1820

William[3]
1801-1822

Monique
1805-?

Alice
1812-?

Dorothea
1813-?

Henrietta
1815-?

PRIMARY SOURCES

[Library and Archives Canada shown as LAC; Bibliothèque et Archives
    Nationales du Québec shown as BAnQ.]

Abbott, J. J. C. *The Argenteuil Case.* Montreal: 1860.

Albright, George Nelson. *Diaries of the Surveys of Montcalm and Arundel
    Townships.* BAnQ.

Ansley, G. D. "City Drainage." *Proceedings of the Civil Engineers' Club of the
    North-West 4.* Chicago: 1878. A paper on the Craig Street sewer.

Arguments in Favor of the Ottawa and Georgian Bay Ship Canal. Ottawa: 1856.

Barker, Edward John. *Observations on the Rideau Canal.* Kingston: 1834.

Bellingham, Sydney Robert. *Correspondence with Alexandre Delisle 1854.* LAC.

____. *Correspondence with Henri-Gustave Joly de Lotbinière, Félix-Gabriel
    Marchand, and Antoine Labelle.* BAnQ.

____. *Correspondence with Louis-Hippolyte La Fontaine, 1842.* Montreal Archives.

____. *Correspondence with John A. Macdonald.* LAC.

____. *A Memoir by Sydney R. Bellingham, c.* 1895. LAC.

____. "Ottawa Improvements." *The Canadian Merchants' Magazine and
    Commercial Review* (December 1857).

____. *Reasons Why British Conservatives Voted Against the Boucherville Ministry.*
    Rouses Point, NY: Lovell, 1875.

____. *Some Personal Recollections of the Rebellion of 1837 in Canada.* Dublin:
    Brown & Nolan, 1901.

____. *Will Executed December 17, 1898.* Public Record Office of Northern Ireland.

Bellingham, Sydney Robert, and Pierre-Édouard Leclère. *Report to Attorney-
    General Ogden.* November 19, 1837. BAnQ.

Bigsby, John J. *The Shoe and Canoe: or, Pictures of Travels in the Canadas.*
    London: Chapman and Hall, 1850.

Bosworth, Newton. *Hochelaga Depicta: or the History and Present State of the
Island and City of Montreal.* Montreal: Greig, 1839.

Bouchette, Joseph. *Description topographique de la province du Bas Canada.*
    London: 1815.

____. *The British Dominions in North America.* London: Longman, 1832.

Bouchette, Robert-S.-M. *Mémoires de Robert-S.-M. Bouchette, 1805–1840.*
    Montreal: 1903.

Brown, Thomas Storrow. *1837: My Connection with It.* Quebec City: Renault,
    1898.

Buchanan, Alexander, H. Heney, and G. W. Wicksteed, eds. *Revised Acts and
    Ordinances of Lower Canada.* Montreal: 1845.

Census of Canada (1851, 1861, 1871, 1881, 1891, 1901). LAC.

Cokayne, George Edward. *Complete Baronetage.* Vol. 5. Exeter: Bollard, 1906.

Colonization Circular. London: 1866.

Courier du Canada (December 20, 1877).

Courier de St. Hyacinthe (February 23, 1878).

Crown Lands Registry for Lower Canada. BAnQ.

Democrat and People's Journal (Dundalk, 1889, 1890, 1894).

Dessaules, L. A. *Six lectures sur l'annexion du Canada aux États-Unis.* Montreal:
    Gendron, 1851.

Dublin Evening Herald (1897).

L'Électeur (Quebec, April 12, 1890).

Filion, Auguste Bernard. *Correspondence with Antoine Labelle.* BAnQ.

Freeman's Journal (1897, 1889).

Hall, Basil. *Travels in North America in the Years 1827 and 1828.* Philadelphia:
    Carey, 1829.

Hawkins, Alfred. *Picture of Quebec.* Quebec City: 1834.

Henry, Walter. *Events of a Military Life.* London: 1843.

Hincks, Francis. *Reminiscences of His Public Life.* Montreal: Drysdale, 1884.

Howison, John. *Sketches of Upper Canada.* Edinburgh: Oliver & Boyd, 1821.

Information for Immigrants. *Settlers and Purchasers of Public Lands.* Quebec City: 1863.

Journal de Québec, 1874 (March 27, 1878).

Journals of the Legislative Assembly of the Province of Canada (1841–66).

Judicial Committee of the Privy Council Case Reports.

Kains, George. *Correspondence with Thomas Kains.* LAC.

Kierzkowski, Alexandre. *The Question of the Seigniorial Tenure of Lower Canada Reduced to a Question of Landed Credit.* Montreal: Lovell, 1852.

Kingston Chronicle & Gazette (February 17, 1844).

Langevin, Hector. *Correspondence with John A. Macdonald.* BAnQ.

Lillie, A. *Canada: Physical, Economic, and Social.* Toronto: Maclear, 1855.

Liste des officiers de la malice sédentaire du Bas Canada, 1862. Queen's Printer: 1863.

Logan, W. E. *Geological Survey of Canada Report of Progress.* Montreal: Dawson, 1863.

____. *A Sketch of the Geology of Canada.* Paris: 1855.

Loranger, T. J. J. *Report of the Committee Appointed to Enquire into the Transactions of the Montreal and Bytown Railway Company.* Quebec City: 1856.

Macaulay, George Henry. *The Proposed B.N.A. Confederation: A Reply to Mr. Penny's Reasons Why It Should Not Be Imposed upon the Colonies by the Imperial Legislation.* Montreal: Daily News, 1867.

Mackay, Robert W. S. *The Canada Directory.* Montreal: Lovell, 1851.

____. *The Strangers' Guide to the City of Montreal.* Montreal: Lovell, 1843.

Mackenzie, William Lyon. *Narrative of the Late Rebellion.* Toronto: 1838.

McDougall, Margaret Dixon. *The Letters of "Norah" on her Tour Through Ireland.* Montreal: 1882.

La Minerve (1837, 1834).

Montreal Illustrated, or, the Stranger's Guide to Montreal. Montreal: Chisholm & Bros., 1875.

Muster Rolls and Pay Lists for Canada (1837 and 1838). Accessed November 15, 2018, at *www.ancestry.ca.*

The New Guide to Montreal and Its Environs. Montreal: Armour & Ramsay, 1851.

The New Standard Atlas of the Dominion of Canada. Montreal: Walker and Miles, 1875.

L'Opinion Publique (January 24, 1878).

Papers Relating to the Removal of the Seat of Government and to the Annexation Movement. London: 1850.

Paton, Colonel George, et al. *Historical Records of the 24th Regiment.* London: Simpkin, 1892.

Prospectus of the Montreal and Bytown Railroad. Montreal: Lovell, 1853.

Register of Acts of Civil Status, Quebec. Accessed November 15, 2018, at *www.ancestry.ca.*

Régistre foncier du Québec en ligne.

Reid, J. H. Stewart, Kenneth McNaught, and Harry S. Crowe. *A Source-Book of Canadian History.* Toronto: Longmans, 1959.

Report of the Commissioner of Crown Lands of Canada for the Year 1857. Toronto: Lovell, 1858.

Report of the Special Committee Appointed to Enquire and Report as to the Condition, Management and Prospects of the Grand Trunk Railway Co. Toronto: Lovell, 1857.

Revised Acts and Ordinances of Lower-Canada. Montreal: Derbyshire, 1845.

Richardson, Major John. *Eight Years in Canada.* Montreal: Cunningham, 1847.

Rubidge, Charles. *An Autobiographical Sketch.* Peterborough: 1870.

Ship Arrivals at the Port of Quebec. Accessed November 15, 2018, at *www.theshipslist.com.*

Shortt, Adam, and Arthur G. Doughty. *Documents Relating to the Constitutional History of Canada 1759–1791.* Ottawa: 1907.

Stewart, Frances. *Our Forest Home.* Montreal: Gazette Printing, 1902.

Tremblay, Ernest. *L'Affaire Letellier et la Constitution.* Montreal: La Patrie, 1879.

The True Witness and Catholic Chronicle (January 9, 1874).

L'Union des Cantons de l'Est (October 1876).

BIBLIOGRAPHY

Achintre, M. A. *Portraits et dossiers parlementaires du premier parlement de Québec*. Montreal: Duvernay, 1871.

Allin, Cephas D., and George M. Jones. *Annexation, Preferential Trade and Reciprocity*. Toronto: Musson, 1912.

Aoki, Jodi Lee. *Revisiting "Our Forest Home": The Immigrant Letters of Frances Stewart*. Toronto: Dundurn, 2011.

Atherton, William Henry. *Montreal Under British Rule, 1760–1914*. Montreal: Clarke, 1914.

Bélanger, Claude. "French Canadian Emigration to the United States 1840–1930." *Readings in Quebec History*. Accessed November 15, 2018, at http://faculty.marianopolis.edu/c.belanger/quebechistory/readings/leaving.htm.

Bishoff, Peter C. "La Société de bienfaisance des journaliers de navires à Québec, 1855 à 1878." *The Canadian Historical Review* 84, no. 3 (September 2003).

Borthwick, J. Douglas. *History of the Montreal Prison, from A.D. 1784 to A.D. 1886*. Montreal: Feriard, 1886.

Boyd, Bevin, and Debbie Boyd. "Boyds in Arundel." In *Arundel Family History Collection* (2007).

Buchanan, Arthur William Patrick. *The Buchanan Book: The Life of Alexander Buchanan, Q.C.* Montreal: 1911.

Burnham, J. Hampden. *Canadians in the Imperial Naval and Military Service Abroad*. Toronto: Williamson, 1891.

Campbell, Robert. *A History of the Scotch Presbyterian Church St. Gabriel Street, Montreal*. Montreal: Drysdale, 1887.

Canniff, William. *History of the Province of Ontario*. Toronto: A. H. Hovey, 1872.

Careless, J. M. S. *Brown of the Globe*. Toronto: McClelland & Stewart, 1967.

____. *The Union of the Canadas: The Growth of Canadian Institutions 1841–1857*. Toronto: Macmillan, 1959.

Casgrain, Philippe-Bâby. *Mémorial des familles Casgrain, Bâby et Perrault du Canada*. Quebec City: Darveau, 1898.

Conklin, Edwin P. "Regional Quebec." In William Wood, ed., *The Storied Province of Quebec*. Toronto: Dominion Publishing, 1931.

Cooper, John Irwin. *Montreal: The Story of Three Hundred Years*. Montreal: L'Imprimerie de Lamirande, 1942.

Corley, Nora. "The St. Lawrence Ship Channel, 1805–1865." *Cahiers de géographie du Québec* 11, no. 23 (1967).

Cross, Dorothy Suzanne. "The Irish in Montreal, 1867–1896." M.A. thesis, McGill University (1969).

Davin, Nicholas Flood. *The Irishman in Canada*. London: Sampson Low, 1877.

Dent, John Charles. *The Story of the Upper Canadian Rebellion*. Toronto: Robinson, 1885.

Dickson, George, and G. Mercer Adam. *A History of Upper Canada College, 1829–1892*. Toronto: Rowsell 1893.

Dictionary of Canadian Biography:
"John Abbott" by Carman Miller
"Archibald Acheson (2nd Earl of Gosford)" by Phillip Buckner

"Hugh Allan" by Brian J. Young and Gerald J. J. Tulchinsky
"Charles Joseph Alleyn" by Marcel Plouffe
"Peter Aylen" by Michael S. Cross
"Jacques Bâby" by John Clarke
"William Badgley" by Elizabeth Gibbs
"Charles Bagot" by Jacques Monet
"Robert Baldwin" by Michael S. Cross and Robert L. Fraser
"James Barry" by Charles G. Rolland
"Jean-Louis Beaudry" by Lorne Ste. Croix
"James Gray Bethune" by Peter Ennals
"John Bethune" by John Irwin Cooper
"John Boston" by Carman Miller
"Charles Boucher de Boucherville" by Kenneth Munro
"Joseph Bouchette" by Claude Boudreau and Pierre Lépine
"Robert Bouchette" by Yves Tessier
"Ignace Bourget" by Philippe Sylvain
"George Brown" by J. M. S. Careless
"Thomas Storrow Brown" by Fernand Ouellet
"James Bruce (8th Earl of Elgin)" by W. L. Morton
"Alexander Buchanan" by Jacques Boucher
"Guy Carleton (1st Baron Dorchester)" by G. P. Browne
"George-Étienne Cartier" by J.-C. Bonenfant
"Joseph-Adolphe Chapleau" by Andrée Désilets
"Pierre-Joseph-Olivier Chauveau" by Jean Hamelin and Pierre Poulin
"Jean-Olivier Chénier" by Jean-Paul Bernard
"Côme Séraphin Cherrier" by Jean-Claude Robert

"Levi Ruggles Church" by Pierre-Louis Lapointe

"John Colborne (1st Baron Seaton)" by Alan Wilson

"William Caldwell" by Edward Horton Bensley

"Lemuel Cushing" by Andrée Désilets

"Eleazar David" by Elinor Kyte Senior

"Pierre-Dominique Debartzch" by Ludwik K. R. Zubkowski

"Alexandre M. Delisle" by Jacques Monet

"Bernard Devlin" by J. C. Bonenfant

"Antoine-Aimé Dorion" by Jean-Claude Soulard

"Louis Thomas Drummond" by J. I. Little

"John Egan" by Richard Reid

"Edward Ellice" by James M. Colthart

"William Ermatinger" by Elinor Senior

"Édouard-Raymond Fabre" by Jean-Louis Roy

"James Moir Ferres" by Lorne Ste. Croix

"James FitzGibbon" by Ruth McKenzie

"Charles Forbes" by John Beswarick Thompson

"Colley Lyons Lucas Foster" by O. A. Cooke

"William Forsyth" by Robert L. Fraser

"Alexander Tilloch Galt" by Jean-Pierre Kesteman

"John Gilmour" by Courtney C. J. Bond

"Amury Girod" by Jean-Paul Bernard and Danielle Gauthier

"Jean-Joseph Girouard" by Béatrice Chassé

"Maximilien Globensky" by Jean-Pierre Gagnon

"Francis Godschall Johnson" by Clinton O. White

"Casimir Stanislaus Gzowski" by H. V. Nelles

"Charles Stephen Gore" by John W. Spurr

"Frederick Haldimand" by Stuart R. J. Sutherland, Pierre Tousignant, and Madeleine Dionne-Tousignant

"Francis Bond Head" by S. F. Wise

"Jean-Baptiste-René Hertel de Rouville" by Serge Courville

"Francis Hincks" by William G. Ormsby

"Andrew Fernando Holmes" by Edward Horton Bensley

"Benjamin Holmes" by Lorne Ste. Croix

"William Holmes" by Barbara Tunis

"Luther Hamilton Holton" by H. C. Classen

"Samuel Jacobs" by Denis Vaugeois

"Henri-Gustave Joly de Lotbinière" by Marcel Hamelin

"Alexandre-Édouard Kierzkowski" by L. Kos Rabcewicz Zubkowski

"Timothée Kimber" by Michel de Lorimier

"Antoine Labelle" by Gabriel Dussault

"Louis-Hippolyte La Fontaine" by Jacques Monet

"John George Lambton (Lord Durham)" by Fernand Ouellet

"Hector Langevin" by Andrée Désilets

"Wilfrid Laurier" by Réal Bélanger

"Pierre-Edouard Leclère" by Jean-Louis Roy

"Luc Letellier de Saint-Just" by Robert Rumilly

"William Edmond Logan" by C. Gordon Winder

"John Lovell" by George L. Parker

"Donald Alexander Macdonald" by Bruce W. Hodgins and Paul W. White

"John A. Macdonald" by J. K. Johnson and P. W. Waite

"James Macdonell" by Elinor Kyte Senior

"Robert Lea MacDonnell" by Jean-Pierre Chalifoux

"William Lyon Mackenzie" by F. H. Armstrong and R. J. Stagg

"Allan Napier MacNab" by Peter Baskerville

"Adam Lymburner Macnider" by Carman Miller

"Félix-Gabriel Marchand" by Michèle Brassard and J. Hamelin

"Gabriel Marchand" by Lionel Fortin

"William King McCord" by Jean-Claude Robert

"Thomas McKay" by E. F. Bush

"Charles Metcalfe" by Donald R. Beer

"John Molson Jr." by Alfred Dubuc and Robert Tremblay

"John Molson Sr." by Alfred Dubuc

"William Molson" by Alfred Dubuc

"Augustin-Norbert Morin" by Jean-Marc Paradis

"Angus Morrison" by Victor Loring Russell

"George Jehoshaphat Mountain" by Monica Marston

"James Murray" by G. P. Browne

"John Neilson" by Sonia Chassé, Rita Girard-Wallot, and Jean-Pierre Wallot

"Robert Nelson" by Richard Chabot, Jacques Monet, and Yves Roby

"Wolfred Nelson" by John Beswarick Thompson

"Edmund Bailey O'Callahan" by Jacques Monet

"Charles Ogden" by Lorne Ste. Croix

"Gédéon Ouimet" by Michèle Brassard and Jean Hamelin

"Pierre-Louis Panet" by Roger Barrette

"Denis-Benjamin Papineau" by Claude Baribeau

"Louis-Joseph Papineau" by Fernand Ouellet

"Edward Goff Penny" by Lorne Ste. Croix

"George Prévost" by Peter Burroughs

"Joseph Gibb Robertson" by Marc Vallières

"William Robertson" by E. H. Bensley

"Peter Robinson" by Wendy Cameron

"Édouard-Étienne Rodier" by Richard Chabot

"John Rose" by David M. L. Farr

"John Ross" by Paul Cornell

"Charles Rubidge" by Wendy Cameron

"Charles-Michel d'Irumberry de Salaberry" by Michèle Guitard

"William Henry Scott" by Jacques Gouin

"Walter Shanly" by Laurie Stanley and John Blackwell

"Nicholas Sparks" by Michael S. Cross

"Frances Browne Stewart" by G. de T. Glazebrook

"Thomas Alexander Stewart" by Alan G. Brunger

"Étienne-Paschal Taché" by Andrée Désilets

"Charles Poulett Thomson (1st Baron Sydenham)" by Phillip Buckner

"Jean-Thomas Taschereau" by Honorius Provost

"Joseph-Rémi Vallières de Saint-Réal" by James H. Lambert and Jacques Monet

"Philip VanKoughnet" by W. L. Morton

"Jacques Viger" by Jean-Claude Robert

"William Walker" by Carman Miller

"George Augustus Wetherall" by John W. Spurr

"John Wilson" by Colin Read

"Garnet Wolseley" by O. A. Cooke

"Philemon Wright" by Fernand Ouellet and Benoît Thériault

Doughty, Arthur G. *Under the Lily & the Rose*. Toronto: Dent, 1831.

Doyon, J. Michel. *Les avocats et le Barreau, une histoire …* Montreal: Corporation de services du Barreau du Québec, 2009.

Ducharme, Michel. *The Idea of Liberty in Canada During the Age of Atlantic Revolutions, 1776–1838*. Montreal and Kingston: McGill-Queen's University Press, 2014.

Fauteux, Aegidius. *Le Duel au Canada*. Montreal: Zodiaque, 1934.

FitzGibbon, Mary-Agnes. *A Veteran of 1812: The Life of James FitzGibbon*. Toronto: Briggs, 1894.

Fyson, Donald. *Magistrates, Police, and People: Everyday Criminal Justice in Quebec and Lower Canada, 1764–1837*. Toronto: Osgoode Society / University of Toronto Press, 2006.

Gentilcore, Louis, ed. *Historical Atlas of Canada: The Land Transformed, 1800–1891*. Vol. 2. Toronto: University of Toronto Press, 1993.

Globensky, Charles-Auguste-Maximilien. *La Rébellion de 1837 à Saint-Eustache*. Quebec City: Côté, 1883.

Grant, George Munro. *Picturesque Canada: The Country as It Was and Is*. Toronto: Clarke, 1882.

Greer, Allan. *The Patriots and the People: The Rebellions of 1837 in Rural Lower Canada*. Toronto: University of Toronto Press, 1993.

Guérin, Thomas. *Feudal Canada: The Story of the Seigniories of New France*. Montreal: 1926.

Guillet, Edwin C. *Early Life in Upper Canada*. Toronto: University of Toronto Press, 1933.

____. *The Valley of the Trent*. Toronto: University of Toronto Press, 1957.

Hamelin, Marcel. *Les premières années du parlement Québécois (1867–1878)*. Quebec City: Université Laval, 1974.

Harrington, Bernard J. *Life of Sir William E. Logan, Kt.*

London: Sampson Low, 1883.

Harvey, Janice. *The Protestant Orphan Asylum and the Montreal Ladies' Benevolent Society: A Case Study in Protestant Child Charity in Montreal, 1822–1900*. Ph.D. thesis, McGill University (2001).

Hind, Henry Youle. *Eighty Years' Progress of British North America*. Toronto: Stebbins, 1863.

Huyshe, G. L. *The Red River Expedition*. London: Macmillan, 1874.

James, Edward. *The Lives and Battles of the Champions of England*. New York: 1879.

Jenkins, Kathleen. *Montreal: Island City of the St. Lawrence*. New York: Doubleday, 1966.

Johnson, Walter S. *Pastor Invictus, or Rebellion in St. Eustache*. Montreal: Quality Press, 1931.

____. *The Rebellion of 1837*. Montreal: 1925.

Journal of the County Louth Archaeological Society 1, no. 4. (1907).

King, Jason. "L'historiographique irlando-québécois: conflits et conciliations entre Canadiens français et Irlandais." *Bulletin d'histoire politique* 18, no. 3.

Kingsford, William. *The History of Canada*. Vol. 10. Toronto: Kegan Paul, 1898.

Kos-Rabcewicz-Zubkowski, Ludwik, and William Edward Greening. *Sir Casimir Stanislas Gzowski: A Biography*. Toronto: Burns, 1959.

Labrosse, Jean. *Canton Arundel Township, Recensement 1901 Census* (2005).

LaGrange, Richard. *La Vallée de la Rouge*, 1981.

Laurin, Serge. *Histoire de Laurentides*, 1989.

Lauzon, Gilles, and Madeleine Forget, eds. *Old Montreal: History Through Heritage*. Quebec City: 2004. In particular, the chapters by Louise Pothier, Alan M. Stewart, Gilles Lauzon, and Joanne Burgess.

Leslie, James B. *History of the Kilsaran Union of Parishes in the County of Louth*. Dundalk: Tempest, 1908.

Lillie, A. *Canada: Physical, Economic, and Social*. Toronto: Maclear, 1855.

Lindsey, Charles. *The Life and Times of Wm. Lyon Mackenzie*. Toronto: Randall, 1862.

Lyne, Daniel Colman. *The Irish in the Province of Canada in the Decade Leading to Confederation*. M.A. thesis, McGill University (1960).

Lynn, Shane, "Before the Fenians: 1848 and the Irish Plot to Invade Canada." *Éire-Ireland* 51, nos. 1–2 (2016).

MacKay, Donald. *The Square Mile: Merchant Princes of Montreal*. Vancouver: Douglas & McIntyre, 1987.

Mackey, Frank. *Steamboat Connections: Montreal to Upper Canada 1816–1848*. Montreal and Kingston: McGill-Queen's University Press, 2000.

Mackintosh, C. H. *The Canadian Parliamentary Companion and Annual Register* (1878). Ottawa: 1878.

Martin, T. Mower, and Wilfrid Campbell. *Canada*. Toronto: Macmillan, 1906.

Monet, Jacques. "La Crise Metcalfe and the Montreal Election, 1843–1844." *The Canadian Historical Review* 44, no. 1 (March 1963).

Morrison, James. "Algonquin History in the Ottawa River Watershed." Report for Sicani Research and Advisory Services (2005).

Mulvany, C. Pelham. *Toronto: Past and Present*. Toronto: Caiger, 1884.

The National Gazetteer: A Topographical Dictionary of the British Islands. London: Virtue, 1868.

O'Hart, John. *Irish Landed Gentry When Cromwell Came to Ireland*. Dublin: 1884.

Olson, Sherry, and Patricia Thornton. *Peopling the North American City: Montreal 1840–1900*. Montreal and Kingston: McGill-Queen's University Press, 2011.

Ouellet, Fernand. *Economic and Social History of Quebec, 1760–1850*. Toronto: Institute of Canadian Studies at Carleton University / Gage, 1980.

____. "Les insurrections de 1837–38: un phénomène social." *Histoire Sociale* 1, no. 2 (1968).

Oulton, Mary. "The Thomsons." *Arundel Family History Collection* (2007).

Penny, Arthur C. "The Annexation Movement, 1849–50." *The Canadian Historical Review* 5, no. 3 (1924).

Pollock-Ellwand, Nancy. "Rickson Outhet: Bringing the Olmsted Legacy to Canada." *Journal of Canadian Studies* (Winter 2010).

Pound, Richard W., et al., eds. *Fitzhenry & Whiteside Book of Canadian Facts and Dates*. Markham, ON: Fitzhenry & Whiteside, 2005.

Rankin, John. *A History of Our Firm: Pollock, Gilmour & Co.* Liverpool: Henry Young, 1921.

Rathwell, Morris. "Arundel 1856–2006." *Arundel Family History Collection* (2007).

____. "The Story of Gore." *Arundel Family History Collection* (2007).

Reid, D. B. *The Canadian Rebellion of 1837*. Toronto: Robinson, 1896.

Rigby, G. R. *A History of Lachute*. Lachute: 1964.

Sandham, Alfred. *Ville-Marie, or, Sketches of Montreal, Past and Present*. Montreal: Bishop, 1870.

Sendzik, Walter. "The 1832 Montreal Cholera Epidemic: A Study in State Formation." M.A. thesis, McGill University (1997).

Senior, Elinor Kyte. *British Regulars in Montreal: An Imperial Garrison, 1832–1854*. Montreal and Kingston: McGill-Queen's University Press, 1981.

____. "The Provincial Cavalry in Lower Canada 1837–50." *The Canadian Historical Review* 57, no. 1 (March 1976).

____. *Redcoats and Patriots: The Rebellions in Lower Canada 1837–38*. Ottawa: 1985.

Shaw, Keith. "Monique Bellingham—Lyme's Canadienne." Accessed November 15, 2018, at *www.lymeregismuseum.co.uk*.

Shortt, Adam, and Arthur G. Doughty, eds. *Canada and Its Provinces*. Toronto: 1914.

Skelton, Oscar Douglas. *Life and Times of Sir Alexander Tilloch Galt*. Toronto: Oxford University Press, 1920.

Smith, W. H. *Canada. Past, Present and Future*. Toronto: Maclear, 1851.

Soucy, Danielle. *La Vallée de la Diable*, 1983.

Terrill, Frederick William. *A Chronology of Montreal and of Canada A.D. 1752 to A.D. 1893*. Montreal: Lovell, 1893.

Thomas, Cyrus. *History of the Counties of Argenteuil, Que., and Prescott, Ont., from the Earliest Settlement to the Present*. Montreal: Lovell, 1896.

Thomas, Pat Flanagan. "The Flanagan History in Arundel." *Arundel Family History Collection* (2007).

Turcotte, Louis-Philippe. *Le Canada Sous L'Union, 1841–1867*. Quebec City: Presses Mécaniques du Canadien, 1871.

Turing, John. "Conservatives and Conditional Loyalty: The Rebellion Losses Crisis of 1849 in Montreal." *British Journal of Canadian Studies* 29, no. 1 (2016).

Various. *History of the County of Peterborough*. Toronto: C. Blackett Robinson, 1884.

Various. *History of Toronto and County York*. Toronto: C. Blackett Robinson, 1885.

Viger, Jacques. *Archéologie religieuse du Diocèse de Montréal*. Montreal: Lovell, 1850.

Willis, N.P., and W. H. Bartlett. *Canadian Scenery*. London: Virtue, 1842.

Wrench, John Evelyn. *Struggle, 1914–1920*. London: Ivor Nicholson & Watson, 1935.

IMAGE CREDITS

1. Bellingham Castle House, photograph from *Struggle*, 1914–1920, by John Evelyn Wrench, 1935

2. *Quebec Viewed from Pointe Lévis*, watercolour by T. Mower Martin, from *Canada*, by T. Mower Martin and Wilfred Campbell, 1906

3. Horse-driven ferry at Lévis, c. 1820, sketch by John Jeremiah Bigsby, LAC, MIKAN 3028509

4. *The Landing at Montreal, c. 1829*, watercolour by James Cockburn, from *Under the Lily & the Rose*, by Arthur G. Doughty, 1931

5. *Durham Boats on the Rideau, c. 1838*, watercolour by Philip John Bainbrigge, LAC, MIKAN 2896135

6. *Cobourg, Upper Canada, in 1840*, watercolour by Philip John Bainbrigge, LAC, MIKAN 2836287

7. The Stewarts' home in the forest, sketch by M. Haycock, from *Our Forest Home*, by Frances Stewart, 1902

8. Timber cove at Quebec, drawing by W. H. Bartlett, from *Canadian Scenery*, by N. P. Willis and W. H. Bartlett, 1842

9. Château St. Louis, sketch by W. S. Sewell, from *Picture of Quebec*, by Alfred Hawkins, 1834

10. *Montreal Viewed from Mount Royal*, watercolour by T. Mower Martin, from *Canada*, by T. Mower Martin and Wilfred Campbell, 1906

11. Hugh Allan's Ravenscrag, photograph by William Notman, McCord Museum 4867, with permission

12. *Notre Dame Street and Church*, watercolour by John Murray, LAC, MIKAN 2836035

13. Papineau's house on Bonsecours Street, photograph by the author

14. Archibald Acheson, Earl of Gosford, artist unknown, LAC, MIKAN 4312918

15. Louis-Joseph Papineau, lithograph by Maurin, Paris, from *Canada and Its Provinces*, by Adam Shortt and Arthur G. Doughty, eds., 1914

16. Reward poster for the arrest of Papineau, from *Canada and Its Provinces*, by Adam Shortt and Arthur G. Doughty, eds., 1914

17. Fort Chambly, drawing by W. H. Bartlett, from *Canadian Scenery*, by N. P. Willis and W. H. Bartlett, 1842

18. The encounter at Booth's Tavern, sketch by Henri Julien, 1888

19. Rebel forces celebrating at St. Denis, drawing by Henri Julien, LAC, MIKAN 2995479

20. Dr. Wolfred Nelson, drawing by Jean-Joseph Girouard, LAC, MIKAN 3635406

21. Lieutenant-Colonel George Augustus Wetherall, artist unknown, LAC, MIKAN 2999105

22. Thomas Storrow Brown in later life, BAnQ, Fonds Armour Landry, P97,S1,P20912

23. *The Death of Colonel Moodie at Montgomery's Tavern*, artist unknown, from *Toronto: Past and Present*, by C. Pelham Mulvany, 1884

24. Sir John Colborne, from *Canada and Its Provinces*, by Adam Shortt and Arthur G. Doughty, eds., 1914

25. *Siege of the Church at St. Eustache*, painting by Charles Beauclerk, McCord Museum M4777.5, with permission

26. Lord Durham, drawing by J. Stewart, from *Canada and Its Provinces*, by Adam Shortt and Arthur G. Doughty, ed., 1914

27. *The Rebels at Beauharnois*, watercolour by Jane Ellice, LAC, MIKAN 2836920

28. Robert Baldwin, photograph, from *Canada and Its Provinces*, by Adam Shortt and Arthur G. Doughty, eds., 1914

29. Louis-Hippolyte La Fontaine, from a painting in the Château Ramezay, from *Canada and Its Provinces*, by Adam Shortt and Arthur G. Doughty, eds., 1914

30. Bonsecours Market, drawing by A. Deroy, LAC, MIKAN 2837616

31. Great St. James Street, c. 1843, drawing by John Murray, LAC, MIKAN 2837616

32. *The Burning of Parliament*, oil painting by Joseph Légaré, McCord Museum M11588, with permission

33. *Papineau Manor, Montebello*, oil painting by Napoléon Bourassa, 1865, LAC, MIKAN 4100537

34. Locks on the Rideau Canal, drawing by W. H. Bartlett, from *Canadian Scenery*, by N. P. Willis and W. H. Bartlett, 1842

35. Carillon & Grenville Railway engine, c. 1895, LAC, MIKAN 3207134

36. Sir William Logan, F.R.S., photograph by William Notman, 1869, McCord Museum 1-42425, with permission

37. *St. James Street and the Bank of Montreal*, 1848, painting by Cornelius Krieghoff, LAC, MIKAN 2895408

38. Advertisement for the St. Lawrence Hall Hotel, from *The Canada Directory*, 1851, from *archive.org*

39. The FitzAlan farm today, photograph by the author

40. A broad stretch of the Rouge River viewed from the southern end of Arundel Township, photograph by the author

41. A farm in the Township of Gore, photograph by the author

42. A political cartoon satirizing Joseph Cauchon, from *archive.org*

43. Joseph-Adolphe Chapleau, photograph by William Notman, 1869, McCord Museum 1-37191, with permission

44. Arabella Bellingham, 1871, photograph by William Notman, McCord Museum 1-64474.1, with permission

45. Bellingham Castle House, c. 1905, photograph from *History of the Kilsaran Union of Parishes in the County of Louth*, by James B. Leslie, 1908, from archive.org

46. Sydney Bellingham in later life, photograph, LAC Ref. No. R7618-0-1-E

47. A.B. Filion, photograph by William James Topley, 1890, LAC, MIKAN 345856

48. The Bellingham-Filion house in Arundel, photograph by the author

49. Auguste Bernard Filion with Curé Labelle in 1889, photograph, LAC, MIKAN 3217897

MAP CREDITS

Library and Archives Canada shown as LAC; Bibliothèque et Archives nationales du Québec shown as BAnQ.

1. Sydney Bellingham's Canada, from a map by S. Lewis and H. S. Tanner, 1823, LAC, MIKAN 3726138

2. The journey from Quebec to Montreal aboard the steamer *New Swiftsure*, from a map by Walton and Gaylord, 1835, LAC, MIKAN 4127087

3. The trip from Montreal to Lachine by stage, and from Lachine to Pointe des Cascades aboard the *Perseverance*, from a map by Walton and Gaylord, 1835, LAC, MIKAN 4127087

4. The journey from Pointe des Cascades to Prescott, from *A Map of the Eastern Part of the Province of Upper Canada*, 1818, by Robert Pilkington, LAC, MIKAN 4129220

5. The journey from Prescott to Kingston, from *A Map of the Eastern Part of the Province of Upper Canada*, 1818, by Robert Pilkington, LAC, MIKAN 4129220

6. The journey from Kingston to Douro Township, from *A Map of the Eastern Part of the Province of Upper Canada*, 1818, by Robert Pilkington, LAC, MIKAN 4129220

7. The route from Cobourg to Douro, from W. H. Smith's *Canada: Past, Present and Future*, 1851

8. The journey from Montreal to Douro, from *A Map of the Province of Upper Canada*, 1836, LAC, MIKAN 3722680

9. Bouchette's map of Montreal, from *The British Dominions in North America*, 1832

10. Geographic context of the Rebellions of 1837–38, from William Kingsford's *The History of Canada*, 1898

11. The march on St. Charles, from part of a map of Lower Canada by L. J. Hebert, 1838, LAC, MIKAN 4127086

12. The march on St. Eustache, from part of a map of Lower Canada by L. J. Hebert, 1838, LAC, MIKAN 4127086

13. Expedition to St. Jean and the border area, from part of a map of Lower Canada by L. J. Hebert, 1838, LAC, MIKAN 4127086

14 The trip to Bellechasse County, from a map by Walton and Gaylord, 1835, LAC, MIKAN 4127087

15. Route of the Montreal and Bytown Railway, from *A Map of Canada Shewing the Railways*, by Maclear, 1856, LAC, MIKAN 4128119

16. Plan of part of the Province of Lower Canada, 1795, by Samuel Gale and John B. Duberger, LAC, MIKAN 4143456

17. Albright's routes from St. Andrews to Arundel, based on an extract from the *Electoral Atlas of the Dominion of Canada*, 1904, LAC, MIKAN 196055

18. Plan of the Township of Arundel, by William A. Crawford, 1879, BAnQ, Fonds Ministère des Terres et Forêts, E21, S555, SS1, SSS1 PA.17A

INDEX

St. Eustache, Lower Canada, 75, 77, 78–80, 82, 83, 93, 97, 102, 122, 123, 128, 136, 137, 151, 178, 190

St. Eustache Loyal Volunteers, 79

St. Hermas Parish, Lower Canada, 136, 139, 140

St. Hilaire, Lower Canada, 69

St. James Street (also known as Great St. James Street), Montreal, xi, 44, 45, 60, 108, 109, 110, 115, 135, 151, 157, 158, 160, 211

St. Jean, Lower Canada, 60, 74, 86–89, 121, 209

St. Jérôme, Lower Canada, 154, 187

St. Lawrence and Atlantic Railroad, 109, 121, 150, 153

St. Lawrence Hall Hotel, Montreal, 158, 159, 161

St. Lawrence River, 7, 10, 13, 15–17, 20, 36, 38, 41, 60, 64, 77, 84, 86, 87, 88, 97, 98, 104, 106, 113, 121, 126, 128n, 143, 148, 163, 203

St. Lawrence Seaway, 19

St. Lawrence Steamboat Company, 38

St. Louis Square, Montreal, 117

St. Martin, Lower Canada, 80

St. Patrick's Society, 2, 47, 59, 133

St. Paul Street, Montreal, 45, 48

St. Placide Parish, 136, 139

stagecoach travel, 15, 16, 18, 138, 139

Standing Committee on Railways, Canals and Telegraph Lines, 130, 141, 148

steamboats, 12, 13, 14, 16, 17, 19, 35, 39, 43, 68, 86, 97, 108, 117, 128, 137, 143, 157, 161, 164, 179, 190

Stewart, Bessie, 27, 28

Stewart, Eliza, 6

Stewart, Frances (Fanny) Browne, 6, 13, 20, 21, 25–27, 35, 36

Stewart, Thomas, 6, 13, 20, 24, 25–29, 32, 35, 36, 111, 135

Stewart, William, 6

Sulpician Order, 45, 102–03

surveying land, 29, 139, 147, 163–68, 170–74,

Sweeney, Campbell, 102, 107

Sweeney, Robert, 884, 85, 102, 107, 156

Sydenham, Lord, 96, 104, 107, 133, 134, 138, 139

Sykes, James, 128, 130

Sykes, William, 130

T

Taché, Étienne-Paschal, 151

Tanneries Affair, 188

taverns, 23, 53, 60, 67, 77, 81, 107, 126

Tecumseh, 36

telegraph, 143, 161

Temiskaming and Northern Ontario Railway, 125

Terrebonne County, Lower Canada, 96, 104, 123, 136n, 139, 140, 152, 188

Thomson, Charles Edward Poulett (see Sydenham, Lord)

Thomson, William, 174, 175

Times and Commercial Advertiser, 107, 211

Toronto (*see also* York), 27, 30, 75, 83, 96, 113, 122, 140, 142, 143, 145, 156, 161, 164, 188, 211

Trent, 157

Trent-Severn Waterway, 22

Trois-Rivières, 11, 14, 64, 98

True Witness and Catholic Chronicle, The, 154

Two Mountains County, 55, 77, 82, 84, 90, 91, 130, 135, 139, 140, 142, 152

Two Mountains Militia, 137

typhus, 33, 106, 111

U

Underground Railroad, 157

Upper Canada College, 76

V

Vallières de Saint-Real, Joseph-Rémi, 103–04

Val-Morin, Lower Canada, 152

Van Buren, Martin, 83

Vancouver, James, 31

VanKoughnet, Philip, 140, 156, 166

Vermont, 63, 72, 83, 84, 92, 104, 121, 157

Victoria, Queen, 82, 147, 192, 196

Victoria Bridge, Montreal, 118, 147, 157, 159

Viger, Jacques, 46, 123

Villeneuve, Louis, 48, 102, 103

Vinet-Souligny, Félix, 48

W

Walker, John Henry, 112

Walker, William, 103, 106–08, 211

Wallis, James, 42, 44, 48n, 48

Walpole, Robert, 42

War of 1812, 17, 20, 29, 48, 82, 151

Warde, Henry John, 70, 73, 84-85, 102, 107, 156

Weir, George, 74, 81, 100

Wentworth Township, 1, 30, 136, 165

Weskarini people, 124, 171

Westcott, James Diament, 158–59

Wetherall, George Augustus, 63, 67–74, 80, 81, 84

William IV, King, 58

Wilson, John, 156

Wolfe, James, 11

Wolfe Township, 136, 136n

Wolseley, Garnet, 189–90

Wright, Philemon, 125

Wright, Ruggles, 125, 128

Y

Yonge Street, Toronto, 76–77

York (*see also* Toronto), 27, 29, 41, 58

York County, 164

Young Irelanders, 111

Yukon, 147

Z

Zouaves, 186